Some of Us

SOME OF US

Chinese Women Growing Up in the Mao Era

Edited by
XUEPING ZHONG
WANG ZHENG
BAI DI

RUTGERS UNIVERSITY PRESS
New Brunswick, New Jersey, and London

Library of Congress Cataloging-in-Publication Data

Some of us : Chinese women growing up in the Mao era / edited by Xueping
Zhong, Wang Zheng, and Bai Di.
    p. cm
   Includes bibliographical references and index.
   ISBN 0-8135-2968-9 (alk. paper)—ISBN 0-8135-2969-7 (pbk.: alk. paper)
      1. Women—China. 2. China—Social conditions—1949-1976. I. Title:
Chinese women growing up in the Mao era. II. Zhong, Xueping, 1956- III.
Wang, Zheng. IV. Di, Bai, 1954-

HQ1767.S598 2001
305.4'0951—dc21

                                                     00-068351

British Cataloging-in-Publication data for this book is available from the British
Library.

Manufactured in the United States of America

To those who made it possible for us to grow
socially, intellectually, and emotionally in a unique historical era

Contents

Chronology

1949   Founding of the People's Republic of China and the All-China Women's Federation.

1950   China enters the Korean War.

1951   Campaign to "suppress counterrevolutionaries."

1955   Campaign to "uncover hidden counterrevolutionaries."

1956   The period of "one hundred flowers blooming," when intellectuals are encouraged to criticize the CCP.

1957   The Anti-Rightist Campaign.

1958   Great Leap Forward. Women are mobilized to participate in social production.

1959–61 Three years of economic disasters.

1966   The Cultural Revolution begins.

        The Red Guards Movement first emerges in Beijing and then spreads to other parts of the country.

        Schools are closed. Free lodging is provided in many parts of the country for traveling Red Guards and students.

Mao has many public receptions of Red Guards in Tiananmen Square.

After years of revising, "model" operas and ballets are promoted.

1968   Massive rustication of urban youths begins. Schools reopen.

1970   A few colleges, as pilot sites, begin to recruit workers-peasants-soldiers (WPS) students.

1971   More colleges nationwide begin to recruit WPS students. Official criteria: performance at job and coworkers', peasants', and local officials' recommendations.

1976   Mao dies. The Cultural Revolution ends.

1977   College entrance examinations are reinstated.

1978   Deng Xiaoping becomes the chief secretary of the CCP.

First group of college students recruited through nationwide entrance examinations enter college.

Acknowledgments

Our thanks go to Elizabeth Ammons of Tufts University for her initial support of the idea for this volume, to the Press's reviewer for her constructive comments and suggestions, and to Leslie Mitchner, our editor at Rutgers University Press, for her wholehearted support for the publication of this volume. We also wish to thank those who encouraged our efforts and cheered us on as we explored the significance of this endeavor and searched for ways to tell and reflect on our stories.

XUEPING ZHONG

WANG ZHENG

BAI DI

INTRODUCTION

This collection of memoirs about the Mao era promises to be different. It offers a counternarrative to the popularly received Red Guards and female victim or sexual repression memoirs found in the West. In telling their stories, the contributors do not represent their early lives through the all-too-familiar lenses of persecution, violence, victimization, sexual repression, and so forth. Instead, their stories, each in its own way, tap into the much entangled dimensions of the social and various public and private domains often overlooked or dismissed by scholars and unexpected by Western reading public in general. In doing so, these stories are poised to raise difficult and challenging questions about a controversial, important period in modern Chinese history.[1]

SOME OF US DEFINING WHO WE ARE AND OUR OBJECTIVES

On an April evening in 1998, a chance meeting brought the three of us together in a hotel room somewhere in Cambridge, Massachusetts. We sat around chatting and enjoying a rare moment of free conversation among peers. As the topics of our conversation flowed from one to another, we stumbled onto one that would eventually result in this collection of intellectual memoirs.[2]

The idea of such a collection formed when we began talking about existing memoirs, those written in English by Chinese and about the authors' experiences in the Mao era, especially during the Cultural Revolution. Because we happened to be talking about gender and women's issues in China, we naturally focused our attention on such well-known works as *Wild Swans* and *Red Azalea*. We wondered why we had often felt the representations in these memoirs and their popular reception in the West to be problematic.[3] Surely we did not expect a few memoirs to tell everybody's story, but what bothered us was not so much that they did not tell our stories (which no one should or would expect), but that they were being treated as if they had precisely done that. As we went on, more questions were asked. If (urban) Chinese women's (and men's) experiences in the Mao era are in fact diverse, what is it about the existing memoirs that do not seem to indicate and speak to this kind of divergence?[4] If it is because these memoirs have in many ways helped reinforce a simplistic view of modern and recent Chinese history, in what ways does one begin to challenge and complicate such a simplistic view?[5] And more importantly, does it matter or is it historically significant to remember that during the Mao era the majority of (urban) Chinese women lived their lives beyond the dichotomy of being either a victim or a victimizer, beyond the assumptions that they were sexually repressed, and beyond a monolithic view of what their lives must have been like? If so, what would be the significance?

Along with these questions, an idea emerged: Perhaps it was time for us to give our own experiences a serious look, collectively. At the end of this accidental meeting, we decided to organize a group of Chinese women who grew up during the Mao era and who were currently working and studying in the United States. We wanted to find out, via an online discussion, if there were shared sentiments among them and if there was interest in our proposed project.

Much to our delight and encouragement, our inquiry met with active and enthusiastic responses. Most called it "a fascinating topic" that they themselves had been thinking about for some time. One participant stated: "My impulse to write about my experiences in the Mao era began when I studied the U.S. women's history in the first few years of my graduate program. The sharp contrast between the social background against which I grew up and that of the U.S. women could not but call into question the 'total negation' of the Mao era. Over the years, I have tried to explore a way to express my reflections on the Mao era. I do not think that I have completed this process, which is why I am highly interested in doing a project which may help me think through a lot of issues." Another echoed this way: "Thanks for inviting me to participate in this evolving and important project. I have personally been thinking about the issues for a long time and also been wondering what would be the most viable means to tackle and represent them. A collective effort is certainly most productive, as it could present to our readers that it was a rather pervasive and culturally embedded past that needs to be articulated in light of the present."

Together, the respondents echoed one sentiment: there is a need to tell stories that present a less clear-cut picture of an era and the people—in this case, women—who grew up in it. Over the years many of us have carried out dialogues with people around us about our past experiences, about what they mean for us, and, sometimes inevitably, about how to understand them in relation to the era in which we grew up and, for that matter, in relation to the time and place where we find ourselves today. We decided that perhaps it was time we raised and discussed all of this in a more public manner. We wanted to do so in a format that most of us had so far consciously resisted: memoir writing. Even though on an empirical level our experiences vary and, given the limited space of our project, we would be able to represent only a tiny fraction of them (not to mention those of millions of other Chinese women out there), we wanted to take advantage of our intellectual positions negotiated and evolved not just through our study in the United States but also, and more importantly, through the questions we felt compelled to ask in our study. As women who grew up during the Mao era, we differ in age and regional and family backgrounds; and while we currently work, study, and live in the United States, we also differ in the fields in which we have received Ph.D. degrees (literature, history, sociology, women's studies, and cinema studies). Together, however, we occupy a unique position— both as individuals who grew up in the Mao era and as intellectuals who have accumulated multilayered cross-cultural perspectives and who share a willingness to explore some difficult issues. One such difficult issue is our interest in responding to the ways in which the relationship between the social condition, women's lives, and women's positions in the Mao era has been understood both in China and in the West.

This position, of course, when perceived from the perspective informed by the now all-too-familiar postcolonial debate, consists of more than the dual aspects identified here. Our experiences coincide with postcolonial histories that consist of, among others, the

Mao era (as one kind of postcolonial context) and the post-Mao era (as another), when China moved into the larger framework of the neocolonial globalization context. And it is within the latter context that we embarked on our journeys traversing to and in the West. It is also within this context that we feel compelled to confront the historical implications of our Mao era experiences. On this level, the desire to tell our stories is, once again, to challenge the existing paradigm or framework of understanding the part of history in which we grew up, and, to echo one of our contributors quoted earlier, to articulate "a rather pervasive and culturally embedded past . . . in light of the present."

Even though we did not always agree with one another, our lively discussion helped shape one thing on which we all agreed: in telling our stories, our purpose is not to produce yet another set of exotic stories that cater to the expectations of Western readers, that is, political campaigns, political persecutions, sexual repression, and so forth.[6] Not only because we do not necessarily have the kind of stories (or want to tell them in the way) that will meet some of the existing expectations in the West, but also, and more importantly, because we do not share some of the assumptions embedded in such expectations. Instead, we want to explore the necessarily more complex dimensions of issues raised and debated in recent scholarship on how to assess and understand twentieth-century China and, especially, the Mao era. Given the specificity of our project, we want to weigh in on the question of historical representation, exploring the relationship between "experience" and "history" and tackling the conundrum of why some people's memories seem to be treated as more legitimate than others. As such, we perceive our collection as a necessary intervention that starts with a set of seemingly simple questions: what does it mean to have grown up in the Mao era? What does it mean to have grown up as a girl and woman in the Mao era? How are we to understand the less clear-cut and seemingly mundane daily existence of our early lives, and how are we to do so in conjunction with the existing views and interpretations of the Mao era?

Along this line of questioning, we hope to rethink and reexamine the underexplored dimensions of that time and space—its ironies, paradoxes, and various contradictions—that were manifested in our lives in various social and personal relationships, in the political and popular culture that we were exposed to, the "high/low" culture that lurked somewhere around the corner of our homes and schools, the familial settings, as well as other domains within and without the state control. We want to factor in the unstable nature of such terms as *qingnian* (youth), *funü* (woman/women), *nan nu pingdeng* (equality between men and women), *lixiang* (ideals), and the contradictions within, especially how they played out in daily life within a state-controlled context while often being subverted at the same time. Through exploring the various intersections between "official ideology" and "lived experience," we want our stories not only to "enrich and complicate" the existing understanding of that era but also to open further discussion of the Mao era and, by extension, its relationship to China's century-long quest for modernity. Our intention, in other words, is not only to argue for the values of individual experiences but also to signify profound, complex social changes whose implications still await further exploration.

Needless to say, writing narratives with so much intended is a daunting task. Throughout we ran into implicit and explicit challenges to the central theme of this collective endeavor and the difficult questions regarding memoir writing, representations, and history.

HISTORY, MEMORY, AND THE MAO ERA

The fifty-first annual meeting of the Association for Asian Studies in 1999 featured a panel discussion on "Memory and Cultural Revolution." Its central theme was that we should not forget the deadly consequences of the Cultural Revolution. One presentation was about finding out how many teachers died in Beijing during the first year of the Cultural Revolution; another discussed the memoirs by such important figures as Ba Jin and Ji Xianlin. The latter presenter vehemently argued that based on these people's memories it was a shame that most Chinese have not taken the step to *qingli* (reflect and clean up) their roles in the Cultural Revolution and that most of them have become accomplices of the state in not wanting to "remember" that ugly past. During the question-and-answer period, someone stated that she had a different kind of memory about the Cultural Revolution, not just the gloomy and dark kind, or of being either a victim or a victimizer, but also of the high and youthful spirit that strongly affected many youngsters. How, she asked, does one account for this kind of memory? In response, the chair of the panel used an analogy: according to him, there were Nazi concentration camp survivors who still get excited upon hearing Nazi music, the kind they used to hear in the concentration camps.[7] The underlying statement is clear: you poor creature, you are so brainwashed that you don't know what's good or bad for you.

Nowadays, it seems one of the easiest ways to arrive at a higher moral ground is to accuse someone of either being like Hitler or his mindless followers or even, curiously, his helpless victims, regardless of whether or not the accusation fits the "crime." While our world has never been in short supply of villains, big and small, such accusations have often themselves become like those *gao mao zi* (high hats) that were readily forced onto the heads of the designated enemies during the Cultural Revolution. If anyone deems this second analogy outrageous, their reaction is expected. And the point here is to argue that a high-sounding (not to mention condescending) labeling is, if not a politically motivated attack, just an easy way to avoid confronting the more difficult task of exploring and examining the less clear-cut and more complex issues involved, or, in Perry Anderson's words, "a lazy exercise of right and left alike today.[8] Why is it that other kinds of memory of the Cultural Revolution (and of the Mao era) can be readily dismissed with a Nazi-related labeling? To be sure, lessons of the Cultural Revolution have yet to be fully learned. But is it to be done only through a dichotomized framework of victims vs. victimizers, namely "helpless" (therefore good) Chinese vs. "evil" Chinese? Is it the only framework, and how useful is it for lessons to be fully laid out and drawn, especially when intellectuals have claimed victim status, thereby effectively canceling out the need to examine the complexity of their own positions? Additionally, who is to say that ordinary Chinese have not been drawing lessons themselves? Their aversion toward language and behavior that remind them of the extremist tendency of the Cultural Revolution, their lack of political fervor and loss of conviction in the official ideology, and their ability and innovative ways to subvert the control imposed by the state can be seen as their ways, rightly or wrongly, of drawing lessons from the Cultural Revolution. Meanwhile, although many intellectuals continue to write memoirs to warn people not to forget, their perspective, as just mentioned, has remained narrowly focused, mostly on the conflict between the state and intellectuals and on the latter being victims. It is precisely this unchanged narrow focus that has itself become blind and exclusionary to issues that are beyond their own sufferings and plight. The irony of this unchanged focus, incidentally, is deeply rooted in the long, often tension-filled relationship between the court/state and educated men/intellectuals, in which the latter exist precariously, finding themselves in or out of favor of the former. And it is the complex nature of this relation that, paradoxically, continues to condition the dichotomized view held by the intellectuals.

On a deeper level, the analogy used by the panel's chair alludes to a fundamental question: whose representations of history are considered legitimate? Or, put differently, whose memories count and why? Zhang Zhen, one of the contributors, ponders on the question this way in the beginning of her essay: "How should I account for my coming of age in the heart of a Chinese metropolis—the home base of the 'Gang of Four' in that area? Why has there always been a sense of unease, or even disappointment, whenever I tell non-Chinese friends in America or elsewhere that my parents and I were not victimized in any dramatic or visible way, as so often described in standard narratives of the Cult[ural] Rev[volution]? Where do answers to these questions lie?"[9] Indeed, where do they lie?

With these questions we come full circle to the ones raised earlier regarding such issues as the relationship between "experience" and "history," the question of whose memories are (il)legitimate, and how to understand representations and interpretations of (women's) lived experiences. We believe the essence of these issues lies "in light of the present" and in conjunction with our understanding of the various subject positions, exerted here in this volume, for example, that cannot be easily identified nor readily be made to fit within the norms of an existing master narrative.

MEMORIES AND THEIR (IL)LEGITIMACY

In the last two decades, a master narrative of the Mao era has existed in and outside China. Inside China, it began in the wake of the Cultural Revolution with the emergence of the "wounded/scar literature" *(shanghen wenxue)*. In the changed political atmosphere of the late 1970s, when Chinese writers began to publish stories of "wounded literature" that exposed personal sufferings endured during the Cultural Revolution, many Chinese responded actively and felt excited by such changes and the stimulation they brought about. At the same time, however, something peculiar was also happening. As Wang Zheng narrates in her essay, for example, she felt confused that almost as a rule "Everyone who was talking, including the once victimizer Red Guards, was a victim scarred by the Maoist dictatorship. But I could not think of any example in my life to present myself as a victim or victimizer. I did not know how to feel about my many happy memories and cherished experiences of a time that the most vocal people now called the dark age."[10] The dominance of the "dark age" narratives, riding on the political mandate "to thoroughly negate the Cultural Revolution," along with the immediacy of the aftermath of the Cultural Revolution, allowed little room for other kinds of memories and for thoughtful reflections.[11] Even though the first seventeen years (1949–1966) were looked upon as better times, the political campaigns waged and the human sufferings inflicted during that time also began to be exposed, and very soon the Mao era as a whole came to be seen negatively in the liberal intellectual discourse that dominated the cultural scene of the 1980s (and beyond).

The dark age master narrative in turn reinforced the long-existing Mao-era-being-a-dark age narrative in the West, especially in the United States, where stories exposing the tragedy of the communist rule found a huge market among Americans, ranging from liberals crusading for human rights to anticommunist conservatives. The successful marketing that secured the popularity of *Life and Death in Shanghai* in the United States in the mid-1980s, for example, most clearly demonstrates what most American readers expected to find in such a book. The popularity of this and other memoirs of the Cultural Revolution has constructed in America a powerful narrative of the Mao era that is charged with violence and persecution. The collective imagination of the Mao era in America, in turn, becomes heavily shaped by these dark age narratives. Not only the general public takes the horror tales of the Cultural Revolution as the entirety of the Mao era, many academics in the China field have been unable to imagine lines of inquiry other than the tragedy of the Cultural Revolution. In many ways, the dark age narrative commands a stronger popular imagination in the United States than even in China.[12]

In both China and the United States, memories of the Mao era have largely been offered by intellectuals or those who frame their memories within the accepted dark age narrative framework. And most of the "nonpublic people" (William Kirby's words) or people who have no means of representations appear to have taken the sufferings and tragedies in the publicized stories as their own and as representative of the times—the Mao era—they themselves also lived through. Meanwhile, there is increasing evidence that people who lived through the Mao era have their own diverse memories which cannot be easily replaced, explained, or represented by a few famous memoirs and well-known intellectuals' suffering narratives. The "Mao Craze" during the early 1990s, for example, though alternately amusing and horrifying to some intellectuals and China watchers who downplayed it as either a marketing scheme or mere nostalgia or political insomnia, has yet to be fully understood. And the memories of the Red Guards or "educated youths" *(zhishi qingnian)* generation, publicized in late 1990s, poses an even more interesting set of questions. The fact that some of the former "educated youths" insisted on a lack of regrets for their youth, or *qingchun wuhui* as the slogan goes in Chinese, effectively expressed the positive nature of their memories. To be sure, one can easily dismiss such memories as a reaction on the part of the older generations of China toward the many failures in the reform era and therefore a mere expression of nostalgia. Still, we believe such dismissal comes a bit too quickly, without willingness on the part of the critics to acknowledge that the public and popular memories of the Mao era are in fact multilayered and complex. The coexistence of the suffering memoirs and the "youth without regrets" sentiments indicates that remembering the Mao era is a contested practice in which different social/class and gender groups stage their negotiations and lay their claims. Memories of the Mao era in China, therefore, are necessarily as diverse as existing social groups and as unfixed as changing social relations and social contexts.

In the United States (and to a large extent in China), mainstream production of memories of the Mao era has continued to ignore such complexity and to be framed within the existing dark age master narrative. Additionally, there is an interesting gender divide that continues to operate within the existing mode of inquiry. For example, in China, most of the suffering memories come from leading male intellectuals such as Ba Jin and Ji Xianlin, while in the United States and the West, the most popular memoirs are those written by women, a phenomenon that indicates the gender dynamics in both countries when it comes to the (il)legitimacy of memories. In China, leading intellectuals' memories have continued to command a moral authority and hence continue to be recognized as more legitimate. And most Chinese intellectuals, while taking for granted the legitimacy (and prestige) of leading intellectuals' memories, have continued to marginalize issues regarding ordinary people's experiences, including those of women. In the United States, on the other hand, it is often Chinese women whose experiences are looked upon as symbolic and representative of China, while at the same time Western intellectuals continue to look to male intellectuals for interpretations, which, we might add, are often framed within a familiar gender-biased paradigm. It is this simultaneous split and combination that constitute the ideological hold shared by Chinese intellectuals and some western China scholars, and, as a result, an underlying assumption about whose memory is more legitimate.

In discussions of John Fitzgerald's article "In the Scales of History: Politics and Culture in Twentieth-Century China,"[13] some commentators responded by questioning how to think of the voices that have not yet been heard. Richard Krause, for example, reflects: "As the circle of participants in exchange expands, we may sometimes mistake a part for the whole, and take worldly authors of memoirs of unpleasant China experiences to represent more than local experience. We should ask ourselves explicitly: do we have special moral obligations toward those Chinese who most resemble ourselves?"[14] William Kirby, on the other hand, contends that there are two reasons for historians' difficulty in writing of the lives of "nonpublic people": "the nature of source materials and the fact that the lives of the least political Chinese became entwined with 'national' quest (for sovereignty, survival, socialism, you name it) in a manner that will not be easy to unravel."[15]

What Kirby implies seems to be that in countries like the United States, the "nonpublic people" may somehow be free from becoming "entwined with" its national quest (patriotism, capitalism, superpower mentality . . . you name it). This aside, one wonders why Kirby is so insistent on having to extract "purity" from the least-political Chinese and believes that without such a possibility, their lives will not offer any additional or equally (if not more) meaningful understanding of (modern) Chinese history. He also seems to assume that the "nonpublic Chinese" do not have their own contexts and that their lives are nothing but always centered around the state-sponsored "national quest." The Mao era (or, for that matter, Chinese history in general), as it turns out, can either only be "objectively" written through collecting archival materials or is impossible to write because ordinary people's experiences are too "contaminated," hence lacking legitimacy and historical significance.

What we intend here is not to exert "experiences" as historical truth but to contend for the need to recognize their historicity. What we have briefly laid out in the above—the different memories and claims with regard to the Mao era and the contradictions within—indicates that memory, as it turns out, is a site of struggle for historical representations and interpretations.

WOMEN, MEMORY, AND THE MAO ERA

On October 1, 1999, the Fairbank Center for East Asian Studies held a two-panel forum centering on the topic "PRC as History." Each panel consisted of about a half-dozen speakers, most of whom were Harvard University China-study faculty, ranging from such fields as history, literature, anthropology, political science, and sociology. From an assortment of disciplinary angles, speakers gave their assessments of the fifty years of the PRC's history. Some commented on it from an ancient Chinese angle, while others commented comparatively between pre- and post-1949 China or between the Mao and post-Mao era. Out of all these speakers discussing PRC as history, however, not a single one focused on women's issues, especially the profound (albeit flawed and incomplete) changes taking place in women's lives during that era. The absence was so conspicuous that the first question put to the panelists from the audience was what they thought about PRC's history in relation to women's issues. When the question was met with silence (because no one appeared to be prepared to answer it) before one of the two female speakers admitted the problem, the audience laughed. And yet anyone who knows anything about the PRC history, or the twentieth-century China for that matter, would know that such a conspicuous silence was actually not funny. How is one to interpret the absence of what should be taken as a major part of the PRC's history (regardless of how one is to assess it) other than to conclude its lack of importance to the world-renowned experts on China?

Although there have been increasing studies of Chinese women and gender issues in the China field, the complete gender-blind discussion of the PRC as history at Harvard continues to indicate the resistance (in the study of Chinese history) to including women and their lived experiences into "the scales of history" and the resistance to acknowledging, to echo Joan Scott, gender in the politics of history.[16] History and women, as Harvard's forum demonstrates, can still be treated as mutually exclusive categories.

It is against the grain of such ongoing resistance and the dominance of the dark age master narrative that we present this volume to English readers. As indicated earlier, unlike memoirs written by the powerful and the prestigious who focused on their relationships with the party-state or by those who wrote within the existing framework of the dark age master narrative, our memories are situated in our diverse and overlapping relationships with family, school, neighborhood, workplace, popular culture, rural China, as well as with the official ideology in the Mao era. Through an intellectual exploration, we want to understand how those relationships and their various dimensions shaped us during our formative years and continue to condition who we are today. As such, our writings are self-consciously reflective, and our experiences indicate an embodiment of contradictions.

Speaking of contradictions, we must recognize some obvious ones at the outset. On the one hand, as urban Han women, there were some of us who grew up in relatively ordinary urban households that, within the Maoist ideology, sometimes placed us in favored positions discursively but not necessarily socially and culturally. There were others who grew up in socially and culturally privileged households that were nevertheless more vulnerable to shifting political winds. On the other hand, being urban Chinese, we collectively benefited from the Mao era policies that favored urban China at the expense of peasants. Most of us lived at the epicenters of the Mao era's politics, where we grew up within an assortment of mundane environments that were at the same time entwined with the polity of the times. We do not pretend to be free from such entwinement—in fact, it is problematic to expect such a possibility. However, we do want to argue, as we have so far in this introduction, that the existing dark age master narrative and modes of inquiry suffer from a lack of basic understanding of the complexity that necessarily underlies not only our own experiences but also the history of the Mao era (and the times both before and after it).

In her *Changing Identities of Chinese Women: Rhetoric, Experience, and Self-Perception in Twentieth-Century China,* Elisabeth Croll writes: "To elicit female perceptions and experience of rhetoric, both historically and in contemporary China, is a daunting task, largely because of the presence of a well-developed and all-encompassing rhetoric explicitly defining female characteristics and a virtual absence of recorded female experience."[17] While Croll fully recognizes the need to find "female perceptions" and the importance of recording "female experience," her observation suffers a similar assumption as that of William Kirby's: they both assume a complete, or "all-encompassing," official or mainstream ideology without any subversive possibilities either in people's daily existence or, in Croll's case, in "female perceptions" and "female experience." What is more, this assumption is also based on a rejection of, or an unwillingness to, acknowledge the positive effects (or the usefulness) of the official discourses in shaping contemporary Chinese women's identities and, additionally, women's agency in maneuvering among various, and often conflicting, political, social, and discursive demands. We argue that unless one is willing to give Chinese women's experience the level of complexity it deserves to be recognized for, their actual experience will continue to be branded as either merely too enmeshed with the official rhetoric to be believed or too mundane to be taken seriously.

Indeed, discussions like ours echo both the changing dynamics in the historiographical debates as well as in the politics of such debates. Ever since feminist historiography began to challenge the traditional historiographical paradigms and put women's experiences and the concept of gender into the politics of history, it has continued to encounter resistance and has also generated active debates among feminist historians themselves. The question, indeed a perennial conundrum, has continued to be "What is history?" Although we did not set out to address this weighty question, our project inevitably encroaches into the realm of this issue when we claim the need to complicate the existing representations of the Mao era. What is at issue, we argue, is not so much as experience vs. history, which is in essence a false dichotomy. What is at issue is who—that is, which social and political group—defines history, represents history, and, above all, decides whose experiences and whose memories count as history, whose do not, and for what reasons.

To complicate the Mao era, of course, is not to whitewash the horrors and catastrophes. Our endeavor is to challenge the black-and-white historical representations that have so far functioned to negate or make invisible (1) important aspects of historical experiences and subject positions that do not fit the either-or historical representations, and (2) the entangled social and cultural dimensions of the era. In this sense, therefore, to complicate the Mao era is to point out that along with disasters there were also changes and achievements. Some of them were profound, while others manifested a continuation of the desire to modernize or the modernizing agenda and attempts that had gone before the victory of the Communist revolution. And all of them have impacted the Chinese individually and China collectively. Just like all the different major attempts throughout modern Chinese history when the Chinese elite struggled to come to terms with modernity, the Mao era was both a disruption and continuation of these earlier attempts, and, as such, it was also a complex era to live through. Individual Chinese, while facing the reality of constant political campaigns and depending on whether they were peasants or urbanites or whether they belonged to the favored classes or not, continued to search, often in their own ways, for means to survive or to better their lives. Many of their daily and personal experiences are both mundane and historical in that together they reflect the changes, the struggles, and the difficulties in China's ongoing, century-long quest for modernity and ways to come to terms with it.[18] Among them, millions of women's diverse experiences help manifest such struggles as well as the changes in women's lives and in their own struggles to become a "modern subject."[19]

Finally, by way of telling different experiences and the contradictions within, our intervention here is aimed at more than challenging historical representations; what we also contend is a need for a counternarrative. Even though it is beyond the scope of this introduction to formulate such a narrative, what we have argued so far has indicated that a counternarrative of the Mao era can be formulated through exploring the profound social changes brought about by the revolution and the subsequent contradictions that emerged within that era.[20] Contradictions include that of liberation vs. oppression and self-repression, "women" vs. "youth," equality/egalitarianism vs. class and other divides, party vs. state, socialism vs. statism, and many more. And it is within this mode of inquiry, we believe, that a more nuanced understanding of the Mao era can emerge.

PERFORMING MEMOIR WRITING: INDIVIDUAL ESSAYS

As already alluded to, our endeavor here involves two overlapping sets of experiences: our experiences growing up in the Mao era and our experiences in encountering, as it were, such experiences again in our diasporic context. The complexity and ironies embedded in the intricacies of these experiences are certainly not up to us to exhaust. Still, from the very beginning, we were aware of the daunting nature of our task. Regardless of who we were before coming to the United States, at the moment, we are Chinese women who have gone through graduate school in this country and have acquired a set of rhetorics, feminist or otherwise, that have shaped the way in which we remember and reflect our past experience. Such a recognition prevents us from claiming our memories to be pure and unfiltered. Additionally, it also reminds us of the need to be reflective on our own positions, which can help us refrain from making sweeping generalizations. In the process of our writing, we grappled with the issue of style, the unfamiliar nature of the genre for this group of women who were never trained to write narratives, and, most of all, the nature of our memory, the meaning of our "production" of such memory, and its relationship with the past and the present.

Furthermore, throughout the writing process we were made to realize another paradoxical nature of our task: to write our past honestly and at the same time critically (meaning reflectively). In conjunction with that, we also came to recognize the meta-issue involved in such an endeavor; namely, the dual nature of our positions: as the writing subject and as the written object. While it was not our task in this volume to tackle the issue on a metaphysical level, our awareness of it at least made it possible for us to be critical readers of each other's pieces and to interrogate the positionality of "the writing subject" of the author. One thing we noticed with great interest was the fact that some of us were able to recognize one another in the remembrances of our younger selves. At the same time, we kept questioning each other as to why some specific events, seemingly insignificant to others, surfaced as the most important part of our past experience and, in turn, became the subject matter of our essays. If any memory is a reconstruction of the past, our "reconstruction" process is one that encouraged the authors to be conscious of the dual nature of their positions. It is a process of constant struggle to fight off sweeping generalizations, ahistorical comparisons, and the tendency to equate individual experience with historical "truth."

The essays in this volume come from nine women and are arranged, for lack of a better way, temporally in the order of our birth. Unlike a usual academic collection of essays, ours will not attempt a summary of the enclosed pieces. To summarize them would limit the scope of interpretations, and we believe that most of the implications are best left to the readers to explore. However, we would like to foreground a few themes in conjunction with the individual pieces, thereby placing the stories and the authors' reflections within the major political events of that era. Our hope is to remind the reader of the need not to overlook the complex dimensions of the social and cultural contexts when they think of the political events they have repeatedly heard, read, or been told about.

Inescapably, our lives could not have been lived outside the realm and impact of such political events as the Anti-Rightist Campaign, the Great Leap Forward, Cultural Revolution, and so forth. However, most of the existing memoirs and various scholarly works about these events focus on such themes as ideological brainwash and state control. They assume a uniformed daily experience and portray life in the Mao era as lacking the possibilities of individual or personal growth. Our authors' narratives, on the other hand, while placing their younger selves and their experiences squarely within those historical moments, challenge these dominant themes and dichotomies by foregrounding and reflecting on the contradictions their own lives demonstrate.

Having grown up under the Mao era's gender equality policies, many of the authors address the impact of such state policies. Did such policies simply produce millions of men-like young women as many have assumed? In what ways did women benefit from the category of "youth" as opposed to "women?" How do we understand young women's preference of the former? Was it a totally gender-free category or did it manage to carry certain gender implications that were liberating to girls growing up female? What kind of social and cultural forces were at work that both mediated official ideology and further complicated these (and by extension many other) young women's lives? Was there a uniform way for women to become aware of their female identity? Our contributors invariably touch upon these questions and they echo and vary from one another as they reflect on their own experiences. Wang Zheng and Lihua Wang directly address the usefulness—and therefore significance—of the category of "youth." They write about the relationship between being a "youth" and being a woman in the production of their own sense of the self. Others, like Xiaomei

Chen, Jiang Jin, and Xueping Zhong, reflect on the role of their mothers in their coming of age as girls and young women. The similarities and differences among their mothers' own social and political positions are clearly reflected in their narratives, indicating the complexity of the gender education these young girls received. Naihua Zhang, Bai Di, and Zhang Zhen, among others, tap into the meaning of female friendship and female-only activities in which they were not forced into a rather rigid gender divide early in their lives. By contrast, we read about Yanmei Wei's reflection on her experience in coming of age as a female in the post-Mao era, in which she encountered a more blatant demand for girls to be "like girls." We leave it to the reader to ponder the implications of these experiences and the authors' reflection.

Quite a few pieces in the collection—Naihua Zhang's, Xiaomei Chen's, Wang Zheng's, and, to some extent, Xueping Zhong's— tell of the authors' experience as a "sent down" girl. Unlike the film *Xiu Xiu: A Send-down Girl* (1999), in which numerous details about Xiu Xiu's experience are represented with problematic assumptions—we point this out precisely because most viewers in the West tend to mistake the film as yet another accurate historical representation of the true experience of the Chinese rustication generation—the authors who write about their own sent-down experiences represent theirs in a much more diverse and less simplistic manner.[21] Naihua Zhang tells a moving story of her friendship with two rural women. Her story both narrates her own positive psychological growth in the northeastern corner of the country and manifests the various contradictions of the times: the rural/urban divide, the ideological fervor whose spell many city youngsters were under vs. the relative lack of ideological control on the part of the peasants even during the Cultural Revolution, the relative freedom she was able to enjoy by being among peasants, the friendship she developed with two rural women and the ultimate rural/urban difference that set them apart, and many more. Wang Zheng also reflects on the significance of the collective experience of groups of young women who did not fail to appreciate their own femininity under the ideological dominance of gender equality, which presumably encouraged women to be like men. These narratives, together with Xiaomei Chen's and Xueping Zhong's, all echo the various voices from the former sent-down youths: many of them believe this experience was especially valuable to their growth as individuals. It is the task of those who have looked upon the rustication of urban youth only as a negative massive movement within the Cultural Revolution that destroyed the lives of the urban youth to fully apprehend the reflections of the ones who experienced it firsthand.

In telling their experiences during the Cultural Revolution, Bai Di, Lihua Wang, and, to a varying degree, most of the contributors, all challenge the simplistic notion of the ideological brainwash in the Mao era. Was the "Mao discourse" always used in the sense that it was meant to be used? What happened when various "revolutionary" clichés and expressions came to be applied by the youngsters in their daily and social activities? How do we understand the complex linguistic transactions that invariably altered the meanings of the political language of a supposedly highly controlled place and time? Our authors do not shy away from these difficult and yet important questions. Nor do they fail to recognize the irony and contradictions their own experiences indicate when it comes to the social dimensions of the relationship between the official discourse and individual's encounter of it.

Culturally, most people condemned the Mao era for unleashing "evil" forces that destroyed the "traditional culture," cultural traditions, and influences of Western cultures. Was it as simple as that? Were there any kind of social forces at work that, for better or for worse, continued certain cultural traditions and mechanisms, leaving a much less clear-cut trace of experiences in people's lives? If so, what were they and how did they continue to exist? And what impact did they have on the lives of these young women? Additionally, what forms of media continued to exist that invariably complicated the life experience of these young women? Conversely, was there anything positive in the Mao era's "new culture" which was much entangled in the lives of our young selves? What kind of contradictions do their experiences manifest? One area where these questions were addressed, albeit indirectly, and where various contradictions existed was the relationship Zhang Zhen, Bai Di, Xueping Zhong, and Wang Zheng had with books. In addition to books, the presence of other forms of modern media and entertainment, such as film or spoken drama, also played a complex role in, to echo Zhang Zhen, the production of the senses of these young women.

In short, reading these narratives against the larger social, cultural, and political contexts in which the various experiences were lived, we hope the reader is able to discover these memoirs' larger social and historical significance and the fact that such significance exists, precisely, in the contradictions these narratives invariably present.

While each piece has a central theme, many of the details and their implications can be seen as echoed, challenged, and at times contradicted by other pieces. Together, they indicate the layers of issues that make them share with and differ from one another, signifying, once again, the complexity of and contradictions within a time when profound and concrete social and political changes affected everyday lives. It is in this sense that some of the seemingly mundane moments in our childhood years become crucial in our memory and, by extension, in our understanding of the Mao era.

We hope that this collection of essays will serve as the beginning of a dialogue for future studies, debates, discussions, and understanding of the Mao era. As such, we hope it will provide some points of departure for further explorations of various difficult issues regarding the very mixed legacy of the Mao era, both in relation to women and in relation to modern Chinese history.

NOTES

1. We would like to thank Rey Chow, David Greenberg, Susan Greenberg, Malcolm Griffith, Dorothy Ko, Lin Chun, and Zhang Zhen for reading and offering valuable comments on the introduction. Thanks also go to the Asian Studies Program of New York University for inviting Xueping Zhong to present the introduction at the "Workshop on History" in March 2000.
2. By "intellectual" we mean the reflective nature of the memoirs. More specifically, we mean our collective awareness or consciousness of the complex questions involved in the writing of our early lives.
3. Between our meeting and the publication of this volume, published articles have discussed the problematic nature of these memoirs. See, for example, Kong Shu-yu, "Swan and Spider Eater in Problematic Memoirs of Cultural Revolution," *Positions* 7, no. 1 (spring 1999): 239–52.
4. As Chinese women, we cannot escape the rural/urban divide that affects the fate of millions of other Chinese women. Knowing this, we must make clear that much of our experience is unique to urban women, especially those from big cities.
5. By "recent" we refer to the Mao and post-Mao eras.
6. By "expectations of Western readers" we refer to the mainstream assumptions in the West about the Mao era, shaped mostly by its Western media, which expect any story about that era to be unfailingly dark and terrifying.

7. Someone wondered if the speaker had meant to say that it was the guards of the concentration camps who might still feel excited upon hearing Nazi music. However, this was not what he said.

8. Perry Anderson, *The Origins of Postmodernity* (London and New York: Verso, 1998), 112.

9. Zhang Zhen, "The Production of Senses in and out of the 'Everlasting Auspicious Lane': Shanghai, 1966–1976," in this volume.

10. Wang Zheng, "Call Me *Qingnian* but Not *Funü*: A Maoist Youth in Retrospect," in this volume.

11. The political history in the post-Mao era, especially after the 1989 student democracy movement, has not allowed an open and serious discussion of the perils of the Cultural Revolution. At the same time, a close look at what has been published in China complicates the general impression left by the much publicized arrest of Song Yongyi, the librarian from Dickinson College who traveled to China to collect publications from the Cultural Revolution. Although there is no openly organized collective discussion and reflection on the lessons of the Cultural Revolution, increasing publications can be found in magazines and even monographs in which untold stories about the Cultural Revolution are being told. Among them is a magazine called *Huang He* (Yellow River), which has published articles related to the Cultural Revolution. What is interesting about the pieces found in this magazine is that some of them are able to present the historical context and individuals' entanglement with the Cultural Revolution in a more complex fashion.

12. Of course, part of the reason is because the CCP's regime continues to bar an open examination and reflection on the Cultural Revolution, which, in turn, results in a weak (not lack of) critical public discourse. At the same time, the dark age narrative of the Mao era in the United States continues to be fed by a popularly accepted negative image of China as a whole. Needless to say, it has to do more with internal politics in the United States than with an informed understanding of China and its complex history.

13. John Fitzgerald, "In the Scales of History: Politics and Culture in Twentieth-Century China," *Twentieth-Century China* vol. 24, no. 2 (April 1999): 1–28.

14. Ibid., 39.

15. Ibid., 42.

16. Joan Wallach Scott, *Gender and the Politics of History,* rev. ed. (New York: Columbia University Press, 1999).

17. Elisabeth Croll, *Changing Identities of Chinese Women: Rhetoric, Experience, and Self-Perception in Twentieth-Century China* (London and New York: Zed Books, 1995), 3.

18. Here we use the word *modernity* without any value qualification but a reference to a historical orientation in modern Chinese history. Whether or not China's pursuit for it should be questioned is not what we are concerned with in this collection.

19. Similarly, by Chinese women struggling to become a "modern subject," we refer to the modern journey Chinese women have taken in modern history. We do not suggest, in other words, that there is a standard modern subject position that Chinese women struggle to become.

20. I would like to thank Lin Chun for this point.

21. *Xiu Xiu: A Sent-Down Girl,* directed by Joan Chen, was released in the United States in 1999. It has been banned in China, allegedly due to the Chinese authority's annoyance toward Chen, who had tricked them during the shooting of the film. It tells the story of a high-school girl from Chongqin who was sent to the countryside in 1975. While the film clearly tries to be a political allegory, it fails miserably in its attempt. It presents yet another victim of the rustication experience without giving Xiu Xiu any agency within that experience. What is more, her overnight change from a pure young girl to a whorelike woman conveniently falls into traditional stereotypes of women—their being either pure or whorelike. This aspect alone adds much insult to the rustication generation, especially the women. It is beyond the scope of this introduction to critique this film, but we do want to state our position on it.

Some of Us

NAIHUA ZHANG

IN A WORLD TOGETHER YET APART
Urban and Rural Women Coming of Age in the Seventies

During the winter holiday of 1998, I flew to Detroit to spend the holiday with my family.[1] After dinner, I picked up *World Journal*, a major Chinese-language newspaper in North America, to read and relax. A half-page advertisement caught my eyes. It was about a writing contest sponsored by the newspaper to mark the thirtieth anniversary for the movement of the 16.23 million urban youths who went to the countryside during China's Cultural Revolution (1966–1976).[2] The writing contest was for the former *zhishi qingnian* (educated youths), or *zhiqing* in abbreviation, to write about their experience in a foreign land.

At first, I could not believe my eyes. I knew the word *zhiqing* is a highly charged term. It covers a highly diverse group of young people whose experience ranged from those working in production teams *(cha dui)*, earning work points like their fellow peasants, to those who were sent to farms *(cha chang)* run by the state or discharged army men earning monthly wages. Geographical locations, living conditions, and personal experiences differed greatly. Yet, to those who once belonged to this group, zhiqing also represents a common identity and immediate bond, a major shift in their young lives, a transition from the city to the country, and an extraordinary experience in that unusual, fervent, and turbulent time. There are numerous fiction and nonfiction accounts of zhiqing and their lives, various zhiqing associations or groups, and stores, farms, restaurants, and products named after zhiqing. I would not be surprised to see more activities organized in China around the thirtieth anniversary of the zhiqing movement. Yet I did not expect that I would see this ad in the United States, a place so far away from where the movement took place thirty years ago.

As I read the ad, it dawned on me that it was only fitting that an event like this was being held in America. The contest asked the participants to write about their *yang cha dui* (literally, to insert into the production team in a foreign country) experience. Yes, to come to a different land and culture to face all the new challenges *is* a major transition in life, just like going down to the countryside; many of us here were former zhiqing, and who we are, how we view and relate to the world, is inevitably shaped by our very experience as zhiqing. This experience has so much affected those who experienced it that its thirtieth anniversary could not be let go without being marked or remembered in North America, or in any other place where former zhiqing disperse.

And the memory of it will never fade; the emotion toward it will never dilute, no matter how many years have passed and no matter where we are. Here in this wintry night, halfway across the globe from China, the ad opened the floodgate of my memory of the eight years I spent away from my home city, Beijing, in a remote village in northeast China.

My memory is a nostalgic one. It is about finding a home away from home. It is about finding myself—as a girl/young woman and as a zhiqing, with my specific family class origin.[3] And it is about taking the journey to womanhood with two young rural women, about the friendship that developed among us, which bound our lives together even though we ended up going separate ways. My story begins in the summer of 1966, with the outbreak of the Cultural Revolution, an upheaval that lasted ten years and changed the lives of millions overnight.

THE CULTURAL REVOLUTION AND "FAMILY CLASS ORIGIN"

In 1966 I was finishing my first year at an elite all-girls middle school in Beijing. The quiet, usual scene of girls reading under peach trees in the campus orchard was suddenly replaced by the energy and excitement of the revolution. One scene that sticks in my mind is a group of young female students storming through the corridors of our classroom building—in green army uniforms with their sleeves rolled up, Sam Browne belts over their jackets— the stomping of their bare feet (a sign of rebellious spirit) on the cement floor resounding through the halls as they passed. They were among the more radical and violent of the Red Guards. They did not show any greater tenderness or mercy than their male coun- terparts in their beating of "hooligans" (people caught off the street who were allegedly engaged in indecent behavior) and their cru- elty toward our school principals accused of being capitalist roaders (a cadre accused of having deviated from the correct line of Mao Zedong).

Many of the students at my school came from the families of the Chinese Communist Party and government officials; among them were the daughters of former PRC President Liu Shaoqi and General Secretary of the Chinese Communist Party Deng Xiaoping, the No. 1 and No. 2 targets of the Cultural Revolution. The school was a mirror reflecting the political struggles at the highest levels. Students formed different organizations based on their political points of view. Whenever a parent was "exposed" as a "capitalist roader" with his or her name appearing on the big character post- ers, the status of the daughter would fall overnight. *Jiating chushen* (the class origin or status of one's family) became a core status for students: it determined whether you could be a member of the privileged Red Guard, join *da chuanlian* (board a crowded train for free travel to other parts of the country to "establish revolutionary ties"), or be outcast from all these activities.

My father was chief engineer and manager of a British-owned coal mine before the Communist Party's takeover in 1949. While he remained a chief engineer afterward, he was termed a "person with counterrevolutionary antecedents" in later political campaigns. As this information was brought to the open at the onset of the

CR in our school, my status changed suddenly—from a popular student in my homeroom class to an outcast, subjected to discrimination and ill treatment. What really shook me to the core was not this status shift, but one single event in the 1968 preparation for the celebration of National Day.

By then, after more than two years' turmoil due to the Cultural Revolution, some order was brought back to school and the initial practice of overt discrimination against people without a "revolutionary class origin" had ceased. The new policy was that people should be judged by their own deeds rather than their family backgrounds. Students also started to graduate or leave school. As universities were closed and employment opportunities were limited due to declined production caused by the disruptions of the CR, a large number of secondary students were sent to the countryside or to state farms to receive reeducation from the poor and lower-middle class peasants. This marked the beginning of the "going up to the mountains and down to the village" movement. We knew that we could soon be leaving Beijing and might never return, so we all wanted to participate in the October 1 National Day parade and celebration in Tiananmen Square for what might be our last time. That year, our school was assigned to be part of the "sea of people" on the square, holding paper flowers to produce changing patterns or words that provided background for the passing parade. After the parade ended, we would surge to the Tower of Tiananmen to see Mao—the dream of most youngsters at the time.

I was elected by my homeroom classmates to participate in the event—by then I was an elected member of the leading committee of my homeroom class, but my participation was denied by the committee leading the whole class. The few of us who were excluded had some "family problems." This incident had a chilling effect on my psyche. Tiananmen Square can hold up to 100,000 people—100,000 people! And I could not be one of them, could not be a drop of water in the sea. I bitterly asked myself, "Am I asking for too much? Did they think that I would engage in sabotage or worse?" I remember the remark of a schoolmate who had a family background similar to mine: "When people learn about your 'class origin,' they would always maintain some degree of suspicion toward you." That remark really hit home. I felt that nobody would ever really trust me and I would never have any future in my life, no matter what I did or how hard I tried.

It was with this deeply buried sense of doubt and hopelessness about my future that I left Beijing on March 22, 1969, boarding a train with four classmates to begin our long journey to a remote village in the Manchuria township of Momoge in Zhenlai County, Jilin Province, in northeast China. I was seventeen years old.

THE VILLAGE AND VILLAGERS

After a twenty-plus-hour journey by train, a ninety-*li* (one li is about half a kilometer) freezing and bumpy ride in an open truck on the dirt road, and then another thirty-li horse-drawn cart ride, we finally arrived at Baxizhao, our village. It was already dark, and we were invited into a team leader's home. The red tea offered to us tasted like alkaline water, and the room seemed so dark that I could hardly see what was not directly under the large kerosene lamp hanging from the ceiling. It took me several days to get used to the lack of light at night. Electricity would not come until four years later.

We soon discovered that our collective production team had a lot of (unproductive) land but not enough hands to farm it. The village was surrounded by stretches of degenerated grassland and fields of sandy or saline-alkaline soil. They did not produce much, which was why our team was poor, and as a result, there was the need to cultivate more land, the so-called *guangzhong boshou* (extensive cultivation with meager harvest) farming method. The villagers were happy to receive five female and three male students to join them. Our welcome was also cushioned by the special grain ration that came with us, which meant that we would not compete with the local peasants for limited and rationed resources. Ultimately, the villagers embraced us because they were honest, down-to-earth, and warmhearted people who came to treat us with a healthy degree of curiosity, and a lot of understanding and encouragement.

Life was hard for us. We had to learn everything about farm

life: how to husk and process millet, *gaoliang* (Chinese sorghum), and corn with a stone roller pulled by a donkey, and how to cook processed cereal in a huge pot on a kitchen range using grass or crop stems as fuel. During summer, work went from sunrise till sunset, more than fourteen hours a day. After a day's work, my muscles ached all over. It was very hard to get up in the morning when the leader's shout of "Time to work!" resounded in the otherwise quiet village as he walked to the field with a hoe on his shoulder. Sometimes, when some of us were too tired to work or were not feeling well, we skipped work for a few days. The team leader would then come, half begging, half urging: "Please go to the field, the crops cannot wait."

It didn't take long for us to get acquainted with the villagers and we got along well. We followed the local customs, addressing our peers by their nicknames, calling middle-aged married persons "elder brother" or "elder sister," and the elderly "grandpa" or "grandma." They addressed us by our full names—just as all students would be called at school. Young girls referred to us as "sister."

We were housed in the "commune house." This house, collectively owned by the team, was part of a cluster of community construction called "commune court." It included a storehouse, stable, pig-feeding house, a big yard to park the horse-drawn carts, and a well in the center for villagers to fetch water and to water draft animals. Peasants gathered in the court before and after work, so we had a lot of opportunity to mingle. They dropped in on our rooms to visit, especially our peers, and they lent a hand whenever we needed help fixing our tools, sharpening our sickles or grass-cutting knives, or doing other farm tasks. Since each had to tend his or her line(s) of crops during hoeing or harvesting, those who finished first often turned back to assist those who were behind, so we would rest together at the edge of the field. On long, cold winter evenings, the young men guarding the threshing ground brought us corncobs and we would light the stove and make popcorn.

After the first harvest came the "idle winter months." We went back to Beijing to spend the month of Chinese New Year with our families. When we came back we learned that while we were away the team had a meeting and ranked every laborer on the team. At that time, all the production teams were learning a new way of recording work points and ranking laborers, which was developed by the Dazhai brigade in Shanxi Province, a model for agricultural production. Based on this system, each person's workday would be recorded throughout the year. At the year-end team meeting, laborers would rank themselves and then they would be evaluated by their peers. The higher the grade, the more work points one would earn for a day's work. Besides factors such as strength and farming skills, attitude toward work was another element of the Dazhai criteria. I was ranked a "first-grade laborer," the highest ranking for all villagers. Not all the male zhiqing got this ranking. I knew I did not compare to the older and stronger farmhands, but I learned farm work fast. I was determined, did not give up easily, and I was also extremely healthy and never missed work. I guess these were the factors that contributed to my first-grade labor ranking by the peasants in my absence.

This incident made me realize that the villagers did not really care what my family class origin was when evaluating my work, nor were their views easily swept by the quickly changing political winds. Living their lives in a remote village in northeast China, with little involvement in the welfare system of the state, they were more independent in their minds and maintained their unique perspective. They watched what a person did and determined whether the person was honest, could "eat bitterness," and was willing to toil. Their groundedness, wit, openness, and trust were sharp contrasts to what I had experienced in Beijing, the center of fierce political struggle and division among people. It was in Momoge that I began to heal from the discrimination I had experienced in Beijing. I began to regain hope, confidence, and trust in people. I also got to know the peasants and the countryside, knowledge essential to a better understanding of agrarian China. In some memoirs or literary works, zhiqing are portrayed as victims of corrupt local officials, and the period in the countryside is seen as a waste of time in their lives. I have always felt a deep sense of gratitude and nostalgia toward the people in my village, a place I devoted a full eight years of my youth and from which I have also gained much in return.

ZHIQING

I have to admit that our zhiqing status granted us some privileges in our lives in the countryside. When we first went to the countryside we had no idea what the future held for us. We thought we would be there forever. But the villagers were very clear on this matter from the beginning: "You are students from Beijing, you are different from us. You will all go back sooner or later."

In many ways, we *were* different from them. We were guaranteed a provision of 650 *jin* (one jin is a bit over one pound) of unprocessed grain a year, while peasants were entitled to only 360 jin in the case of a bad harvest. Many peasant families were poor and in debt. They had no cash to spend and had to rely on the sale of a few eggs from the chickens they raised to buy household necessities such as salt. Since we only needed to support ourselves, and because we had support from our families, we could occasionally treat ourselves to the thick, hard crackers sold at the village store. This was a welcome alternative to our staple foods: sorghum, corn, and millet, and they were a treat that villagers' children could hardly afford.

We were different also because we had no personal connections to the local people or families of our own to support. We were conscientious about work and loyal to the collective. Our shrewd team leader thus soon learned to entrust us with certain tasks. He assigned one of my friends to keep watch in the melon field, as muskmelon was a hot item from the team vegetable garden and many of them disappeared before they could ripen and be distributed to peasant households. My friend was so conscientious about her job that she not only did not touch the muskmelon herself (it was the common practice for melon watchers to treat themselves with melons—after all, this was one of the incentives!), but she also refused anybody who stopped by the team vegetable garden demanding a treat (a too common practice contributing to the loss of melons). A frustrated and mean-spirited woman thus cursed loudly when passing by our open window: "Little Stingy! They are not your family's (melons)!"

The team once needed somebody to make tofu for the villagers and to feed the team's pigs using the tofu residue and other feed. The team leader told me about this job after we returned from our vacation in Beijing and I agreed to do it. I later learned that the man who had been making tofu refused to take on the additional task of feeding pigs. The team leader did not want to confront him directly, and it probably would have been difficult to get another villager to risk offending the tofu maker and take on more work. A willing and unsuspecting zhiqing was a perfect solution to the deadlock. I received a lot of support for taking on this assignment. The team's stockman taught me how to make tofu. Since he was up all night taking care of the horses, he would begin the long process of grinding soaked soybeans after midnight. When I got up early the next morning, the grinding would almost be over, and I could continue the tofu making along with my other chores.

Because I had to use the mill to grind pig feed frequently, I needed to catch an elusive donkey from the herd to pull the mill. I often got help from older boys or grandpas for this task. An old grandpa also trained a young donkey for me so that I would not have to compete with other women, who needed the donkeys to process their grain. He would often drop in, watch the donkey pulling the mill round and round, and tell me stories about his youth when he was a master carter driving a cart drawn by seven horses (today a cart is drawn by four horses).

Zhiqing were also assigned to do other tasks, such as working as barefoot doctors or elementary school teachers, tasks that made use of their education and training. In the 1970s, "scientific farming" (adoption of new farming techniques) was promoted as a means to increase grain production, and Zhiqing became active participants in this effort. Among the new techniques was a newly developed bacteria manure called "920." Some zhiqing, including the zhiqing at the other production team of our brigade, began to cultivate the bacteria using glass jars and makeshift sterile boxes made from cardboard boxes. All the brigades were required to set up structures for scientific farming experiments. Our brigade thus established an experimental farming station in 1972 staffed by six people—two older men and four young women. One elder man was the deputy party secretary, who oversaw the affairs of the station while carrying out his duty at the brigade; the other older man handled draft oxen and our cart. The four young women, myself, another Beijing zhiqing from the nearby village, and two rural women, did the farmwork and other tasks, including making "920." The two men stayed with their families in the village while the four of us, from other teams, lived together in the brigade's house. The other zhiqing soon left to attend a vocational school for teachers, leaving me and the two young rural women to live and work together at the brigade.

Northeasterners often use the expression "sleeping on the same *kang*" or "ladling out of the same pot" to describe the closeness of relationships among people. This refers to the living arrangement in the northeastern countryside, where the major feature of every room is a huge kang (occupying half of each room), heatable bed used for eating, resting, sleeping, and doing other work while in a sitting position. This arrangement really brings people close to one another, and thus Guirong and Lifeng, the rural women, and I became close friends.

WORKING WITH MY FRIENDS, THE YOUNG RURAL WOMEN

Both Guirong and Lifeng stood out among their peers. Guirong , a year older than I, was the head of the Brigade's Women's Federation. Lifeng, a year younger, was head of her village's women's team. Both were skilled at farm and needlework. Guirong looked thin and frail but was known for the farming skills she learned from her uncle, a master farmer. To watch her thin out sorghum seedlings was a treat. In her hands, the long-handled hoe moved with high efficiency and accuracy; a few agile and neat strokes would clear out a seedling. There was never a wasted or redundant move. She was equally adept at sorghum harvesting, another farm task that sets farmers apart in terms of their skills. She was quick, yet extraordinarily calm and graceful, leaving behind small bundles of sorghum in the exact same shapes and intervals, making a well-patterned design if viewed from the edge of the field. I tried to learn her way of sorghum harvesting but could never quite get it.

Lifeng was sturdy, with a round face, round arms, and a shy little grin whenever she opened her mouth to speak. She was versatile in farmwork and had greater strength than both Guirong and me. She would vie with us for the most strenuous tasks. She was especially good with the draft animals—the oxen just responded to her commands better—so she became the natural carter for our oxen-drawn cart.

We often said to one another that there must have been some kind of lot or luck that brought us and kept us together. After a year at the brigade's experimental station, we were transferred to the brigade's small orchard, with me in charge. The orchard was located on a hillside next to Guirong's village, with a two-room earthen house overlooking rows of little Chinese pear-leafed crabapple trees. We had three oxen and an old-style cart with wooden wheels. We grew short crops such as beans and vegetables in between the small fruit trees. After working at the brigade orchard for a year, the commune wanted to establish an agricultural experimental farm on the site of the commune, with me as its head. I told the commune leaders that I wanted Guirong and Lifeng to go with me, and they happily agreed. We remained together along with a dozen other people—farmers from various brigades and a few local zhiqing—until I left the countryside to attend university three years later in 1977.

The five years we were together have left me many fond memories. My experience would have been quite different without them. From the time we got together, they showered me with the affection and generosity typically displayed by the country folks. Both Guirong and Lifeng were good cooks. Their plain husked gaoliang and maize cakes tasted much better than those we zhiqing made. There were no vegetables in the long, cold spring in our area, and villagers would eat their meals with uncooked Chinese green onions dipped in thick soybean sauce. I was not used to eating uncooked green onions at the time, so they brought from home dried vegetables and made dishes out of them just for me. I soon learned to eat the way they did and grew fond of northeastern home cooking, which, to my delight, has gained popularity in Beijing in recent years. They made cotton-padded jackets, cotton-padded pants, and numerous pairs of shoes for me. They made these shoes from scratch. They twisted hemp thread, pasted pieces of old cloth or rags together, and then stitched several layers of those to make soles, then they put the soles and the uppers together. I was still wearing these comfortable cloth shoes after I returned to the city, and I later had to tell them to stop sending me new ones because they wore out too quickly on cement. But I still remember the comfort these shoes brought to my feet and the warmth they brought to my heart.

Guirong and Lifeng were very knowledgeable and resourceful about farming and country life. They were also eager to learn and try new things and were extremely diligent in their efforts. I think we were alike in this respect. All three of us were enthusiastic about and fully devoted to what we did; we had a perfect mutual understanding in doing things and the three of us made a great team. During the first winter we were together at the brigade's experimental station, we were up at the break of dawn to collect manure for fertilizer. We first gathered the pigs' manure in the village, as pigs were not confined when there were no crops in the field. After breakfast, we would go to the grassy marshland to collect frozen cow dung. Since we were away from home and could not look after the "920" bacteria cultivated in the test tubes, we sewed small pockets inside our cotton-padded jackets and put the test tubes in them to keep them warm. We spent the entire day in the grassy marshland in order to collect a full cart of cow dung. For lunch, we would light a small fire to warm up and to soften the corn cakes that had turned as hard as stone in the subzero temperatures.

The winter of 1973 was very cold; my nose was frostbitten despite the warm fur hat I wore. My nose would turn pure white if I stood facing the wind. Clear, watery mucus would drip from my nose unnoticed. One day, when we were having supper, Guirong put down her bowl and stared at me sadly. I asked her what was the matter. Shaking her head, she said, "A young woman with a runny nose, how can you find your mother-in-law's house in the future?" A drop from my nose had fallen into my bowl as I was eating and I did not know it. Her seriousness and her saddened voice actually made me laugh. Fortunately, I recovered from the frostbite by the end of the winter, so Guirong did not have to worry anymore.

Together, the three of us did all kinds of work—one of the most strenuous tasks was throwing up mud and troweling the roof of a house. Once, the three of us troweled a five-room house in one day. After that, both Guirong and Lifeng had chest muscle pains from handling the mud, and the wrist of my right hand was swollen from pressing the trowel too hard for too long. I had to get an injection of medicine from the commune hospital. We did our work under various conditions. I still remember vividly how numb and cold my feet felt when they broke through the thin ice as we cut reeds in the pond at dawn, or when we rode on the horse-drawn cart on long trips related to our sideline production activities in the winter. It was always the feet that got cold first. They felt like two lumps of ice on my body, and the chills crept up to my heart and lodged inside my bones. I felt frozen from the inside out, and it took a long, long time to recover and warm up. There were also many obstacles to overcome. Our heavy, narrow wooden-wheeled cart got stuck in the muddy marshland easily when it was fully loaded with dried grass we had cut in the rainy fall season. When this happened, we would have to unload an entire cargo, get the cart out, and then reload it, wishing all the time that our cart had rubber wheels.

All this may suggest we had a hard time. Yes, we encountered many difficulties and endured hardships, but, all in all, we were happy. At that time, all organizations or projects had to be self-reliant. We had to support ourselves before we could have money to do experiments or other tasks. We were proud that, as a result of our efforts, both the brigade orchard and the commune experimental farm were doing well economically. We had our sweet harvests. For example, among the vegetables we grew between small fruit trees were three huge squashes born on the same vine, the largest was more than thirty jin. The local farmers joked with us: "Better keep a good watch over them. It would be like losing your heart if they got stolen!" Most important, we liked the challenges and we rose to meet them. The specific time and circumstances under which we lived provided opportunities for us to engage in a variety of activities and made our experience fulfilling, enriching, and empowering.

Because we were completely immersed in what we were doing

at the time, I don't think we gave any specific thought to what led us there. Now, in retrospect, I have begun to see how the CR ethos of equality and "men and women are the same" rhetoric, our autonomy in an all-girl setting away from home, and the prolonged, much protected, and privileged stage of youth all worked together to allow us to have these special and remarkable experiences.

GENDER AND YOUTH

When I first began pondering my experience of growing up as a girl, it occurred to me that unlike family class origin or zhiqing, gender was an aspect that I was quite unconscious of in my youth. This did not mean I was unaware of the fact that I was a girl. In some ways I was aware of gender and so were my peers. When writing compositions on what they wanted to be when they grew up, many female students dreamed about being "female scientists," "female engineers," "female pilots," and "female tractor drivers," etc. It was apparent that we were aware of occupational segregation, and we were inspired to take nontraditional gender roles—thus the emphasis on "female" for all the occupational roles mentioned above. No one mentioned anything about growing up to be a mother. One of the students wrote about wanting to be the wife of an ambassador in my middle school. This incident was picked up during the CR as evidence of how the bourgeoisie education of our school had corrupted innocent young minds: this female student desired a social status acquired through marriage to her husband rather than by her own making.

I guess my insensitivity toward gender came from the fact that as a girl I was never made to feel that I was inferior to or different from boys, either at home or at school. In both situations, the central criterion for evaluating a school-age child was whether the child was a good student. At school, girls took similar classes and engaged in all activities with boys. I was the elected head of my homeroom class from first grade on and later became the chairperson of the Young Pioneer Brigade for our elementary school of more than two thousand pupils. The Cultural Revolution's popular slogan, based on Mao's quotation, was "Time has changed. Men and women are the same. Whatever men can do, women can do, too." These words inspired girls and women to take unconventional roles and to enter male domains. For example, our commune's well drilling team was made up of young girls, following Dazhai's "iron girl" model. They worked on heavy equipment, moving from village to village to drill deep irrigation wells. Our all-girls brigade orchard and the commune experimental farm led by a female zhiqing were also the products of this specific historical context. In retrospect, I actually benefited from being both a zhiqing and a woman. My formal education as a zhiqing granted legitimacy to "scientific" farming experiments, and, in the "can do" atmosphere of the CR, women were encouraged to do what men did and more women were appointed to leadership positions.

Since I was the leader of a small autonomous group, we were even less restrained by the conventional sexual division of labor and so engaged in farming tasks typically carried out by men: highly skilled tasks such as sowing, plowing, winnowing, hand-feeding the fodder chopper, and strenuous tasks such as ramming home construction, earthen brick making, and cart loading. This enriched our experience. One of my most enjoyable experiences was riding the commune's riding horse. It knew how to "walk." When it took quick, steady steps, it felt as steady as sitting on a bench. And, when it ran, its long, shiny, black mane flew back, and the rapid clatter of its hoofs sounded like beating drums, adding to the excitement. I still remember the sense of freedom I felt when riding this beautiful red horse. Few women could have the luck I had to ride a horse in our area because access to horses was very limited.

The "men and women are the same" slogan also had a direct impact on the construction of my gender identity—in particular, my sense of femininity. Like many of my peers at the time, I wore baggy gray or blue outfits. I really did not like dressing up and was drawn to a simple, unadorned appearance and spirited images of girls and women typical of that time. Unlike many young people who grew up in the post-Mao China surrounded by increasing emphasis on differences between men and women, high interest in fashion and beauty, and commercialized sex in the media, I was actually quite "ignorant" about my body and the traditional sense of femininity. Among the many things Guirong and Lifeng made for me was what they called "little garment," a strip of white cloth worn like a bra except that it is flat and it tightens and flattens the breast. I knew local people consider it indecent and ugly for young women to show big breasts. But what Guirong and Lifeng told me was that the "little garment" would help me gather strength, especially when doing strenuous tasks such as raising a heavy bundle of millet to load the cart. I tried it and that seemed to be the case. So I wore it when I was there and even after I left the countryside. The first time I had any concrete idea about the concept of bodily shape was around 1982, when I was already back in the city and teaching in a university. I was on a trip with a younger student who had been in the countryside for a couple of years. Recalling her past experience in the countryside, she complained to me: "I really hate cha dui, it ruined my shape!" As she said it, it suddenly dawned on me that there existed such a thing as shape—it reminded me of myself hoeing in the field under the hot sun in the countryside—sometimes bare-footed and never wearing a belt. Matters such as looks and shape were just not things I was very keen on when I grew up.

I have to admit that while I was in the country I had little consciousness of gender division or gender inequality. It was easy to take gender equality—an ideal that was widely promoted—as the reality and regard problems as reminiscent of old systems and ideology that would erode with time. When I was in the countryside, I did not have the strong sense of women as a category and group as I do now. For example, as much as I sympathized with the peasant housewives, observing all the backbreaking and endless work they had to do, I viewed their sufferings as all rooted in the economic backwardness of the countryside, which I thought I was helping to eradicate through my work at the experimental farm. It never occurred to me that they and I were all connected as women.

All three of us, Guirong, Lifeng, and I, were also clinging to our youth, which, in a way, blocked us from developing a greater gender consciousness. Youth is not strictly a reference to age. Most important, it is marked by specific roles and status. In our area, a girl becomes a woman when she is married. The local people often referred to the three of us as *"san ge xiao gu niang"* (three little girls). Once a girl is married, she joins the ranks of *"lao niang men"* (old wives). Young women can be called *da gu niang* (big girls), or *da gui nu,* as the dialect goes, when emphasizing the maturity of a young woman and the qualities she is supposed to possess. But the fundamental difference is between gu niang (girl or young woman) and *xi fu* (wife). A common saying is: "it would be the end of it if a female marries" *(nu de yi jiehun jiu wan le).* Gu niang, especially da gu niang, is in a privileged position at her maternal home. She has a say in the household, wears better clothes, and is still doted on by her parents. Yet, as soon as she marries, she immediately becomes an adult, a xi fu—somebody's wife, a marginal figure in her husband's household. Guirong came from a large family of thirteen—her widower uncle and his three children lived together with her parents' family and her grandmother. She was the second oldest of nine children and the eldest daughter. When she went home (I often went with her), her younger sister and two cousins would visit with us, and her sister-in-law, who was Guirong's age or younger, would help her mother cook and do other household chores. She never mixed with us. It is no wonder that northerners use the term *gu nai nai* to refer to both the sister of one's paternal grandfather (for example, grand-aunt) and to the married (and unmarried) daughters of the family. In the case of the latter, it symbolizes the higher status of daughters in her maternal family.

To the young women in our part of the countryside, becoming a xifu also meant losing their identity. A married woman was commonly referred to as "so-and-so's xifu" by the parents-in-law, relatives, and other villagers. That was the way Guirong's mother addressed her sister-in-law. And the life of a peasant's wife was extremely hard. She had to get up before dawn to make breakfast for those going to the field. Besides preparing and serving three meals, she had to process the cereal; gather and prepare feed for the pigs, chickens, and other household animals; tend crops and vegetables in their own plot and garden; find time to make shoes and clothes for family members; and, of course, take care of the children. In summer, they also had to weed the millet field for the production team. Rural women had to endure more than impoverished lives in our area. For example, one of the local customs was to have hospitable hostesses at meals to make sure the guests' dishes and bowls were never empty and people could eat to their hearts' content. Guirong's grandma told me that for her generation of women, "If you had a husband who liked to drink, you would have to stand on cold floor for two or three hours on bound feet while they sat on hot kang drinking liquor."

Guirong and Lifeng desperately wanted to be like me, to have a paying job (nobody had any doubt that I would have a job in the future, even though we never talked about it) and enjoy the free standing and economic independence it would bring. With that, everything would follow. If this could not be actualized, their fate and future lives would be determined by whom they married. In that regard, their first choice would be to marry a wage earner rather than a peasant. Next best would be to marry someone with special skills or a position in the countryside, such as a rural doctor, vet, accountant, and so on—so at least they would not have to get up in the dark to prepare breakfast for him. These types of young men were the cream of the crop and were better matched with young women of high aspirations such as Guirong and Lifeng. To be a peasant wife would really mean no future for women like them.

In any case, none of us were thinking about marriage at the time. To me, it seemed to be too early and embarrassing to even think about such personal matters as marriage and dating. The uncertainty of my whereabouts in the future might be another factor that subconsciously made me brush away the issue of dating. Lifeng's mother wanted her to engage in an exchange marriage for her elder brother—that is, marry a man whose sister would marry Lifeng's brother in return, as agreed upon between the two families. Lifeng's brother was already over thirty at the time, way past the prime time for marriage. Lifeng' s mother was afraid that he would never be able to find a wife on his own because he came from a poor family headed by a widow. Lifeng rejected the arrangement vehemently. We wanted to achieve something with our experimental farm at the commune. I was a true believer in scientific farming as the way to improve productivity and the standard of living for peasants and felt that I could contribute to this end. We all wanted the farm to develop into a viable institution that would provide a future for all of us. So long as we postponed marriage and all the issues that came with it, we did not have to directly confront these aspects of being a woman. Years later, when I first experienced gender discrimination and inequality, it was also around the issue of marriage.

It was in the mid-1980s when I was doing graduate work in Beijing that I suddenly found I had involuntarily become part of a "social problem" identified by then Chinese Communist Party Secretary Hu Yaobang. I was part of the large number of young men and women displaced by the CR who remained single into their late twenties and early thirties. Hu called on all organizations to pay attention to this matter, and suddenly matchmaking services and organized activities aimed at bringing these people together boomed. The interesting thing about it was that in urban areas there were many more women than men in this group, and they were better educated and more accomplished. Though equally as displaced as their male counterparts, women had delayed marriage to pursue their education and careers and were therefore as old or older than many of the single men. This created a problem, as men often marry women younger than themselves. Moreover, in the changing political and social atmosphere of post-Mao China, the concept of "iron girls" or "superwomen" started to carry a negative connotation. What used to be these women's strength now turned into their disadvantage in the dating and marriage arena, where the majority of men wanted a woman who was weaker than and inferior to himself. And women usually desired a husband of equal, if not of better, quality or education and would not want to compromise their pursuit of career or other goals. I remember feeling annoyed when concerned leaders or elder acquaintances whom I hadn't seen for a while asked me, "Have you solved your 'personal problem' *(geren wenti)?*,"[4] meaning was I engaged or married. I often did not know what to say because I was thinking to myself, "What problem do I have?"

Well, that was another story that happened much later. When we were together, Guirong, Lifeng, and I had our minds set on what we were doing. However, we would find out that while we had shared aspirations and goals, we would end up with different fates.

THE RURAL-URBAN DIVIDE AND DISPARITY

Once, when I was home for my winter vacation, a Beijing friend was curious about my life with Guirong and Lifeng: "You live with them, are they dirty?" I was caught off guard by the question because the three of us blended naturally and easily. And they were definitely not dirty. As a matter of fact, when I was with them, my cotton-padded quilt and mattress had been taken apart and washed more than ever before. As either Guirong or Lifeng would stay at home to cook and do other work for the team, and they would find time to do things for the three of us, including washing all our clothes. I seldom got to wash clothes except when I was home on rainy days.

Our life together had an impact on all of us, we had all changed. I learned to do all kinds of farmwork and considered myself a good farmer. I planned and arranged farm activities year round (of course, with the help of my peasant partner) and took the lead in doing them (I was a *da tou de*, meaning "the one who takes the lead"). I adopted the local dialect and the peasants' ways of living and chatting to the point that I could pass as a northeasterner. One such episode took place in the winter of 1974, during a trip that our commune organized to have the production team leaders visit Dazhai, the agricultural model brigade. One of the team leaders got separated from the group during our stopover in Beijing, so I went to the Beijing train station to look for him. I was upset that I got scornful looks and slighted responses from the train station employees. When I told a cousin of mine about my experience, she said, "Didn't you know that Beijingers look down on northeasterners? You dress like a northeasterner, you speak with a northeastern accent, they must have mistaken you for a northeasterner." Yes, I had changed. I discarded the vanity and sense of superiority typical of city folks and became more down to earth. My life in the countryside changed my way of looking at the world and at life. Even today, my love for crops and other plants, my respect for and easy bonding with physical laborers, and my cherish of grain and other foods have their roots in the time I spent in the countryside.

Guirong and Lifeng changed, too. They adopted the personal hygiene habits of urban folks, such as teeth brushing and daily washing. They had clothes that were popular on Beijing streets: leather boots, long and wide woolen mufflers, and Dacron clothes that I bought for them in Beijing. They also made a trip to Beijing themselves, staying with me, touring the city, and shopping. As our experimental farm was much better off than their villages and since they did not need to pay for their families' expenses or debts out of their income from our farm, they had money to spend on themselves and had the autonomy and exposure to the outside world that few of their peers had. We studied together in the evenings. Guirong picked up books I had. Lifeng, who had very little schooling, began to learn to read and write. She had a little notebook with her and often took it out to review the words in it when she had a chance. We had shared dreams and aspirations and we had lived together like I would with my zhiqing friends.

But we were all aware, even though we did not talk about it, that our final destinies would diverge because of the fact that I was from the city and they were from the countryside. Due to the strict household registration system aimed at restricting rural migration to cities, it was extremely difficult for them to leave the countryside and change their rural status, while zhiqing were much more mobile, even though they did not have much direct control over where they would go, either. For my sake, Guirong and Lifeng wanted to see me get out of the countryside sooner because they did not see it as a place where zhiqing belonged. By 1975 the zhiqing movement had lost its momentum, many zhiqing were reassigned jobs in towns and cities, and Beijing zhiqing began to be allowed to return to Beijing for "health reasons"—in reality, a way to let Beijing youngsters go back to their home city. I stayed, not for some lofty or abstract ideal (I was extremely healthy, too), but because I had concrete things to do. My heart was tied up in the experimental farm to which all three of us had devoted ourselves.

But our dream was hard to realize. We had to give priority to economic self-sufficiency and experiment and research could come only after providing for the members of the farm. The conditions were also inadequate. For example, the small amount of land we had next to other production teams' fields limited our ability to produce hybrid corn seeds. Besides, the peasants did not recognize those seeds. I spoke at a commune meeting of production team leaders, urging them to buy them, but only a few did. I felt the peasants were just too conservative in their thinking and not open to new ideas. Progress was made, but very slowly.

The overthrow of the "Gang of Four" in October of 1976 signaled the end of the Cultural Revolution; even people in the countryside sensed big changes were coming soon. The university enrollment began again. I was already the last Beijing zhiqing in the commune. Many urged me to go to college, including Guirong and Lifeng. I realized that there was not much I could do for the experimental farm, and higher education had always been my goal, so I decided to apply. As I still wanted to do agricultural experiment and research, I put down the provincial agricultural university as my first school choice in my application form. Due to disruptions caused by political changes related to the overthrow of the "Gang of Four," the planned college entrance exam did not take place, and applicants were finally assigned to various schools by the local authorities. I was thus assigned to the provincial normal university, becoming one of the last group of "worker-peasant-soldier students."[5] When I asked a commune leader why I did not get the agricultural university, he said, "All agricultural colleges and universities [have the policy of] *she lai she qu* [recruiting students from rural areas and sending them back to where they came from after graduation]. You are a Beijing zhiqing, why make you come back to the countryside?" As a matter of fact, I knew I would be able to go to an agricultural research institute after graduation because I knew people at the regional agricultural research institute would want to have me. I was sure that I would make a good agricultural researcher and that would also allow me to remain connected to what I had been doing and to the place to which I felt deeply indebted.

Guirong and Lifeng were more on the side of the commune

leaders than on mine on this matter: "You can do anything well. It is time you go. Why would a zhiqing stay in the countryside?" My imminent departure was hard for all of us. Even though it was not totally unexpected, when it came it still seemed sudden, and it was hard to believe that this would be the end of our five years together. We had seemed inseparable. But Guirong and Lifeng were truly happy for me—and relieved, as they had begun to worry I would be left behind with them, which they felt would have an ill effect on my future. They immediately plunged themselves into preparations for sending me off, taking apart and washing my cotton-padded coat and my cotton-padded quilt and mattress and making me a new pair of cotton-padded pants, which were light with a thin layer of cotton and a checkered flannelette lining that neatly fit my legs. "Back in the city, you won't need to stay outdoors all day long and wear bulky cotton-padded pants," Guirong said.

They never showed any trace of jealousy, not even a tiny bit of resentment over the unequal opportunities and fate lying ahead of us, even though it was at that very point that I began to see clearly the privilege I had, the naked inequality and gulf laying between us. I knew that they were as capable as I was, if not more so, and deserved to have whatever chances I would have in life. This made me feel all the more guilty about leaving them behind with an uncertain future. The desire to help Guirong and Lifeng find a job preoccupied me completely before I left, and this was also the main reason I went back to Momoge during my first summer vacation. I talked to the commune leaders, one by one, about what would happen to Guirong and Lifeng. I emphasized to them that Guirong and Lifeng had worked for the commune for more than three years. If there were any chances for employment—for example, if the commune store needed new shop assistants or the county-run factories recruited workers—they should be the first to get the job. The commune leaders all agreed with me. Nobody could dispute the fact that they were outstanding and had delayed marriage and given their utmost to their work. But chances for employment for rural youths in our poor and remote area were extremely slim, and, despite their hard work, neither Guirong nor Lifeng had any personal connections to the commune leaders. Nor did I have any clout. If an opportunity ever came up, could Guirong and Lifeng beat the children or relatives of influential leaders in the competition? I refused to give up hope. As a matter of fact, I had never hoped so earnestly and hard that they would be granted their wishes; yet deep down I also felt hopelessly helpless, for there was nothing else I, or we, could do.

I left Momoge in January 1977 with nostalgia and a sense of guilt. The experimental farm was dismantled at the end of 1977, after all crops were harvested and accounts were settled. Guirong and Lifeng went back home and subsequently married. Guirong married the agricultural technician of our commune, a young man of Mongolian nationality who was a graduate of the prefecture agricultural college and a state employee. It turned out that he actually took the only quota our commune had for an agricultural college, the one I would have gotten if given the chance. I felt it was fate that he was given the opportunity I had desired and that Guirong had married him. Lifeng married Wanyou, a fine demobilized serviceman from my village. Wanyou was a good friend of us zhiqing, a frequent visitor of zhiqing's house before he join the army. He took delight in helping others and had a bright smile and hearty laughter. We all liked him. In pre-reform China, when there was very little mobility, joining the army was one of rural youths' few routes of upward/outward mobility. Servicemen were able to see the world. After marriage, Lifeng and Wanyou settled on a state farm in Heilongjiang Province, where the soil is richer and people's lives easier. I was comforted by the fact that both Guirong and Lifeng were happy with their husbands.

In the summer of 1992, during my first trip back to China since coming to the United States, I went to Momoge, a place I would never forget. Now a township, Momoge had changed a lot. The township (previously the commune) was new and the dirt road that ran through the center of the town was replaced by an asphalt road. There was even an ice-cream stand by the roadside. I was thrilled to visit Guirong, her husband, and their two children, now residing in the township. Guirong had just returned from a four-li bicycle trip to a pond where she had been catching fish to sell to help her family. Her face looked darker and thinner than before but immediately lighted up when she saw me.

I also went back to my village, where I made a point to see the crops. The land was all under family farming now. I found that hybrid seeds were now widely used and the crops were better tended than when I was there. I had to admit that science and technology in farming alone, as I had believed, could not solve the issue of poverty and other problems in the countryside. Land ownership, leadership, state and local policies, and many other factors must all play a role.

It hurt me to find that the peasants there were still living in great poverty. Most of them still lived in cracked earthen houses and wore ragged and faded clothes. After I had been to more places, I could now better assess the local living conditions. Zhenlai County is acknowledged as one of the five poorest counties in Jilin Province. And as I went from place to place during my trip, I discovered that there was a large gap between the prefecture city, county, township, and the village. There was more poverty every step down to the village, even though things were improving. Villagers now all had enough grain to eat. Our former production team leader told me, "Now every family has wheat flour to treat their guests, nobody eats millet when they have guests in their household." True to his words, in the two days I was there, I never ate millet. I actually missed it. At Guirong's maternal home, her married cousins and sister were all back because of my visit, and they slaughtered a sheep to treat me. Her uncle, the patriarch of her family, said to me, "guinu ["daughter," the way he addressed me, treating me as one of his own] have returned home, [we] slaughtered a sheep. Our family now owns sheep."

It hurt me to see that the rural-urban divide and the material gap between Guirong and me were still there after a decade and half. But I took comfort in the fact that time and distance had not affected our bonds, and we were as close as ever. Sitting on the kang at Guirong's house, with our legs crossed, we talked and talked as if continuing an unfinished conversation left from yesterday. Her two children, a boy and a girl, were fast asleep on the bare mattress, stretching out their arms and legs, wearing only their shorts. Her husband, Tiegang, was in the kitchen cleaning a big basin of small fish and doing other household chores. I had already gotten to know and like him. Guirong and I laughed when recalling the funny incidents of the past, and I shed tears when she told me about a tragic event in her family. That was one of the most cherished nights of my life. I had never felt so close to her and to that piece of land. I knew I would go back again and bring my American-born daughter with me. I wanted her to know the place and the people there, a place that is part of her mother's past and roots.

NOTES

1. I am indebted to my friends Susan Joel and Paula Palmer for their reading and editing of my drafts, and to Bai Di, Wang Zheng, and Xueping Zhong for their comments.
2. Called the movement of "going up to the mountains and down to the village" (shang shan xiaxiang), it was one of the most ambitious and drastic mass movements in the history of the People's Republic of China. It was propagated as a way for the youth to transform the backward rural China and to reform their own petty bourgeois world outlook. Scholars have pointed out that it was a means of reducing the unemployment pressure exacerbated by the disruption of production during the Cultural Revolution.
3. Jiating chushen in Chinese, determined by the political and economic status and the occupation of one's parents and grandparents. The Red (good) family class background included "revolutionary cadres," "revolutionary military officers," workers, poor peasants, and lower-middle peasants. The Black (bad) family class background included capitalists, landlords, rich peasants, counterrevolutionaries, and "rightists." This distinction was used as a way to stratify people and was seen as an indicator of one's political trustworthiness.
4. In Chinese, wen ti can mean either "problem" or "matter."
5. An educational practice during the Cultural Revolution when prospective students for colleges and universities were not selected directly from the graduating high school class but from young people who had served as workers, farmers, and soldiers for some time after graduation from high school.

WANG ZHENG

CALL ME "QINGNIAN" BUT NOT "FUNÜ"
A Maoist Youth in Retrospect

A few days before Women's Day, March 8, 1978, my five roommates and I were in our college dorm after class.[1] Each of us had just received a movie ticket from the administration. To celebrate Women's Day, our college was showing a movie free to all female faculty, staff, and students.[2] Staring at the ticket in her hand, Qiao, the youngest among us, protested: "Yuck! How come now we are counted as *women [funü]*?! It sounds so terrible!" Her strong reaction amused us. But we all agreed that we did not like to be categorized as women. For us, the contemporary Chinese term for women, *funü*, invoked the image of a married woman surrounded with pots and pans, diapers and bottles, sewing and knitting needles, and who hung around the neighborhood gossiping. Her world was filled with such "trivial" things and her mind was necessarily narrow and backward. We were certainly not women. We were *youth (qingnian)*, or, if you like, female youth, to which we had no objection.

Our discussion of the meaning of the label *woman* did not go much further that day, but it has emerged from my memory again and again during the past decade of my study of feminism. Each time, the scene in my memory has generated different questions for me to ponder. Did we internalize male cultural values to such an extent that we denigrated women the same way men did? What were the specific meanings of *funü* in the Mao era? Did our rejection of the term suggest any facets other than our internalization of patriarchal values? What shaped my perceptions of the terms *youth* and *women* in my early years? What was implied by the word *youth* to which we tried to cling? Scholars of Communist societies have often emphasized the manipulation of youth by the totalitarian states. But when "youth were identified most fully as agents of change for the whole society," how did this emphasis affect gender production?[3] Since in most societies young women are seldom identified as "agents of change for the whole society," how did Communist female youth fare with the officially sponsored identity of major agents of social change? These and many more questions led me to revisit my life in the Mao era.

Funü, women, who were they? When the word *funü* was used in the Mao era, it was often used in, or associated with, the compound noun *jiating funü*, family women-housewives. The rest of the women were in other categories, with respective proper names, such as female scientists, female workers, female engineers, female teachers, female drivers, female shop assistants, female students, female cadres, and female revolutionaries. Women in these categories with a prefix *"nü"* (female) enjoyed a much higher social status than housewives. The state mobilization of women's participation in socialist construction was accompanied by popularizing Engels's theory, which held women's participation in social production as the measure of women's liberation. When most urban women were thus "liberated" in the dominant political discourse, jiating funü, who had to devote their energy to family responsibilities, were excluded from the glorious rank of socialist constructor. They were seen as relics of the old feudal society. Accordingly, the term *jiating funü* soon acquired such derogatory connotations that one could not utter this word without contempt. My mother was among this marginalized, degraded, and rapidly shrinking social group in the Mao era.

But there were still many jiating funü-housewives when I grew up in the 1950s, and they were all mothers or grandmothers. On the first floor of a four-story row house in downtown Shanghai where my family lived, the four families sharing the tiny space were run by four housewives. My mother was illiterate and had small feet *(xiaojiao)* that used to be bound. Of the four housewives, only one could read, and she had small feet, too, even smaller than my mother's.

Since my mother was home, I did not have the opportunity to go to daycare or kindergarten. I always envied kids who held onto a rope to form a line when walking in the street with their teachers. They sang and laughed and had great fun with their little friends. I just stayed home and watched the four or more housewives in the neighborhood wash, cook, shop, and gossip.

The world of housewives was not without excitement and joy. Indeed, they had to go to their battlefield every morning, the market. Even with all kinds of coupons that rationed food equally for city dwellers, the quality and quantity of everyone's meals were not equal. If a housewife could manage to be first in line in the market, the best cut of pork would be hers. Otherwise, she might have to purchase a piece of lousy meat from pig breast with her half a jin monthly ration. Vegetables and fish were not rationed, but sold on a first-come first-served basis. The markets usually did not open for business until 7:00 A.M., but many housewives began to lining up as early as 4:00 A.M. Each took a little wooden stool and one or two bamboo vegetable baskets. Shoppers had to run between several lines, since each line was for just one item. A stool, a basket, and even a brick could hold one's place in the line. But she had to go to each place constantly, to chat with the women both in front and behind her to secure recognition of her place while she was away and to check if it would soon be her turn.

My mother, with her small feet, ran from line to line every morning. Often, she came back from the market with baskets of meat, fish, and vegetables that were too heavy for her to carry, especially on Sundays. I could always tell without her saying a word whether or not she got good stuff. She had a joyful smile if she got what she needed for her planned menu. And she was elated if that day the market had some rare delicacy and she was the lucky one who got it. Getting enough good food was a major part of her life. She had eight children and a husband (a picky one) to feed. Without guests, lunch was usually three to four courses (my father and some of my older siblings did not come back for lunch) and dinner was five to six courses. To feed such a big family well in a time of scarcity was a remarkable achievement.

In those years, I never consciously associated my mother with the term *jiating funü,* though I knew she was a housewife. The term *jiating funü* suggested many negative attributes that I did not see in my mother. I placed her in a different category. She was illiterate and could not read the newspapers that gave us new ideas. In fact, she did not even know how to say any of the new expressions, although she showed wonderful verbal memory by telling me many folktales and nursery rhymes. I have searched hard in my memory and can only think of one or two occasions when she said *renmin zhengfu* (people's government) and *Gongchandang* (Communist Party). That is all. Ignorance of the new socialist ideas should have qualified her as a backward woman, but I never judged her that way. Instead, what I saw in her was hard work and self-sacrifice. In my early teens, I once asked her, "Why didn't Mom go out to work when most women did? Mom could be selected as a model worker easily!" She replied, "Well, if I had gone out to work, you all would have had to eat in the canteens. The meals there are poor and more expensive." She paused a little, adding, "No one who went out to work has small feet." I lost words to continue the conversation. I knew her small feet physically tortured her daily, but I had never realized that they were also such a terrible burden on her mind. The oppression of old feudal society is still with Mom, I thought. Mom is a victim of the old society. I am a new person of the Mao Zedong epoch (a set phrase of the time).

My mother's small feet and illiteracy made it easy for me to identify her as the "oppressed." When my father blamed my mother for trivial things like forgetting to sew a button back onto his shirt and upset her, I would protest to my father. "Stop oppressing Mom, Dad! This is the new society. Dad should not oppress Mom any more." (In my family, the central content in children's moral education and the strictest rule held by my father in discipline was never to address seniors by pronouns "you," "they," "she," or "he." To show respect, to know your place, a junior should always address or refer to the older ones by kinship terms. This Confucian

etiquette became my second nature and mixed with my revolutionary speech.) Sometimes I would try to instigate my mother to re-
volt. "Mom, don't be afraid of Dad. Men and women are all equal.
Mom should say this sentence to Dad loudly." But Mother smiled
at me with a little embarrassment. "I don't know how to say those
words," she said. "I have a clumsy mouth." I could not understand
why her mouth was so clever when she told me all those fairy tales,
folk songs, and stories from her life. Since new phrases came out
of my mouth easily, I decided to be my mother's mouth whenever
new words were needed. Sometimes after I defended my mother,
she would say, "Fortunately, I have a little daughter to speak for
me." Father called me "a little protector of Mom." My fourth sister once told me, "Dad laughs when you criticize Dad. But once
when I tried to do the same, Dad got mad at me and scolded me
terribly. You are Dad's favorite. You can do whatever you want to."
I knew my father pampered me, his youngest child, his little pet.
Even my criticism sounded amusing to him. He must have seen
humor and irony in his little daughter's mastery of revolutionary
language.

Mother was the youngest daughter of a worker's family, and
she herself became a worker in a lace factory owned by Germans
at eight years old. She worked in the factory until she turned
twenty, when she married my father. Father was the youngest son
of a comfortable gentry family. Both of them were from Shandong,
the native place of Confucius. Their fathers, though of different
classes, shared a friendship based on a similar taste for wine and
an appreciation of each other's character. Drinking and chatting
in a bar one day, they found that one's daughter was two years
younger than the other's son, neither engaged. They delightedly
decided the marriage of their children right away.

My parents got married in 1930, when my father had already
acquired a desire for the new style of women, women with an education and natural feet. My father always openly complained about
this arranged marriage, which he had tried to resist. One day he
complained to me in my mother's presence, "Look, my greatest
misfortune is to have married your mother, who does not know
the pleasure of reading. She always interrupts me when I am totally

absorbed in my book." I replied right away, "That is the result of Dad's selfishness. If Dad taught Mom three characters a day since the day Mom married Dad, instead of just asking Mom to wash and cook, Mom could have long been literate. Didn't that Communist in the movie teach his wife to read? So no one is to blame but Dad self." Both my parents laughed. They knew what I referred to and what I meant.

We had all seen "The Revolutionary Family," a very popular film with a cast of first-class actors. The story was about a woman's life from the day she was carried on a wedding sedan chair in the late 1920s. She was illiterate and marrying a man she had never seen before, just like my mother. But her educated husband was a Communist, unlike my educated father, who was a Nationalist. The underground Communist husband taught her to read and write. After he was killed by Nationalists, she carried on his revolutionary task and brought up her three children as revolutionaries. When I saw on the screen that handsome Communist husband holding his young bride's hand, patiently and lovingly teaching her to write with a brush pen, I wished that that were the relationship between my parents. The only difference between my parents and this couple was that my father was a Nationalist. I concluded after viewing the movie that all the consequent huge differences between the two couples hinged on that one crucial difference. I assumed that there would not be such inequality between my parents if my father were a Communist. But if my father were a Communist, I would have been totally confused and would have lost the ability to direct any revolutionary words at him. Since he used to be a Nationalist, all the ideas and concepts that I learned from books and movies could be applied to our family case consistently.

Movies constitute a large part of my childhood memory. There were four movie theaters within a ten-minute walk from my home. The price for a movie was fifteen or twenty cents for adults, eight or twelve cents for children and students. When the whole school booked a movie, the discount price for each student was five cents. The Cathay Theater, one block from my home, had Sunday morning children's specials. Since my early elementary years, I spent many Sunday mornings there. Our school often booked movies there, too. Watching movies was a part of the teaching curriculum. All of the students lined up and went together to the theater. After each movie, our teacher would lead a class discussion, and then we were required to write an essay about what we had learned from the movie. Heroes and heroines in the pictures were our role models, and revolutionary movies were a guide to a revolutionary life.

My experience in film education had begun even before I started school in 1958. My second sister, Xiujuan, nineteen years older than I, was a factory worker. On her day off, she liked to spend time with me apart from helping my mother with housework. One warm, sunny day, she took me to see *Tens and Thousands of Rivers and Mountains*. This was a hot new movie about the Long March of the Red Army. I must have been four or five years old. It was the first time I had ever seen a war movie. I still remember the scene in which Red Army soldiers tried to cross the suspension bridge over the Dadu River. The bridge was made of cables connecting two cliffs high over the roaring river. The Nationalist army had removed the planks on the iron cables to prevent the Red Army from crossing the bridge. But the Red Army soldiers tried to cross it anyway. One after another, they grabbed onto the thick cables to crawl over the river. Bullets came at them from the fortress on the other side of the bridge. One after another, wounded soldiers who could not hang onto the cables any more fell into the swift current below. Having never seen death before, I was astounded by the violent, agonizing deaths amplified on the huge screen. My heart pounding madly, I struggled desperately with each soldier trying to hang onto the cable. Their ordeal became mine. They died but I remained alive.

On the way home from the theater, Sister Xiujuan took me to a food shop for a snack. She ordered a delicious fruit soup. It was a rare treat for me. I took a sip of the warm, sweet, refreshing soup and said, "The Red Army soldiers never had such delicious soup!" Sister Xiujuan smiled at me and replied, "No, they never had it. They endured all the hardships and sacrificed their lives for the sake of our happiness." It dawned on me that I owed my enjoyment of this bowl of fruit soup to those soldiers who had fallen into the river.

My indebtedness to revolutionary martyrs was reinforced after I began school. Movies, storybooks, and textbooks all described how revolutionaries sacrificed their lives so that we could live happily in the new socialist China. The red scarf that we Communist Young Pioneers wore was "a corner of our red flag that was dyed with the blood of martyrs." Wearing the red scarf over a white shirt, we Young Pioneers loudly sang our theme song, "Communist Successors:" "We are the Communist successors. Inheriting the glorious tradition of our revolutionary predecessors, we love our country and love our people."

I was obsessed with the idea of becoming a revolutionary. There was no other choice, since I definitely did not want to be the enemy of the revolutionaries or the despicable renegade. I wanted to be like the many heroes and heroines in the movies and novels. The most dangerous work in the revolution was underground work. Underground Communists were often arrested and horribly tortured to force them to talk. I fantasized about becoming a Communist underground worker. Taiwan was not yet liberated, and two-thirds of the people in the world were still living in darkness. I thought it very likely that I would be sent to do some underground work when I grew up. But, I wondered, can I endure the torture if I am arrested? I could not give an affirmative answer to my own question. I was afraid of many things besides pain. My mother used to raise chickens in our backyard. Once a rooster suddenly charged at me. I was so frightened that I climbed through a window to escape. In school, when our teacher placed sample trays of frogs and earthworms on our desks for us to observe, I closed my eyes tightly, feeling as if I were in hell. How can *I* pass the test of torture? This disturbing question generated the biggest anxiety in me until one day I found a solution.

In the third or fourth grade, I read many detective and spy stories. One story from the Soviet Union was about a German spy caught by the Soviet Intelligence. When the Soviets began to interrogate the German spy, he bit on the corner of his collar and died instantly. The Soviets found out that there was a tiny lethal pill sewed into the tip of his collar. I had never read anything like that in stories about Chinese Communist underground activities.

"The foreigners are more advanced," I thought. "I am sure when I grow up, our country will have this technology, too." The new finding relieved me immensely. My innate weakness could not inhibit me from becoming a revolutionary any more!

Why am I recalling these childhood experiences with fondness, the experiences that prove how thoroughly "brainwashed" I was by Communist propaganda, to use American mainstream language? Why are my feelings connected to these memories so different from those I experienced twenty years ago? Twenty years ago, when Chinese intellectuals began to expose and critique the horrible deeds of the Communist Party's dictatorship, I was thinking of those soldiers falling into the river and seeing their tragedy multiplied.[4] The party had betrayed all those martyrs and they had died in vain. I questioned the meaning of their sacrifice. I saw myself among a whole generation of youths who were cheated and used by Mao because he called on us to devote our lives to the revolution while he devoted his to power struggles. The ugliness of the actual process of revolution relentlessly mocked my naïveté in taking the beautiful dream of revolution as reality. I found myself reviewing my childhood dreams and adolescent efforts to be a revolutionary with deep ambivalence.

The overwhelming amount of literature exposing Maoist crimes both enlightened and confused me. The older generations were condemning the Maoist persecution. Many of my generation were repenting their inhumanity when they were Red Guards. Everyone who was talking, including the once victimizing Red Guards, was a victim scarred by the Maoist dictatorship. But I could not think of any example in my life to present myself as a victim or a victimizer. I did not know how to feel about my many happy memories and cherished experiences of a time that most vocal people now called the dark age.

Twenty turbulent years have passed since then. Changes in the world, in China, and in my location have all helped me to walk out of my confusion. There is no need to hide my positive feelings for much of my life in the Mao era. Instead, I have a historian's intense curiosity for understanding the historical and social background that shaped my positive feelings and enabled me to express my feelings against the dominant voices in the American post–Cold War discourse and Chinese post-Mao discourse. This presentation of my memories is the result of a twenty-year external and internal transformation that cannot be expounded in the limited space here. Perhaps one brief example can illustrate some experiences that assisted my reassessment of the Mao era.

Not long after I arrived in the United States, I met an American woman at a friend's home. She told me with apparent pride that her daughter was a cheerleader. I did not know what kind of leader that was. Hearing her explanation, I could not bring myself to present a compliment, as she obviously expected. I just hoped that my eyes would not betray my disdain as I thought to myself, "I guess this American woman has never dreamed of her daughter being a leader cheered by men." I feel fortunate that I was "brainwashed" to want to be a revolutionary instead of a cheerleader.

In the fourth grade, teacher Jiang asked us to write an essay on the topic of "What I Will Be in the Future." I am sure that all the schoolchildren in China were asked to write more than once on topics such as "My Dream" or "My Wish for a Career." But this was the first time I had written an essay of this kind. I liked the topic because I had much to say. I did not write about my fantasy to be a Communist spy in that essay. I guess by that time I already understood the party's expectations of the younger generation. Battlefields, guerrilla wars, and underground works were the past glories. My generation, born in the new society, definitely missed out on those romantic and adventurous experiences. Now we were expected to devote ourselves to the socialist construction. Chairman Mao said that our country is as poor as a sheet of blank paper, but that will allow us to paint the most beautiful new picture on it. Building a beautiful new China sounded like a pretty exciting project to me.

The essay reflected my mood quite well. I wrote that I wished to be a geological prospector who explores the mysterious primeval forests or uncharted land to find long-buried treasures (natural resources) for our country; or a farmer who makes our homeland a gorgeous tapestry; or a textile worker who weaves the most beautiful fabrics for our people; or a teacher who spreads the seeds of wisdom and fosters the growth of a forest of talented students; or an actress whose performance inspires her audience; or a doctor who cures the sick and rescues the dying. I concluded the essay by saying, "Whatever occupation I take, I will be a socialist constructor." I was pleased with my flowery essay because it genuinely expressed what was in my mind. I could not decide which one to settle on, and I wished to have a taste of all those occupations. These occupations (and many others that did not appeal to me, such as that of a scientist) were glamorously propagandized, and the descriptive words I used were widely circulated clichés at the time. We learned to write in the language of official discourse quickly. I believe many little girls and boys of my generation dreamed of being a geological prospector. Facing the Western embargo, China desperately needed to exploit its natural resources. Propaganda for recruiting young people to work in this area was very effective. When my neighbor's daughter was accepted by the geology department of a prestigious university, we all envied her for her future prospects of an adventurous life. The government's directory on the career choices of youth certainly shaped my desires.

But my desires seemed to be too extensive. Teacher Jiang read my essay loudly to the whole class as an example of poor writing, though without mentioning my name. "It is unfocused without a theme," she criticized. "No, I have a theme," I disagreed in my heart. "The obvious theme is that I want to be a socialist constructor!" Of all my essays in the elementary and middle school, I only remember this one because of the humiliation of winning the prize for the worst essay. To me, a historian, this valuable piece of historical evidence in my memory is illuminating. Before I had reached ten years of age, the subject position of a socialist constructor was solidly established. The socialist constructor was no doubt heavily constructed by the dominant political discourse. But to a girl, was this discursive position more oppressive and limiting than that of a homemaker, a position no less powerfully constructed by the dominant discourse in the United States during the same period? Was brainwashing girls to become young vanguards in socialist construction more oppressive and limiting than brainwashing girls to become cheerleaders for football games? No.

The image of a socialist constructor was gender free. Coexisting with traditional gender expectations of labor division, this dominant gender-free discursive position created legitimacy for women to cross gender boundaries and enabled girls' personal development. The theme of my essay was to be a socialist constructor, a category that would allow me to go in any direction. In fact, I seldom thought of myself as a girl, a category that did not mean much to me when the prevailing slogan was to be a "socialist new person." Once I was striding on the wall of our backyard to get a good view of our neighborhood. My mother called, "Get down! How can you little girl climb the wall? What terrible manners!" I looked at her without budging an inch, retorting in my mind, "Mom is just feudal. Why can't a little girl climb the wall?" At school, girls and boys shared in all activities, including sports. I jumped and ran like boys. I got into fights with boys. Nothing in the formal curriculum reminded me of my gender. I was a student and a member of the Young Pioneer League, who was going to be a new youth of the new China.

Despite my sheer unawareness of gender, a gendering process was taking place quietly in the realms beyond the reach of official ideologies. Much that I experienced in the subcultures or outside of the public institutions shaped my subconscious sense of femininity. My strong conviction in the official ideology that "male comrades and female comrades are the same" and my perception of being a nongender youth coexisted with an unconscious conformation to feminine norms and an eagerness to establish my femaleness in a heterosexual world.

When I walked into the hallway of our row house one day, I saw my neighbor Mother Huang tell something to three women on the first floor, one of whom was my mother. Mother Huang spoke in a low, secretive voice with a sneer. The other three women listened with apparent fascination. I passed by indifferently, but when I turned the corner of the hallway, where they could not see me, I stopped and listened. I have excellent hearing. My ears were especially sensitive to whispers and secretive tones, perhaps a result of training by Mother Huang, who was an informed source since her husband was the gatekeeper in our lane. Gossiping about neighbors' personal troubles and family feuds gave a sense of moral superiority to Mother Huang, who used to be a washerwoman in a brothel and was still washing clothes for some neighbors to subsidize her husband's meager income.

Mother Huang was now gossiping about Peiying! Peiying was a high school girl living with her paternal aunt in the number 7 row house in our lane. I never talked to her, but I liked her a lot. She walked in and out of the lane with a gentle sweet smile. She was always dressed neatly and in good taste. Fair skinned and slender, she was very pretty. What had happened to her?

"Her teacher asked her to coach a naughty boy in her class. The boy, who is one year younger than Peiying, often went to her home to do homework with her help. But who would expect, he made her pregnant! Now she has to marry that little rascal!" Mother Huang's sarcastic and vindictive tone implied, "That serves her right!"

At the time, I was about nine years old and knew that a man could make a woman pregnant, but I did not know how. Of course, this gossip did not help solve the puzzle, a puzzle I had nowhere, or no way, to ask for an answer, a puzzle I had to figure out someday by myself. When I was seventeen, I finally put pieces of the puzzle together and reached a moment of revelation. But many of my friends did not learn the answer until their wedding night, just like my mother. At nine, I was unimaginative. I could not imagine what Peiying did with that boy. But judging by these women's reaction, I could tell right away that her pregnancy was disastrous. Soon, events confirmed my assessment. On Peiying's wedding day she was dressed up like a bride, but unlike other brides, she was sobbing in such deep grief it seemed like she was going to a funeral. I can still see her vividly today, wearing a bright red flowery silk scarf and holding a white handkerchief to wipe away her tears. Peiying sobbed her way out of the lane, under the stares of many women and children. She broke my heart. Such a lovely girl to end up like this!

Worse still, that little rascal soon proved to be an abusive husband. Each time he hit her, she cried back to her auntie's home. Sometimes Peiying would run out of the house screaming and yelling, with her hair all messed up and her clothes crumpled. I never saw her gentle maiden smiles again. Peiying divorced the man when her son was two or three years old. Hers was the only divorce in our lane of eighty-two households.

Later, whenever I came across the word *zhencao* (chastity), I would think of Peiying. I knew all too well that losing zhencao meant a girl's doom. I don't remember if I vowed not to let a man ruin me like Peiying did, but I suspect her experience had something to do with my aloof manner toward boys.

I never saw Peiying's case as feudal oppression, a phrase I effortlessly applied to my mother. Peiying was an educated youth in the new socialist society, an image that had no association with feudal oppression. There was no new language to describe Peiying's trouble. Even if at the time I did come across official material on marriage and love, the common cautionary tales to guard women against the pitfall of losing chastity would not help demystify the taboo, but only reinforce it. There was certainly no such term as *sex-gender system* available to me. Peiying's trouble was described and commented on by housewives in the neighborhood, who were a large part of her trouble. I felt extremely sorry for Peiying for subjecting herself to so many gossips and so much shame. But at no time did I wonder why she had to endure such humiliation for her pregnancy or why she had to marry that rascal. Every adult took it for granted that that is the way of life. A little revolutionary like me could not think otherwise. Although I disliked Mother Huang's and other gossiping housewives' pettiness, their gossip demarcated clear boundaries for me.

Little girls became successors of the old sexual morality as easily as they became successors of revolution. After years of free association with boys in elementary school, we self-imposed gender segregation in the junior high school. We no longer played with boys and seldom talked to them, except for deskmates in absolutely necessary situations. No teacher or parent had a hand in creating this segregation. We adolescent girls initiated it for a simple reason: to avoid gossip.

One girl at a senior level often talked merrily and lengthily with boys. My classmates and I commented on her behavior disapprovingly, "Look at her! She is so flighty." "Look at the way she curls her bang. She tries to be pretty!" Trying to be pretty was a derogatory description of a girl. We often openly expressed our admiration of pretty girls and disdain of those who were not but were trying to be. Trying to be pretty revealed one's intention to draw attention. We were not shy of standing out in our academic performance or extracurricular activities, but we definitely did not want to attract any attention to our appearance. Decent girls were supposed to behave this way. We had established this set of behavioral norms before we learned about political terms like *bourgeois lifestyle* in the Cultural Revolution.

One summer it was getting hot earlier than usual. But because it was not yet the usual time to change into skirts and short sleeves, all seventeen girls in my class kept waiting for someone to be brave enough to change into summer clothes. No one wanted to be the first to change because she would attract unbearable stares. We rolled up our long sleeves and waited. Finally, one girl could not put up with the heat anymore and came up with a smart idea. She talked to each girl in our class and we all agreed delightedly that we would change into summer clothes together the next day.

What was in our active compliance to the norms of female modesty, which had close affinity to female chastity? Was it simply out of our fear of being seen as indecent? Why did I feel a strange excitement in my compliance?

When I was working on the farm in my late teens, we girls would often swim in the river two hundred feet away from our dorms. Boys went to the river topless. We girls changed into our swimming suits in our dorms and then put on our long, opaque gray plastic raincoats to cover our bodies. We took off the raincoats right before we jumped into the river. Never was there a moment that I envied the boys' convenience. Quite to the contrary, wrapping the raincoat over my body, smiling meaningfully at other girls doing the same thing, I felt a mysterious sacredness. It is a ritual belonging only to girls. Performing this and other female rituals constituted my gender identity in a social environment that lacked significant distinction between male and female youth.

Half a block away from my home was a picture bookstand that

I frequented often before my third grade year. Throughout the 1950s there were numerous private picture bookstands in Shanghai. They did not sell books, but loaned them to kids to read there (sometimes old men read there, too). The stands were usually located at the entrance of a lane that had a second-floor apartment built over the entrance. The entrance's roof sheltered the young readers at the bookstand from the rain and sun. With shelves of picture books against the wall and a few low benches squeezed together, this stand was the place where I found immense pleasure, second only to movies.

My parents never bought any books for me, nor for my siblings. Not many of my friends' parents bought them books, either. We went to bookstands. Picture books usually lent for one cent each. Thicker ones, or those made from movie scenes, cost two cents each. I rarely could afford those. I wanted the quantity, so I often opted for the cheaper thin ones that cost one cent for two. Often, after I had purchased a box of matches, a cake of soap, or a pack of toilet paper for my mother, I would ask if I could go to the bookstand with the leftover change in my hand. My mother usually let me keep the change if it was less than five cents. With more children in school than in the workplace, she did not have more than a few pennies to spare.

The picture books were all about four and a half by six inches in size and were in black and white. Except for the ones made from movie scenes, the rest contained exquisite illustrations on each page, with two or three lines of words below explaining the story or dialogue of the characters. Most of them, interestingly, were not about revolutionary heroes or heroines. Perhaps because of the bookstand owner's taste, there were many mythologies and ancient stories from either Chinese ancient times or foreign countries. I loved them. I am not sure if I was attracted more by the exotic stories or by the beautiful illustrations. In sharp contrast to revolutionary heroines, the ladies in these ancient stories wore gorgeous dresses and fancy hairdos. The dangling hairpieces and earrings and long, silky, wavy sashes around their delicate shoulders and waists emitted a sensuous femininity and accentuated the female characters' gentle and coy manners. Inevitably, a male character would fall in love with the beautiful female character.

One illustration etched deeply in my mind. The setting is in the garden of a Mediterranean aristocrat. A beautiful young lady in a dress similar to a sari leans against a flower fence. She wears fresh flowers in her black hair, thick and shiny and tied in a loose bun. Her dangling earrings, sparkly necklace, and bracelets are made of precious stone. Her dress is thin and tight, exposing her sensual figure. She raises one slender arm to hold onto a vine covered with blossoms. She lowers her head and turns her face halfway away from the man talking to her. She is soft, gentle, and shy. The well-built man is strong and firm, but also gentle, and his upper body leans forward as if bowing. He is confiding his love for her. I re-member my heart pounding rapidly when I turned to this illustra-tion, as if I were that lady. I gazed at this picture for a long time. I cannot recall the story at all, but the image remained a quintes-sential love scene for years in my childhood romantic fantasies.

One afternoon, when I was in the third grade, I was hiding in our small dark bedroom reading. Suddenly, my third brother burst in and snatched the book from my hand. "How dare you!" he shouted. "You are stealthily reading my book again!" My brother was four years older than I and was very mean to me in those years, a result of my parents' undisguised partiality toward me. The cru-elest thing he ever did to me was forbid me to touch the books he borrowed from friends. Although the supply of books from my classmates and the children's library was plentiful, by the third grade I was more interested in my brothers' and sisters' books. My fourth sister, who was seven years older than I, also forbade me to read her books, though for different reasons. "You are too young to read these books!" she chided me seriously. "Your mind would be too complicated." "A complicated mind" was a negative phrase meaning that one thinks what one should not think. In my case, she meant that at my age I should not show interest in love sto-ries. But I could not help it. The book my brother snatched away was *La Dame aux Camélias* by Alexandre Dumas. Before he returned the book to his friend, I had already read it several times. Our two-room home was too small for my brother and sister to successfully hide any book from me.

I developed an insatiable appetite for romantic stories. Under my peculiar circumstances, I also developed special skills to read fast and trace the line of romance quickly out of a novel's multiple themes. In the fifth grade, it took me only two afternoons before my sister and brother came home to finish *War and Peace*. It was a thick book even in Chinese, but I skipped all of the parts on war and focused on the pages when ladies appeared. It was not until the Cultural Revolution that I had more security to read romantic stories leisurely.

The Cultural Revolution began in 1966 at the end of my second year in junior high school. Girls in my class formed a Chairman Mao thought-propaganda team. We boarded buses after rush hour and sang revolutionary songs and recited Chairman Mao's quotations to the bus riders. It was a great treat to have free rides on buses. We giggled a lot each time we got off a bus, as we were amused by the comical contrast between the quietly indifferent passengers and bus conductors and our blatantly enthusiastic performances. "The adults don't like us being there, but none of them dares to tell us to get off the bus!" But our festive mood soon changed when Shanghai students began following Beijing students to form Red Guard organizations. Only students from Red families were allowed to join the Red Guards.

One day my two best friends and I were talking outside my home about the troubles on our minds. We revealed to one another for the first time our not-so-Red family backgrounds. Ying's father used to be a small business owner; Feng's father used to be a member of the Nationalist Youth League; and my father used to be a Nationalist Party member. At thirteen, I only understood that this was the first time I was disqualified for something not by my behavior and performance, but by something over which I had no control. I felt humiliated but did not know with whom I should be angry. But my low mood did not last long. Who cares about Red Guards anyway?! Humph! I don't even want to join you! I despised those Red Guards in army uniforms walking around with self-conceited airs. Big deal! I don't see anything special in you. At no time did I associate those teenage Red Guards with the image of a true revolutionary in my mind.

My fourth sister, a devoted young high school teacher, was criticized by some of her students. Her students thought she had a

permanent in her hair, which was naturally curly, and she was criticized for having a bourgeois hairstyle. The students also ordered
her to turn in her outlandish clothing, a jean jacket with a sailor
collar. She was miserable in those days. I was angry with those ri-
diculous and ungrateful students, because I knew how much my
sister cared about them. Largely because of my sister, my sympa-
thy was with the teachers. Once I saw two male students beating a
teacher in my school. I was totally disgusted by the gross and ugly
scene. I stopped going to school after that. There was no school
anyway.[5]

Except for a trip to Beijing to see Chairman Mao, I spent the
first two years of the Cultural Revolution doing my favorite things
at home, singing and reading. It was like a never-ending summer
vacation. No school, no worries about math tests, and no homework. I could read as late as I wanted and sleep in the next morning. Books were plentiful. My third brother's friend, the one from
whom he used to borrow books, offered to give my brother many
books. His father was a translator of novels and worried about a
house search by Red Guards. His collection of books was evidence
of his love for Western bourgeois literature, and he wanted to get
rid of them. This was similar to my father's situation. He sent his
lifelong collection of rare editions of Chinese classics to a recycling
station to destroy evidence of his love for feudal texts. I remember
my father's shaking hands touching each book before he parted
with them, and I worried about his high blood pressure as his veins
popped out on his forehead. I did not feel very sorry about my
father's books, though. There was rarely any romantic story in
them. Besides, who would want to learn about feudalism?

My siblings and I all loved nineteenth-century European literature. Before the Cultural Revolution these world classics had a
legitimate place in socialist China. Supposedly, they would enhance
our knowledge of the evils of capitalist society. I suspect it was a
pretext invented by a huge body of intellectuals and translators who
loved Western literature or made a comfortable living from it. To
gain legitimacy in publishing such literature, intellectuals also published articles to guide young readers in reading these classics the
"correct way." Often these guides presented a historical context of

the capitalist society in which the story took place and attributed the protagonists' limitations to their bourgeois class background. Glancing over these "guiding" essays that frequently appeared in youth newspapers, I knew I did not read in the "correct way," though my pleasure in reading was no less.

My brother stopped being mean to me in his high school years. My fourth sister was busy attending condemnation meetings organized by Red Guards in her school. No one was monitoring what I was reading. Surely my mind became more "complicated." I started to make my own romantic stories every night before falling asleep. In my fantasies, the beautiful and feminine heroine, me, and the handsome hero inevitably fell in love with each other, although we did not necessarily confide our love for each other. Many times I cried over a touching story in which I sacrificed my love for the sake of the man I loved, or vice versa. There was rarely any physical contact between the lovers. I did not yet know what sex was and could not imagine it even in my wildest fantasy. My love stories were fully charged with emotions, restrained emotions. The hero I loved was metamorphic, shifting from a well-mannered and reserved English gentleman from Dickens's, Hardy's, or Jane Austin's novels, to a passionate French lover created under Dumas's pen, to a sentimental melancholic Russian aristocrat in Turgenev's short stories, and finally to a devoted and loyal Chinese Communist revolutionary. Of course, I also tried to mix different qualities together to make the ideal type for myself. My hero wrote love poems like Robert Browning, confided his love in a sensuous voice like Cyrano's, and sang serenades beneath a marble balcony, where I stood, bathed in moonlight, wearing a long white dress. He has the physique and internal depth of Rodin's "Thinker." And he would bravely sacrifice his life for a noble cause like a Communist revolutionary, which was why I often cried over my stories. This project of fantasizing my ideal lover kept me preoccupied for the first two years of the Cultural Revolution, before I was sent down to the countryside. At the peak of Chairman Mao's endeavor to eradicate all bourgeois, feudalistic, and revisionist influences, I eagerly opened my heart and mind to a world of heterosexual romance imbued with Victorian gender discourse that blended well with Communist sexual mores. Who could have thought that my acquired passion for Victorian romance and "bourgeois taste" would assist me in becoming a Communist Party member?

At eighteen, two years after I had worked on a state farm in Chongming Island, I was accepted as a party member, one of the first four on the farm when the party began to recruit young members in the Cultural Revolution. I had not expected that my party membership would come so easily. The party leaders never even mentioned my father's political problem. It was not because they were too short of applicants to discriminate against me. Our farm had a population of more than twenty thousand young people, and many former Red Guards rose to become prominent activists. My best friend, Lin, had applied for a party membership much earlier than I, but she was not among the first to be accepted.

Lin was four years older than I, and a high school graduate, while I was only a junior high school graduate. We were assigned to the same dorm and shared a bunk bed. I was immediately attracted to her eloquence, quick mind, capability, and devotion to revolution. She had a lovely handwriting and wrote beautiful articles. Compared to mature high school graduates, we junior high students felt like kids. Lin stood out among all of the high school graduates in our brigade, and she was soon promoted as a team leader.

Lin and I talked all the time in the fields, whenever we were not out of breath. Actually, she talked mostly, and on one topic: the significance of the Cultural Revolution. Apparently sensing my apolitical naïveté, she patiently explained to me the history of the Red Guard movement, the great historical significance of the movement sending educated youths to the countryside, and the importance of guarding against revisionism. She enlightened me within only a couple of months. Her description of the goal of sent-down youth (zhiqing) fit well with my childhood utopian dream, that Communism aims to make the whole world a beautiful garden where everyone lives happily without exploitation and oppression: "From each according to one's ability and to each according to one's needs." Now we revolutionary youths were in the position to make our country a beautiful garden. We should make this barren island a beautiful Communist garden as the first step. It seemed feasible to me, as long as we youth all devoted ourselves to that common goal. It cannot be more difficult than the Long March. It required only our sweat and hardship, not our lives.

I enthusiastically began to work toward this glorious dream, imagining myself among the ranks of revolutionaries who heroically endured hardship and pain for the sake of all people's everlasting happiness. Snow flew into our straw hut through holes in the walls. Muddy boots were frozen fast on the dirt floor in our dorm. Rain leaked through the straw roofs and onto our beds. Blisters on my hands bled from digging canals with a spade. Broken skin on my shoulder stuck to my shirt after carrying heavy loads on a shoulder pole for a whole day. My backbones felt as if they were broken from bending for long hours in the field transplanting rice seedlings. The pain was a test to see if I could become a true revolutionary. I confronted each test in high spirit. When the farm increased our salaries, I wrote a letter to the brigade leader sincerely asking for the lowest rank of salary. I reasoned, "When the Red Army soldiers were on the Long March, each had only five cents a day for food. I have no reason to ask for more than what I need to feed myself since our country is still poor." I was soon identified by the party leaders as a promising "revolutionary seedling."

I was striving to be a selfless revolutionary, and so was Lin. She influenced me greatly with the many revolutionary texts she passed to me. But why was I the chosen one and not she? There was only one significant difference between us: She switched boyfriends frequently, while I was without one. Her revolutionary image was severely tarnished by the succession of her boyfriends, while my reputation was impeccable. In fact, before I was accepted as a party member at a routine meeting, where I was to hear the evaluation by the masses, there was only one criticism: "Somehow Wang Zheng has a kind of aloofness. She does not make approaches to the masses." The criticism was a familiar one and came mostly from young men. Once when I was home on vacation, I told my father that some guys in my brigade criticized me for being aloof (*qinggao*, a term often applied to bourgeois intellectuals in the CCP language, connotes bourgeois disdain for the masses of workers and peasants).

I wondered if he saw that in me. My father replied immediately, "What qinggao? Any guy saying that wants to approach you. Just ignore them! I know what's in men's minds." I did not expect such a sexual interpretation for what I perceived as a personality problem in me. I found it quite illuminating.

The party leaders on the farm must have seen my "aloofness" in a different light. To these married men in their late thirties, this pretty girl was innocent, pure, serious, and hardworking. They adored this moral paragon who showed no interest in boys, let alone attract gossip. The first group of party recruits were role models for all of the youth on the farm. They had to be morally flawless.

Chairman Mao said, "The eyes of the masses are sharp." Those young men's complaint of my aloofness was perceptive. I sized up each of them at first glance. No one was even close to the ideal type in my fantasies. Why bother to approach them? My love has to be reserved for the one who deserves it. This was a firm conviction based on both the Chinese concept of chastity and the exaltation of romantic love in Victorian literature. Love, in my mind, was as sacred as the goal of Communism, if not more. The difference was that you could take action to build the perfect society of Communism, but you had to wait patiently or, rather, hopelessly, for your perfect love to appear. I was aware of the impossibility of obtaining my ideal love, and it caused me profound agony. Even before I arrived on the island I had thought about the barren Chinese rural setting with despair. Nothing could be more distant from my dream of a cosmopolitan romantic world permeated with music and flowers. Did I unconsciously translate my longing for a romantic garden into passionate action for a Communist garden?

The Communist utopia was my religion. As Marx said, "Religion is the spiritual opiate for the people." A large dosage of this special "opiate" effectively relieved the pain of my hopeless romantic longing and made me "high" in an environment that many without the spiritual opiate found hard to bear. It transformed my despair in finding the ideal love into hyper energy for building an ideal society.

The road to a Communist youth was imbued with gender. However, the subject position of Communist youth was not gender specific. Clinging to this position, young women like me sensed few gender constraints in our devotion to the revolution. Numerous young female leaders emerged on this island with eight farms. This cohort never believed in female inferiority and were free from social expectations of the roles of wife and mother. Femininity was not defined as performing the traditional roles of wife and mother. To be a good *female* youth was to devote herself heart and soul to the revolution. This criterion implied a rejection of the role of wife and mother, which was embodied in the term *funü* and entailed positive appraisal of young women's remarkable ability and strength. We never worried about being seen as unfeminine for surpassing men in our job performance. When young female and male leaders got together at meetings or training sessions, we talked about our work and discussed Marxist theories on equal terms. Being the same idealist type, young leaders of both sexes shared a comradeship in our concerted efforts to build better farms. A utopia seemed within our reach since the atmosphere was already there. In those intoxicating moments with many young likeminded dreamers, I was a revolutionary youth, a Communist Party member. My gender was irrelevant.

On the day when my college roommates and I were discussing the meaning of *funü* and *qingnian*, I had already worked at various posts for a decade. Experienced as a farmworker, brigade leader, editor and director of the broadcast station on the farm, guide to national and local exhibitions, curator of an exhibition hall, and a movie actor, I regarded myself as a seasoned veteran in a bankrupt revolution. I could no longer identify with the party as a result of my disillusionment, which was intensified by the increasing knowledge of the power struggles within the party after Mao's death, a familiar experience shared by many of my peers. We were ready to discard Mao. But *qingnian-youth*, a term charged with Maoist connotations, was still dear to us. In 1978 the term no longer connoted a Communist dream. Identifying with this Maoist social category, we, the first class of female college students after Mao's death, unconsciously acknowledged our privileges and empowerment in being a youth in the Mao era.

Two decades had passed before I was able to examine the meaning of Maoist qingnian at a conscious level. In China at the end of the twentieth century, qingnian has long been replaced by *nüxing* (female sex or femininity) as a dominant subject position for urban young women. Now femininity is in vogue instead of revolutionary youths. Nüxing connotes no revolutionary zeal as qingnian did, and it is not promoted by the party-state. However, nüxing spurs strong consumerist zest in the market economy since femininity requires, first of all, many feminine products, with cosmetics at the top of the list. Via new means of media, advertisements that have both reflected and contributed to the contemporary gender discourse of femininity have shaped gendered desires and identities more effectively than state propaganda in the Mao era. Does nüxing signify more freedom and space for young women's social advancement than qingnian? I don't think so. Nüxing helped a generation of young women in the post-Mao era acquire a legitimate sexual identity, unlike qingnian, as a dominant subject position in the Mao era that had dismissed sexuality. However, the recognition of female sexuality is double edged. Accompanying contemporary young women's greater degree of sexual freedom, the sexualized female body has been portrayed as inevitably inferior to the male body in the discourse of femininity. The innate weaknesses of nüxing have become the rationale for overt gender discrimination in employment and education in the post-Mao era. More seriously, young women who have been constructed by the discourse of femininity willingly choose feminine occupations, and those few who dare to cross or challenge gender boundaries appear unfeminine and unattractive in public opinions.

As a scholar studying gender discourse in twentieth-century China, I find myself frequently reflecting on my own gendering process when writing about gender before and after the Mao era. It has become increasingly clear to me that the gender-neutral subject position of Maoist qingnian has significant gender implications. My generation lived through a political era preoccupied with creating socialist new persons. Together with socialist constructors and Communist successors that defined what a revolutionary youth ought to be, these state-promoted gender-neutral terms marginalized many gendered terms in public discourse. Such discursive

practices did not aim at liberating women. Rather, they demonstrated the party's attempts to situate citizens in a new kind of social relationship, to pull both men and women out of the web of
Confucian kinship obligations and to redirect their ethical duties
from their kin to the party and the nation. Scholars of Communist societies may call this statist scheme manipulation or domi-
nation, but few have noticed that the enforcement of this scheme
disrupted conventional gender norms and created new discursive
space that allowed a cohort of young women to grow up without
being always conscious of their gender.

Middle-aged, a mother of two, and residing mostly in the
United States, I am no longer a qingnian. But deep inside, I recognize that temporal and spatial changes have not succeeded in re-
moving subject positions formed in my youth. My interest in
feminism is generated by its critical power, and it is also conditioned by my qingnian ideal of gender equality. I am delighted to
have found in feminism a cause of my own, for the demise of
Maoist revolution did not extinguish my youthful dream of a society of equality and justice, a dream shared by numerous feminists worldwide. Feminism also provides me with a critical position
and feasible means to carry on a revolution on my own terms. No
longer a qingnian, I still want to be a revolutionary nonetheless. I
am stuck with the identity of "agents of social change" endowed
by the Maoist state.

NOTES

1. The author wishes to thank the following friends and colleagues who gave comments
   on early versions of this essay: Bai Di, Paula Birnbaum, Grace Eckert, Gail Hershatter,
   Emily Honig, Loretta Kalb, Dorothy Ko, Sheila Lichtman, Nikki Mandell, Karen Offen,
   Raka Ray, Abby Stewart, Marilyn Yalom, and Xueping Zhong.
2. In the fall of 1977 the first nationwide college entrance exams took place after an eleven-
   year interval. Those who passed the first exams did not begin their class until February
   1978. We were all brand-new college students at different ages.
3. See Claire Wallace and Sijka Kovatcheva, *Youth in Society* (New York: St. Martin's Press,
   1998), 66.
4. When Deng Xiaoping took power after Mao's death, there emerged a nationwide Intellectual Emancipation Movement by the end of 1970s. Sanctioned by the new party
   leadership, intellectuals began to openly critique many practices of the Communist
   Party during the Mao era and to investigate the political and intellectual roots that led
   to the calamity of the Cultural Revolution.
5. All teaching in Shanghai schools from junior high and up stopped in early June 1966.
   All of the teachers and students were supposed to devote their time to the Cultural
   Revolution.

XIAOMEI CHEN

FROM "LIGHTHOUSE" TO THE NORTHEAST WILDERNESS
Growing Up among the Ordinary Stars

In September 1981, when the autumn leaves were turning brilliant colors, I became one of the first students from the People's Republic of China to enroll at Brigham Young University. A few parties and gatherings later, in the course of which my fellow students and I got to know each other, I was urged by my new American friends to write what they called my "incredible stories" of growing up in an elite theater family in Maoist China, especially the events that occurred during the Cultural Revolution. "You may never have to worry about graduate school once you strike it rich publishing a best-seller like that," they predicted, evidently feeling pride in their new friend who was a "Red Commie," and someone they would have never dreamt of meeting a few years earlier.

Moreover, my first week of teaching freshman English composition (as a graduate teaching assistant) made me an instant celebrity in the local evening news, much against my will. On camera, I distinguished between the American and British spellings of *aesthetic* and *esthetic* and convinced an all-American class that they could learn something from me about such topics as the six critical approaches to *The Scarlet Letter*. Oddly enough, however native my English might have seemed, it was the first time I really learned the meaning of *celebrity*, a word that, though I might have encountered it in English class in China, had slipped out of my active vocabulary. This was in spite of the fact that its Chinese counterpart, *mingren*, had played an important part in my teenage years, when I was growing up in a family of theater stars who constantly sought the acceptance of ordinary people.

Writing this essay seventeen years later, I feel fortunate that I did not jump at the first opportunity to construct my autobiography. Perhaps I held back because I feared becoming a celebrity of any sort. I probably also sensed that this kind of attention should not come at the expense of tarnishing what I still treasure: the memorable years that laid the foundation for my being who I am. My pride in my identity as a woman from the People's Republic of China, in spite of my experience in China—or perhaps precisely because of it—prevented me from "selling out" my stories to Western consumers before I'd had the chance to acquire the critical skills I needed to present an account fair to both my culture and outsiders interested in a rounded picture of China.

My background as a privileged teacher of English in Beijing, a graduate student in comparative literature at Indiana University, and a tenured professor at Ohio State University has compelled me to question the many lives I have led so as to determine the boundaries of my own knowledge of China, the object of my teaching and research. Moreover, my experience in the United States has constantly offered new perspectives on my memories of growing up in Maoist China. My treasuring of these memories is bound up in an appreciation of how the Maoist era shaped my cultural and personal identities—an appreciation that grew as I came to understand better my adopted culture. After all, it was from post-Maoist China that I learned about the mysterious West, which became my target culture, both from the standpoint of academic career and personal adventure.

It must be said that my appetite for this adventure was minimal at first. In 1973, when I ended up as an English major at Beijing Foreign Language Institute, I lamented the fact that I would not be fulfilling my childhood dream of pursuing a creative writing career in the Chinese Department of Peking University. Not until after I had read the many fascinating English-language materials that became available to me did I vigorously pursue my ambition of going to graduate school in the United States. To recover an affirmative experience in China, therefore, is not to dismiss an equally positive experience of living outside China, where global perspectives provided me with a unique way of valuing my own culture, no matter how negatively it had been portrayed in scholarly works and the popular media.

This essay provides a different perspective, I hope, from that of the autobiographies by writers from Maoist China that were current in the West in the post–Cold War, post-socialist era. Looking back, I must admit that I benefited from teaching these memoirs of the Cultural Revolution, especially the ones written by women writers of my own generation. I was among the first to bring into the classrooms of the Ohio State University *Wild Swans* and *Red Azalea,* which I used as springboards for teaching the history and culture of modern China. At the same time, however, I became increasingly troubled by the paradoxical impact of these books on the American public, especially at a university campus in mid-America. In a land with little history of educating its people about non-Western experiences, how does one go about depicting modern China without biases, without sounding like a Cold Warrior or a radical Maoist?

The responses of Ohio State students who enrolled in my class "Women in East Asian and Asian American Literatures" may shed some light on that difficulty. The students' in-class essays expressed their enthusiasm at being introduced, via *Wild Swans,* to a world in which generation upon generation of Chinese women had fought for their emancipation and happiness in a way that they as Americans would never have imagined. Their lives had changed, some claimed, after reading about these people and events outside of Ohio. And more than ever before, they had come to appreciate what America had to offer them in terms of individual freedom and choices.

While delighted that my students' horizons had thus been expanded to encompass other literatures besides the traditional Anglo-American span from Beowulf to Virginia Woolf, I was nevertheless made uneasy by the realization that I was unwittingly contributing to a discourse of China bashing occurring in America and the rest of the West. I was taken aback, for instance, by the occasional outbursts from my students who swore never to go to China, because, among all nations, it had the worst record in the abuse of human rights. Our discussion of *Wild Swans* and other stories seemed only to confirm the disparaging information about China that they had already picked up from the American media. Tibet, forced abortion and the country's one-child policy, Chinese spying on American nuclear secrets, illegal contributions to the Democratic Party, and so forth—these were the issues that represented China to them and that had taught them to see it in an unfavorable light.

To redress the situation, I would begin talking about growing up in China. My purpose was to set out the positive values and useful lessons with which I was imbued and which contributed to what I believe to be my strength, while not discounting the destructive nature of the Cultural Revolution, which I experienced along with the authors of those women's autobiographies. However, this attempt to provide my students with a balanced view of China further complicated my critical position. Sometimes I was shocked by my own voice, which began to resemble the China-bashing stories I was striving to rectify when I would speak of being disqualified from joining the Red Guard because of my elite family background, my parents' persecution as theater stars, and my life on a farm in rural China. These were, after all, experiences common to many who lived through that period. Moreover, when intent on holding the attention of freshmen new to the challenge of serious learning in a university setting, didn't I make a special effort to tell a gripping story? In critiquing others' stories, therefore, I also needed to acknowledge my own shifting positions, which might have jockeyed to be the voice of authority. But after occasionally receiving Christmas letters from China sent by former students (sometimes from the least likely ones, who had, at one point, been turned off by my stories), I was encouraged to seek an affirmative way to describe the complex, special era I lived through. Thus, my goal, in this brief memoir and elsewhere, is to arrive at a balanced perspective that can honestly reflect my native experience and, in so doing, both affirm and interrogate that experience.

I can honestly say that I had a happy, even an exhilarating childhood, although I was not spared some growing pains. While I had many of the same experiences recollected in this anthology, such as that of being a *qingnian* (youth), a *funü* (woman), and a *zhiqing* (educated youths living in rural China, full of the spirit of *wusi* [selflessness]), I want to focus on my experience as the daughter of two luminaries of the theater, who at times filled me with pride and other times mortified me, depending on where I was and the circumstances. I came to realize that this paradoxical type of response shaped much of my personality and the way I interact with people. When it felt safe to do so, I could easily be sensible of my elite background and the certain superiority I associated with it; conversely, I could as easily identify with the many different types of "common" people whose lifestyles and careers were far removed from anything to do with my family. These dual identities often provided me with a sense of security that allowed me to function at my best. On other occasions, however, I felt subjected—at least in my young mind—to the scrutiny of the two worlds, which seemed to me to be worlds apart. I suspect that many Chinese offspring of artists and intellectuals or those of petit bourgeois family background had this same problematic relationship to the common people—a conflict and an accommodation that formed for them (and me) much of the drama of the Maoist era.

I was born in January 1954, rather inconsiderately on the eve of my mother's launching of her career-making role of Yelena in Chekhov's play *Uncle Vanya*. The production was a national event to commemorate the fiftieth anniversary of Chekhov's death and to promote friendship and cultural exchange between the Soviet Union and China. Later on, I was told that when I was four weeks old, my mother had to breast-feed me four times a day in a nearby daycare center between rehearsals. Among my earliest memories were the long hours I spent waiting for my parents to pick me up Saturday afternoon from the nursery, which was actually a boarding school for preschool children where I stayed from seven months old to age seven (we got to go home only from Saturday night to

Monday morning). I also remember waiting by the window of our second-floor apartment, hoping to see my mother appear any moment in the alley *(hutong)* that led from the back door of the theater to our courtyard. My heart would bound with joy when my mother finally appeared, sometimes holding a bouquet of fresh flowers that her fans had presented her with. Frequently I would beg my mother to promise she would wake me at midnight after she came back from the performance, because otherwise I might wet the bed, I told her. Of course the real reason was that I longed to spend some more time with my parents before I returned to the nursery the next day. I remember how delighted I was when I was sick for two weeks, since this meant I could play in my mother's warm, duck-down quilt until late in the mornings without worrying about going back to the nursery. I would also have plenty of time to wait for her return home by the window, anticipating her fragrance, her smile, and her touch.

When I grew a bit older, I could sometimes become quite embarrassed by my mother's colorful, shapely dress and high-heel shoes, which were regarded as "bourgeois" trappings in a socialist China that was urging its artists to follow the example of the common people in sticking to a simple lifestyle. But when she explained that her elegant clothes and her jewelry were very much appreciated at social functions frequented by diplomats and foreign friends, I felt a sense of harmony and security, for I understood perhaps that as an artist her province transcended national boundaries. Her stage roles of Yelena in Chekhov's *Uncle Vanya* and of Nora in Ibsen's *A Doll's House,* for instance, resulted from artistic collaborations with Soviet and Norwegian stage directors. Moreover, foreign critics often marveled at the modern Chinese drama as performed by my parents, who had dedicated their lives to promoting this art form. From this and other examples of artistic dedication and excellence, I learned to appreciate the glamour associated with the stage and the rewards for exceptional theatrical gifts such as my parents had. I also became aware that my mother's commitment to her art could never be eclipsed by anything else, not even her personal life.

I remember, however, heaving a sigh of relief not too long before the Cultural Revolution, when my mom dressed, for the first time in her life, in the then fashionable green uniform in imitation of the People's Liberation Army, like a truly proletarian woman. By then, in her mid-forties, my mother had lost some of her youthful allure. She also switched from her stylish wavy permanent to a short haircut that was popular among women. Although it had been her goal all her life to serve and to identify with ordinary people, it was only when she adopted external forms that turned her into one of them that she succeeded in dispelling that sometimes uncomfortable sense of privilege I had.

The Maoist rhetoric that privileged the common people (for example, workers, peasants, and soldiers) ensured that any sense of elitist glory such as had once been planted in me as a child would be uprooted because of the contemporary insistence that an acting career was no more glorious than any other occupation. In fact, long before the revolution was won, Mao Zedong had already laid down, in 1942, his principles in regard to literature and art. They should serve the ultimate interests of the working classes, then considered the backbone of the Chinese Communist Revolution and, later on, the masters of a new, socialist China. Thus, whereas heretofore my head had been turned by my parents' scintillating careers and star status, I now noticed that in their midnight conversations they spoke with excitement about their upcoming tours to the factories, mines, and remote rural villages, which had never seen drama by a renowned national theater. They also thoroughly enjoyed tutoring the local people in all parts of China on creating their own modern spoken drama.

I still remember my mother telling me about a girl from a wealthy Shanghai family whose parents had been classified as capitalists before 1949 and who on that account had not been allowed to go to Xinjiang Autonomous Region. The girl insisted on going, however, and she eventually proved herself a capable farmer whose contributions to constructing the socialist countryside drew favorable notice. During Premier Zhou Enlai's visit to Xinjiang, she was received by him and other statesmen as a model worker and a representative of youth with undesirable family backgrounds. "She was not that much older than you," my mother said, "when she left her comfortable home in Shanghai to forge a successful career

against all odds." During her tour in Xinjiang, my mother encountered numerous young people like this girl and enjoyed coaching
performing groups consisting of brilliant youths. To be able to live
and work with them, and be finally accepted as if she were one of
them, answered a cherished dream of hers. I remember my mother
writing letters far into the night to maintain connection with young
people she met who had been sent a long distance away from the
city and from the homes in which they were born. She would show
my brother and me pictures of them that she had pasted to the
diaries they gave her as souvenirs when she left Xinjiang.

When my parents returned home from those trips, sometimes
after a year-long separation from me, I was supremely happy. I absorbed the inspiring messages they gave, chief among which was
their ardent desire to travel again to the remote regions of the country, to experience again rejuvenation by the spirit of the common
people. It was the responsibility of socialist artists to be accepted
by the ordinary folk, for only this approval could qualify them to
depict the latter's revolutionary acts on stage. My parents' passionate belief in ordinary people, and their sincere efforts to reform
themselves into revolutionary artists, deserving of the working
class's trust, remain among my most prized impressions from the
time I spent with them at the dinner table. For a small child seeking her place in the universe, the communication of such messages
afforded allure and profound reassurance. During their subsequent
trips away from Beijing, I would sit after dark on a small stool
in the middle of the courtyard of my home, counting with my
nanny the numerous twinkling stars in the sky while imagining
what play my parents might be performing and in what remote
region they might, perhaps, be seeing the same brilliant stars I saw.
I longed to grow up to be just like them—to be a star, but not a
lonely, aloof star, rather a star surrounded by equally bright stars.
To be just one of them—but still a star. This paradoxical yet perfectly harmonious desire to be a "celebrated ordinary person" captured my imagination during adolescence, when I felt comfortable
relating both to ordinary celebrities (for example, my parents) and
to the much-celebrated ordinary people my parents were attempt-
ing to emulate. My parents embodied both, forming for me a

unique amalgam—contradictory yet harmonious—of the ordinary and extraordinary. They did this by straddling two worlds: the special life of theater stars and glamorous career and the world of the working class, whose tribulations in the old society they represented in their theater productions and whose aspiration of building a socialist China they enthusiastically shared. Thus I learned early to shift among multiple identities.

Yet growing up in my mother's shadow, I felt an inevitable sense of inadequacy such as any teenager under similar circumstances might experience in any culture: the fear of the proverbial ugly duckling that she will never become a beautiful swan. Fortunately, this anxiety was short lived. Later on in elementary school, I soon learned the value and even the rewards of being an ordinary person. It was really all right not to be gorgeous, for beauty came from within, and that was what really mattered, since it would shine through whatever was external. My mother reinforced this homely lesson, telling me once, when I was dancing in the middle of the room, trying to imitate her Nora in Ibsen's *A Doll's House,* not to try to become an actress. "An actress shines only for a brief period, at the height of her beauty and youth," she said. "Be a teacher," she advised, "for then the older you become, the more knowledge you will accumulate, and hence, the more respect people will have for you." Of course she did not anticipate that I would end up a professor teaching in the United States, which, in the 1950s and 1960s, was one of socialist China's two deadliest enemies (the other being the Soviet Union); some of the dramas staged by her theater company proclaimed that unambiguous political message.

My sense of multiple identities did not spring entirely and solely from my relation to my parents. In fact, I did not feel the full impact of this experience until I myself became "famous" in my own right at age eleven. On June 1, 1965, International Children's Day, an essay I had written to mark the occasion, entitled "Mingdeng," or "Lighthouse," was published in the *People's Daily,* the quintessential CCP newspaper. Aside from the usual festivities and getting the day off from school, this June 1 was particularly memorable since it marked for me the beginning of a more complicated journey for myself. For even today, after eighteen years in the United States, I still encounter former schoolmates now living in California or New York, who, upon hearing my name, ask if I am the Chen Xiaomei who wrote the "Mingdeng" essay that brought so much honor to our school. Moreover, in 1983 I was invited to speak as a celebrity alumnus at the ceremony commemorating the founding of Beijing Jingshan School, where I was introduced to the young audiences as "the author of 'Mingdeng.'"

In the aftermath of the publication of my essay, I experienced fame at first as any child would. The doorkeeper of my school would often welcome me with a broad smile: "Xiaomei, more letters for you, from all over the country. Must be all about that wonderful composition you wrote." Neighbors, relatives, playmates, and friends competed in complimenting me on my "literary talents." However, I did not want to seem different for having written "Mingdeng" any more than for being the daughter of a theater star. I did my best to shy away from any suggestion of superiority and difference. It was, again, uncomfortable to be regarded as different, to be above my peers. As if to justify my concerns, some of my classmates became jealous and rose in protest: "Did she really write this essay? No one our age could possibly have written something like this. Either the teacher, or teachers, or her parents must have helped her, one way or the other!" They wanted the truth. Of course I knew the truth: I did write it, all by myself.

It had not been all that hard. One day on a bus ride home, I saw the evening light along the Central-South Lake (Zhongnanhai) of the Forbidden City, where Chairman Mao lived and worked. Thinking of what our teachers and the news media constantly told us, I fantasized that every evening our great leader burned the midnight oil poring over plans to guide the Chinese and other peoples all over the world in their efforts to achieve national and world revolution. With sincere passion, I wrote that each time I passed by Zhongnanhai, I meditated on the significance of those glimmering lights from the other shore of the lake. They were indeed the brightest stars in the sky and the freshest flowers in the garden. It was perhaps under these lamps that our great leader, Chairman Mao, was drawing up the blueprints for our motherland. Indeed, he might be penning his statement in support of the national struggles for independence waged by the peoples of Asian, African, and Latin-American countries. He might be tuning in on central and local radio stations for news from rural and urban China. With pleasureful ease, I continued writing, imagining that the never-extinguished lamp from the "lighthouse" across the lake had lit up the paths for workers, peasants, soldiers, and other peoples of the working classes, inspiring them to accomplish unprecedented miracles. It occurred to me that under their own lamps in the motherland, workers were studying Chairman Mao's selected works. Peasants were listening to young people who read to them Chairman Mao's essay "Serve the People." PLA soldiers on the border were receiving radio transmissions from faraway Beijing. Under yet other lamps, red-scarved young pioneers were helping the sick and the old with their housework. I listed, at random, several widely publicized national achievements of the time, such as the successful explosion of our first atomic bomb and the completion of one of the longest bridges ever built across the Yangtze River in Nanjing. I even mentioned our victorious record of winning five championships in the Twenty-eighth International Ping-Pong Tournament. My palpable pride in growing up in this golden era of a vibrant China caused my imagination to soar freely. To boot, I enjoyed expressing myself in the way that felt most comfortable to me while engaged in writing, which was itself a challenging act.

As it turned out, my teacher came to my rescue, reassuring everyone that I wrote the essay as part of the homework assignment given everyone in class and that I received no extra help from any teacher. She also informed the class that right then my mother was touring Xinjiang Autonomous Region to promote an ethnic play, while my father was in Hebei Province, where, as leader of a team from the Ministry of Culture and Art, he was participating in the socialist education movement in the countryside. In truth, my teacher deserved much of the credit for inspiring me to write the essay, and, indeed, for initiating my desire to write. I was impressed by the feeling with which she read to us Lu Xun's stories and by the way she encouraged us to expand our imagination around any object we encountered in our daily lives and to write something meaningful and beautiful about it, both for practice and to enrich our minds and hearts. I remember, in the fourth grade, when I was most inspired by her instructions. I was standing in front of the display window of the Xinhua (New China) Bookstore, staring at the covers of the elegantly designed books and imagining what stories a single picture from one of these volumes would suggest to me. I remember seeing the jacket of *Hongyan (Red Crag)*, the story of the CCP martyrs who sacrificed themselves during the war for their revolutionary beliefs. I stood there for hours, taking notes of what came to my mind and what kinds of other stories I could generate from that particular illustration, which depicted Sister Jiang (Jiang Jie), the heroic protagonist and local CCP group leader, respected and loved for her skills for working with ordinary people. I drew courage from Sister Jiang's story during the period when I was confronted by my classmates, realizing that there was no comparison between what I was going through in our bright socialist country and the difficulties she had to overcome at a time when her life was often in danger. I told myself that I just had to trust my peers, who would eventually pass fair judgment on me and my writing.

Contrary to what some Western child experts might anticipate, I was not too deeply affected, much less traumatized, by this disruption in my sense of the inherent justice and harmony in my world. Growing up in Maoist China, I had been taught to admit my own vulnerabilities and weaknesses by being open and receptive to the criticism of others. Both at home and at school, I had been taught the value of sincerity and humility. Even when I might have gotten the idea that I excelled, my parents and teachers told me that I might not really be the best of all, since there were so many people around me whose strength would build on my own strength. I was used to the "criticism and self-criticism" meetings, where we "little leaders" (class president and other "servants of the people" in charge of various aspects of our school life) would open up each session by inviting criticism from our classmates that we might use to improve our work. If we were to become leaders one day, our leadership would not be effective without the support of the masses. Thus, listening to the "little masses" was an important component of our education; it would enable us, when we grew up, to better serve the masses in the real world, those ordinary people who, by the sweat of their brow, ensured our happy way of life.

Thinking about all these things while I was being "attacked" by my peers took the sting out of my resentment. I even experienced a sense of tranquillity and groundedness, since I remembered being told that no matter how muddy the waters might seem to get sometimes, the truth would eventually come out, and my classmates would trust me again, as long as I continued to believe in them. Bewildered as I might be, this knowledge nonetheless rendered me master of the important moments of my life, and I knew that that strength did not come from just within myself. For me, this was another lesson in "believing in yourself and in the masses," one of the many positive lessons I learned in Maoist China that later I could apply to my career in and out of China. The episode also illustrates another dimension of my identification with celebrated ordinary people: that is, one is not really a celebrity until one truly identifies with the ordinary people, which, in my situation, were the "little masses" in my class that I, as a "little leader," was supposed to help. Furthermore, one is not a leader until she sees herself as able to be led and regards herself as an equal member of her team, and not in the least superior to the masses in the first place. In this seemingly contradictory world, I nevertheless felt powerful within the sphere of my limited power, belonging as I did to an infinite universe, with unseen but real power being exerted all the time among the little masses.

I returned to my "Mingdeng" essay some thirty years later, in the fall quarter of 1997. For a graduate seminar at Ohio State University, I photocopied it in the original Chinese and presented it as an anonymous piece that reflected the Maoist discourse in the print culture of the earlier 1960s. Reading it aloud to my class in the same poetic way with which it was recited for numerous parents and visitors at Beijing Jingshan School, I tried to give my students a sense of the cultural fever of those times which inspired a generation with dignity, pride, and a passionate belief in an exciting future. Whatever else I was able to achieve in that class, I hoped at least to have imparted to my students my sense of responsibility for having helped shape a Maoist discourse that had as much to do with our willing acceptance of the government's actions as it did with the government's actions themselves. I wanted to make it clear that many people, including myself, became enchanted with the government's vision and wholeheartedly embraced the new culture. Thus "Mingdeng," in a small measure, became a creator of a Maoist discourse, after itself having been created by the Maoist culture. Coming straight from the heart of a child of that time, it demonstrates the seductive power of culture and its persistent appeal for even the nation's youngest citizens.

My uncertain attraction for, and concomitant fear of, the spotlight, continued to characterize much of my childhood in Beijing and teenage years in the wilderness. I still remember how exciting it was to dance, with fifty other girls and boys, in the welcoming ceremonies for the state head presided over by the late Premier Zhou Enlai—and how heartbroken I was, after the Cultural Revolution started in 1966 and my father's past was being investigated, to have my name removed from the list of performers from Beijing Jingshan School slated to dance for the state leaders and distinguished foreign guests in the Great Hall of the People. Artist and team leader of the national China Youth Art Theater's stage designers, my father created setting, lights, and costumes for two dozen productions in socialist China. However, none of these achievements could spare him punishment for his past affiliations with theaters sponsored by the Nationalist government before 1949. After being rejected several times for membership in the "propaganda team formed to spread Mao Zedong Thought (Mao Zedong Sixiang xuanchuandui)," I went home and organized my own team with children who lived in my courtyard. Ranging in age from six to thirteen, we presented a curious line-up of all sizes and shapes. What we had in common was that at least one of our parents (all of whom had once been performing artists) was undergoing investigation. Without our realizing it, our performance, in addition to blending in with the activities that supported the mass movement, probably expressed our desire to carry on the artistic tradition of our parents. To demonstrate our pride and passionate commitment to the movement, we made our own team flag by embroidering golden thread on a piece of red cloth. Joining the street theater of the Cultural Revolution, we were able to attract crowds to watch our ensemble, and no one ever questioned us about our family background or whether we were politically qualified to perform. Now when I look back on that experience, I see that our popular performances undoubtedly benefited from the skills that we had picked up and the abilities we had inherited from our families. At this time there was indeed in me an intense desire to be on stage, just like my mother, perhaps because my mother was no longer able to act owing to the government's accusation that she was one of the *sanming* (three famous groups of actress, directors, and writers) and *sangao* (three "high" groups of professionals who were distinguished by their salaries, living standards, and income from royalty, all remnants of the bourgeois culture and opposed to the interests of the common people).

While organizing the performing group, though, I realized I was still functioning in the pre–Cultural Revolution mode of a "little leader" and decided that at our first meeting, when a group leader was supposed to be elected, I would strive to convince my friends that I was not right for the job. I pointed out that since the first grade I had been a "little leader" in Jingshan School, a small "capitalist roader," so to speak, from a once-elite school now under attack for training its students for the "bourgeoisie road." Also, coming from a less desirable family background as I did, I, more than anyone else, needed to be helped and reeducated by my peers. However trite those words may sound, I truly believed what we heard via the official media at the start of the Cultural Revolution, despite the fact that, growing up in the same courtyard among parents who worked for the same theater, no one had more politically correct family backgrounds than we did. In any case, rather than have a leader, we decided we would be a team of true equals and would educate ourselves and each other. Walking on the street with my homemade *xuanchuandui*, therefore, I felt relief and pride: I had my own team without having to be a Red Guard. It was not without a certain sense of being celebrities that we performed for the public, but since we had not been trained in the performing arts, we were not burdened, like our parents, with the professional artist's fear of being criticized by the masses. I was delighted to play the actress, and yet I did not have to be a leader—I was just as ordinary as anyone else. The experience may have come to my aid later when I auditioned successfully for the xuanchuandui in my middle school.

Since no serious learning took place in schools during the Cultural Revolution, I devoted most of my two years of middle school to the performing arts and consequently almost became a pro at it. We would perform in the street, on various stages in squares after public gatherings, and in rural areas not far from Beijing before local peasants and fellow students who had come to help with the autumn harvest. Each time a new quotation of Chairman Mao's was released regarding the Cultural Revolution, I would stay up all night with my teammates, writing scripts, adapting old songs to new lyrics, and producing new dances and skits for it. We competed with other teams in these activities, anxious to be the first to give expression to the new idea in street parades and celebrations. Intent on being the best, we worked hard and played just as hard. In hindsight, I view my xuanchuandui days today as one of the most exciting times of my adolescence, when fun and duty intertwined so well as to render perfectly natural my role of little player in the larger scheme of political theater. In all this, my mother was my most ardent supporter, especially when she had no work of her own and had to divide her time between criticizing, along with the masses, the bourgeois theater and art she had once been a part of, and sorting out things to be sent to my father, who was in detention. I was not so much aware of her predicament as I was of the thrill and freedom in riding a bicycle to wherever my performing duty called me. For the first time in my life, I even had enough pocket money for snacks and cookies before and after performance (for I could not always be home in time for dinner).

In 1968, the latest new quotation from Chairman Mao radically changed the course of my adolescence. It was the one in which he proclaimed the countryside an enormous arena where educated youths from the city could fully tap their talents while being reeducated by local peasants. Joining the national movement of repairing to the countryside, my class of 1969 went to Beidahuang, the northeast wilderness bordering the Soviet Union, then regarded as a threat to the Chinese nation. The twin glories of defending the border while throwing in my lot with the peasants to reclaim the fertile land of the frontier appealed to me. Said to be only thirty miles south of the border, the village I was to be sent to had only recently seen some military conflicts. It was moreover a fabled region, not far from the Heilongjiang River, where only the bravest ventured and where Siberia-like temperatures sometimes fell to thirty degrees Celsius below zero. Although I was one year younger than the minimum age posted for these exploits, and thus did not have to volunteer, I insisted on going.

On September 9, 1969, my sister arrived just in time to see me off after traveling almost two days by train, without much sleep, from Yunnan Province, the southwestern tip of China. We had only a few hours together before we set out for the train station. My brother also returned home for the occasion from a small village in Inner Mongolia, where he had been working as a peasant for one year. My father was still in detention. Studiously going about her household chores as if it were just another day, my mother tried not to betray her emotion and sadness. A few years later she told me how hard it had been for her to make preparations for the long journey of her youngest child, after her two older children had already been sent thousands of miles away.

To lighten the mood, my sister, who had never had a chance to see me perform, asked me to do a xuanchuandui skit. It was interesting that I chose a dance based on the image of "Mingdeng," which was called "The Red Army Soldiers Long for Mao Zedong." I performed the story of the protagonist, who, during a trying period, beheld the twinkling northern star in the dark sky, which reminded her of the oil lamplight from Mao's office in the Jingguangshan Soviet area. Recalling the journey in which she had followed Mao from victory to victory, she was able to gather her spirit and march on. My sister praised my solo act and was glad to see me in high spirits, wearing my green xuanchuandui uniform, with its red band on which was embroidered my team's name in gold

thread. I was ready to join my teammates in the Beijing train station and looked forward to our going together to the wilderness
to spread our performing tradition. My sister, brother, and mother
must have known what was in store for me on the frontier. As for
me, although I felt sad to be leaving my family, friends, and school,
I was excited by the prospect of a new life in a faraway land that,
as the folksongs said, was covered with the footprints of exotic animals. I was also excited that we would be adapting our performances to the local audiences of the new environment, for I wished
to continue my parents' recent work in serving the ordinary people
in Xinjiang and Henan.

At Beijing train station, I was tearless as I waved to my family and friends. My mind was occupied with the work we had to
do: keep up the morale of our schoolmates; help the train atten-
dants serve food and hot water and clean tables and floors; and pitch
in as "little helpers" in whatever other ways needed. I had even
brought a medicine box in case of emergency. I hoped that, depending on the space available, we might also be able to perform, or at
least conduct a few singing sessions when the time was right.

As soon as the train moved out of the station, however, something I had never anticipated happened. People around me began
to sob loudly, and I could not help but feel sad. My greatest despair,
however, came with the sudden realization that my xuanchuandui
had ceased to exist! We were not sitting together, and I was not
able to find our team leader, even after a frantic search for her. Finally, I was told that now that we were leaving Beijing, our middle
school had lost its purpose or function as an organization. We were
Bingtuan zhanshi now, soldiers of the military farm—that is, adults
waiting for orders from our work unit supervisors. In the face of
this profound disappointment, I tried to maintain the spirit of optimism with which I had set out and to persist in my original plan
of "doing good deeds" for the people around me. I hoped against
hope that somehow the members of my xuanchuandui would find
their way to each other soon. It was not that I longed to be ac-
corded any special privileges, but rather that I felt willing and able
to endure any hardship, as long as a xuanchuandui of some sort
existed.

When, on my first day in the northeast wilderness, I learned that all of our team members had been assigned to different villages hundreds of miles apart, I was devastated. In a region whose means of transportation consisted of ox carts and tractors, we might not see each other for a long time, let alone perform together. I remember being totally confused and heartbroken when a truck dropped off a dozen of us in the middle of the wilderness, in front of a pile of lumber, with which we were to build our own lodging. Luckily we had been preceded by fifty educated youths of our age from Tianjin, Shanghai, and Harbin who had settled there in the past year. Otherwise, we would have been obliged to cut down trees and clear the ground before building. Although I was not yet deterred by the hard labor, I was really frightened to realize that, for the first time in my life, I was alone, without my team and without my family. Until then, my team, which defined my very existence, had seemed more important to me than my family. Now, for the first time since leaving Beijing, I missed my family terribly.

Whereas before I had felt and behaved as though I were invincible, I now felt vulnerable, seeing part of my childhood dream shattered. I still worked hard both in the fields and also in the dining hall, where I used a blackboard to report my peers' accomplishments in reclaiming the wilderness. I got up earlier and stayed up later than my peers to write articles and copy them on to the blackboard with colorful chalks, making use of the writing skills I had acquired when I was composing my "Mingdeng" essay. But deep in my heart, I longed for the real spotlight. It did not have to be on a formal stage, I argued inwardly; I would have been glad to perform in the open fields, as my parents had done for the local peasants. Many times while tilling the land or harvesting wheat or soybean, I would look off into the horizon at the dirt road stretching to faraway places and I would yearn to see a truck coming toward us that had been dispatched from farm headquarters to recruit "new blood" for its own xuanchuandui, whose mediocre performance had not impressed me.

In those days, I wanted to visit Beijing, but even more than that, I fantasized about being recruited by a performing troop. Yet when a rare opportunity presented itself two years later, I shied away from trying out for serious parts in the headquarters' xuanchuandui. I was more comfortable adhering to my commoner status on the farm, dancing in holiday celebrations and feeling no pressure to occupy center stage. On other occasions, I was pulled the other way by my desire for star status. I volunteered to imitate a cock's crow at the beginning of a drama depicting a model farmer who got up well before dawn (even before the cock crowed) to see to the farm community's needs. From behind the curtains, where I felt most comfortable, I accomplished what a Chinese proverb calls *yiming jingren*. This may be translated literally as, "A single rooster's crow alerts the world," or figuratively, "An obscure person amazes the world with a single brilliant feat." My unusually realistic rooster crowing fetched me so many compliments that it became my favorite and, sometimes, only contribution when asked to participate in impromptu party skits (and so it remains to this day). I had discovered a way to enjoy the spotlight without having to take center stage. From such a concealed position, one might become a *wuming yingxiong*, or anonymous hero, the type most celebrated in Maoist China, from an ideological standpoint, because of his or her desire to remain nameless. For all who lived through that era—and especially the children—the preeminent role model was the ordinary soldier Lei Feng, famous for the countless good deeds he performed anonymously. He had recorded his actions in his diaries, but his identity would have remained unknown had he not died in an accident; thereafter his fame quickly spread as Chairman Mao called on the entire nation to learn from the spirit of the "Comrade Lei Feng."

Curiously, my rooster-crowing act resolved matters for me. Once accepted by my farm's xuanchuandui as one of its own, I no longer wanted to be one of them. Performing, if one had to do it everyday, could be a bore, I realized. Somehow, I did not belong to that world anymore, and I began to understand why my mother never wanted me to be an actress. My childhood dreams finally gave way to reality as I considered the more pressing things there were to learn and the new horizons to explore. For my last two years in the wilderness, I became a reporter for the farm, traveling to local villages to write up the good deeds of educated youths and their ideological models, the local farmers. By publishing my articles in local newspapers, I participated in the representation of a local experience that still supported the idea of *mingdeng*, the power of Mao Zedong Thought. I learned to conceive of the negative aspects of our experience as temporary and isolated events that we could eventually overcome. Moreover, I recognized that I was blessed with the opportunity to be in touch with all kinds of people, from whom I could learn a variety of qualities and skills. To write convincing articles, for instance, I lived with farmers, shepherds, veterinarians, brick makers, mechanics, combine drivers, production team leaders, and old settlers, winning their trust and friendship while writing their stories and telling them my own. I seemed to be experiencing my own version of the ideal life of the literati: traveling thousands of miles and reading ten thousands of books *(xing qianli lu, du wanjuan shu)*. Writing kept me in touch with reality but also offered an escape from it, a space in which I could fantasize a better life. Writing granted me an intellectual life that made it possible to celebrate the ordinary people while being accepted by them as a star. This dual position later helped me gain admission to the English department of Beijing Foreign Languages Institute, another elite school, which I joined on September 9, 1973.

Writing also found me a soul mate, a handsome man who was my first crush. Born into a peasant family in a rural area outside Tianjin, Xiao Guo was indeed a *caizi* (a talented scholar), a brilliant mind, and a flair for writing. He also attracted me because he was as down-to-earth as the local peasants. When we traveled together to the villages, he always knew what to say to the farmers of different backgrounds and could do their particular tasks as well as they could. Time passed all too quickly when I was with him. My heart leapt when one snowy day on our way to a village in an oxcart, he gently placed his cotton-padded coat around my shoulders. I treasured the nights that we chatted until morning, facing each other across a table while reading and writing under the same lamp in our office. My "Mingdeng" story only came up once as we reminisced about our childhoods. For I was a different person now, one who understood that most Chinese peasants and other ordinary people still struggled to secure the basic means of existence for themselves and their families without caring much about what happened under Mao's lamp in Zhongnanhai.

Xiao Guo and people like him sheltered me when I lived in the northeast. I remember in particular one event during my first two years in the village in which people unexpectedly stood by me. Although my peers had selected me for commendation as an "outstanding" farmer, I was nevertheless barred from becoming a member of a Youth League because my father was still under investigation for his past. I felt rejected and disappointed, but I was touched on hearing that the older members of the Youth League had argued my case, pointing out the unfairness of a party policy that rejected children on the basis of their politically suspect family backgrounds. More than ever, I revered these veteran farmers of an earlier generation (some of whom were illiterate), who had settled in the wilderness, answering the CCP's call to reclaim the frontier for collective farming after having fought courageously during the civil war. What recognition or reward did they receive after years of sacrificing in the wilderness? In view of their contribution, what reason had I to resent the fact that my hard labor brought me no visible "payoff"? When I was invited to their homes, which were devoid of the comforts that urban dwellers would have regarded as necessities and taken for granted, I felt warmth, love, and trust from these people, who, in turn, envied my education and even my family background. They sometimes urged me to tell them about my parents' acting careers and wanted to know how they were faring during the Cultural Revolution. (Some of their questions might have been deemed politically incorrect, since my father was still being investigated as an enemy of the people.) They treated me like a daughter and cherished me for being down-to-earth like them, but also for coming from a family of "celebrities" that differed from theirs. While I would not deny the sometimes dispiriting effect on me of back-breaking labor and my longing to return home, I can still say that spiritually and emotionally I was not as devastated as many authors of Cultural Revolution memoirs would have us believe everyone was. I never felt totally alone. Caring and supportive people accepted me for who I was. Thus in that cold, wintry, and snow-covered northeast wilderness I knew a kind of real love that gave me hope and brought warmth to my heart.

In 1973, four years to the day after I had departed from Beijing, I left the wilderness for good. All day Xiao Guo helped me pack without saying a word. As I shook his hand to say good-bye, I thought of our favorite novel, *Niumeng* (*The Gadfly*, written by E. L. Voynich and published in 1897). One of the most popular Western novels in the People's Republic of China during the fifties and sixties, it told the story of Arthur, the protagonist, and Gemma, his "comrade," childhood friend, and secret love. Together they fought courageously for the revolutionary cause they shared without ever expressing their love for each other. But before the authorities executed him, Arthur wrote to Gemma, telling her that when she was a little girl, he had kissed her without her permission: "It was a scoundrelly trick to play, I know; but you must forgive that: and now I kiss the paper where I have written your name. So I have kissed you twice, and both times without your consent." Of course I did not kiss Xiao Guo's hand, nor did I ever reveal my love in the many letters I wrote him after my departure.

On the day I started back to Beijing, I felt despondent at leaving behind my many dear friends. I felt no need now to look for my teammates from my xuanchuandui (as I had on leaving Beijing): they were all right there, standing next to me and around me. Xiao Guo saw me off at Jiamusi City, where the local bus system finally connected with a small train station. It took us a whole day to get there, during which we hardly said anything to each other. At this moment of farewell, no words could be sufficient to express how much we shared, not only our dreams but also memories of the hardships we had faced, the friendship we enjoyed, and the countless sleepless nights we spent writing, under dim lamps, accounts of the idealistic endeavors of our generation.

To Xiao Guo and to numerous unsung heroes and heroines who never left the northeast, I dedicate this essay. I know that a good part of me was left behind in the wilderness, perhaps because he and his family never left the northeast. My wish is that I might preserve a real mingdeng story that speaks for those ordinary people still tilling the land in the Chinese countryside, who never had the chance to return to their birthplace. This nostalgia for the energy, youth, and idealism of those times I feel more keenly with each day away from China.

BAI DI

MY WANDERING YEARS IN THE CULTURAL REVOLUTION
The Interplay of Political Discourse and Personal Articulation

---

IN THE 1990s

While I studied for my Ph.D., there was a photo of Mike, my son, on my desk at home. It shows him when he was about six, just coming from China to join me in Columbus, Ohio. His cute smile on those round, chubby cheeks gave me a great sense of pride. I was the mother of a well-behaved son. That photo washed away the physical fatigue and mental frustration generated by my forever-hectic schedule in American academia. Being a mother was not easy. But how could I complain? Mike was just a nice boy.

"Mike, it's time to take a shower, and don't forget to floss your teeth." Every night I gave the same undisputed orders. Like most Chinese families in the United States, we communicated in Chinese at home.

"*Hao* [OK], mama," my obedient boy would answer.

This routine would soon be disrupted once his chubby face became more square and edged. Mike started to resist my orders. His official declaration of independence was announced one evening when he was about ten.

"Mike, it's shower time," I said habitually.

"*Deng yixiar* [Just a minute]!" His eyes were fixed on the TV screen.

"Wait for what? Your hair smells. Go take a shower." I was a very persistent mother.

"Mom, can you ever stop? When you watch TV, I never bother you! I know what to do and when to do it!" He blasted back in English.

"Oh, give me a break. Exactly because you don't know what to do and when to do it, I am here to take care of you." A mother had to have the upper hand.

"You are so unfair! Can't you just leave me alone? It's going to be over in a few minutes, gosh, why you are so controlling!"

Since then, this has become a pattern. Mike's choice of using Chinese or English in response to my requests is a good indicator of whether he plans to obey me or not. As time goes on, he has enriched his vocabulary of resistance: "freedom," "democracy," "I have the right to . . . ." But I am convinced that what we usually argue about are not issues of democracy or personal choice. He has a lot of choices. Overall, I am as reasonable as a mother can be. He just likes to watch TV instead of washing his hair.

One day in an after-dinner conversation with a visiting professor from China who specializes in comparative cultural studies, I mentioned these issues of the American discourse of personal freedom and rights, my concern over Mike's inadequate Chinese, and our increasingly confrontational mother-son relationship.

"Well, it's only natural." As always, Professor W had a ready answer. "Chinese is a language of obedience, and English one of democracy. The Chinese language, whether as Confucian rhetoric or Maoist discourse, is not a language that promotes the notion of 'self.' To think about it, we Chinese are the victims of our own language. Self, freedom, personal rights, all these are basically Western concepts, and they are embedded in Western languages. Imagine this, it sounds awkward in Chinese if a child says to his parents, '*Nimen yinggai zunzhong wo geren de xuanze*' [You should respect my personal choices]." Professor W's newly learned postmodern theory on the hegemony of language seemed to have found its applicability.

This casual conversation touched upon some issues deeply important to me both academically and personally, issues that continue to baffle as well as interest me. In the fall semester of 1999, I was invited to give a guest lecture in a women's studies class at Iowa State University. After my talk on the effect of the spread of global capitalism on Chinese rural women, one student asked me a seemingly irrelevant question: "I wonder how you became a feminist since you had never been exposed to freedom and had never enjoyed free speech?"

These two instances very much point to one problematic which is characteristic of a popular, yet rarely critically challenged postmodernist assumption that discursive practices have the all-containing power to constitute the speaking subject's ideology. This linguistic determinism, when applied to the (mis)understanding of modern China, is tinted with an Orientalist/essentialist simplicity; while Western languages help create freedom, people living in mainland China are regarded as mute or incapable of personal articulation because of the hegemonic discourse. They are said to live in a discursive "matrix," to borrow the name of a recent Hollywood film, where official language always succeeds in brainwashing each and every one.

I was born and had most of my schooling in the People's Republic of China. Does that mean I have been doomed since my birth to become a self-effacing robot? Has the Communist rhetoric with which I was brought up deprived me of expressions of personal desire? If so, how could I have become what I am now: an opinionated career woman with strong feminist beliefs, an educator encouraging critical thinking in my students? As I recall my childhood experiences, I am pretty sure that I was no less disobedient at heart, even though I was a well-behaved and well-versed girl. In fact, my own official demonstration of so-called agency came when I was about Mike's age.

IN THE 1960s

When the Cultural Revolution had started in the summer of 1966, my father, a party official at a university in Harbin, a city in northeastern China, was "struggled against" and was labeled a *Zouzipai* (capitalist-roader). A zouzipai was a bad person, and a bad person, as I understood then, did not love Chairman Mao. However, I was pretty sure that my father loved Chairman Mao—and that my father was a much better person than my mother. My mother was a harsh punisher who only noticed me when I did something wrong, or something she could interpret as wrong, such as not getting a perfect score on a math test. Her way of punishment and showing disapproval was to sulk. Her silence created in me self-disappointment, guilt, and loneliness. My father, however, seemed ready to accept me as I was; he was the parent who recognized my achievements. It was my father who encouraged me to recite Chairman Mao's poems when the collection was published in 1964. During family friends' visits on Sundays, my recitation of Mao's poems became a routine performance designed by my father to entertain the visitors. On these occasions, his appreciative smiles told me he was proud of me.

It was beyond my comprehension why my father was labeled a bad person and was struggled against. However, my capitalist-roader father now seemed more like a father than the busy member of a cadre he had been before the Cultural Revolution's onset; he now came home every night and the family ate together. What's more, Mother suddenly had the motivation to prepare nice dishes.

To be with my father was a new luxury for me. Prior to his new labeling, I seldom saw him. I was at a boarding school and only came home on Saturday nights, and he often had meetings late into the night and sometimes into Sunday morning. Now he was at home like all the other fathers, back from work punctually every day, and I was free from school. Our school was closed at the beginning of the Cultural Revolution.

One wintry evening in January 1967, my father, mother, younger brother, and I were sitting around the kitchen table having dinner. I was trying to finish my bowl of rice, which would not go down easily. My throat was tight with anxieties, and my heart was pounding. My eyes rested on my father. This time I was not trying to figure out whether he was a good person or a bad one. I had something more important in mind.

Those days, my father wore a swimming cap at home, a red-and-white striped cloth cap for beginning swimmers indicating they should stay at the shallow end of the swimming pool. He looked funny in it because it was winter. Later I learned that his hair had been cut into a *guitou* (devil's hairdo) by some Red Guards during one of the struggle meetings. Now with his swimming cap on, he hummed some tunes as he chewed. His favorite song, also the only one he could sing, was "Women nianqing ren you ke huore xin" (We Young People Have Fervent Hearts), which always baffled me, because in my eyes he was not young at all. My father did not have a musical ear, his singing was forever out of tune. But that out-of-tune tune had a soothing effect on me. Even today, the thought of that song brings tears to my eyes. I believe that, at that moment, my father's singing represented stability, familiarity, permanence, and ultimate optimism in a time of radical uncertainty.

My mother sat at the other end of the table. She was more patient with us now because my father was home. She kept saying that she had to thank the Cultural Revolution for giving back her husband. She often said, "Huaishi bian haoshi [A bad thing can turn into something good]," quoting Chairman Mao.

As dinner drew to an end, and as my mother's newly learned dish, fried pork loin, settled in our bellies, my father's out-of-tune humming serenaded us. Overcoming my intense uneasiness, I finally mustered up the courage to announce to them that I would like to *duoquan* (seize power) in our family.

"What? What power?" Mother shouted back.

"We should have a power seizure struggle in our family," unable to explain myself, I merely repeated my statement.

Why did they need an explanation? I wondered. They surely understood the meaning of "seizing the power." Outside, the deafening sound of gongs and drums celebrating the victory of Shanghai's January power seizure had been going on for nearly a month now. Following Shanghai's example, *geming zaofanpai* (the revolutionary rebels) in at least ten provinces tried to gain provincial power, but only our Heilongjiang Province rebels had succeeded. Besides, my mother was trying very hard to join the power-seizing Red Guards in her school, and my father's power had been taken away by the students at his university. Actually, power seizure was one of the main topics at the dinner table between my parents those days if they ever talked at all in front of me and my brother.

"Seize what? Cooking is the power here. All right, from tomorrow on, you cook!" My mother concieved of a way out partly to deal with my rebellion, partly to gain relief for herself from the pain of kitchen work. Our family nanny had left at the outbreak of the Cultural Revolution.

Father was quiet during my mother's counterattack, but the bewildered look on his face clearly showed that he needed some clarification from his adored daughter. Clarification I gave, but I cannot recall the exact words I used. With some revolutionary mumbo jumbo, I managed to make my point: I wanted to have some power, economic power, which boiled down to money. Yeah, I needed some pocket money. In the end, my mother's anger ebbed, thanks to my father's mediation, and a middle ground was found among all the parties. I would have some pocket money under the condition that I take charge of buying food for the family, which meant I was responsible for going to the market each day. "Money is earned," Mother said, not forgetting to throw her motto at me when the ordeal had ended.

Power seizure at home was a collective action. While I was negotiating with my parents for the first time in my life, I knew I was not the only one being rebellious *zaofan* toward my parents. A somewhat similar situation was staged in two other households in our big residential courtyard. Two other saboteurs were asserting the same demand to their parents, using similar political rhetoric. How can I describe the sensations that swamped me when I had retreated to my room knowing that the next morning three of us would gather in SY's small bedroom and celebrate our victory? It was joy, but, more than that, it was a newly found confidence in myself. I had a face-off with my parents, especially my mother, and I won the battle. For me, nothing could be a greater achievement than having my own voice heard and my desires recognized and satisfied by my parents, the ultimate authority figures in my life.

Thanks to this well-thought-out plan in which we had decided to satisfy our personal needs under the guise of fashionable politics, we got what we wanted from our miserly parents. To be honest, I hadn't the faintest idea then what *duoquan* meant. It was just a powerful word with which one could get what one ordinarily could not. How we translated the personal into the political while plotting our power seizure, I have no recollection. However, I am pretty sure that it must have been SY who initiated the whole thing.

SY and I attended the same boarding school, and we had been in the same class since we were four. Before the summer of 1966, I never liked her. I was a good student and usually got good grades in all subjects. I thought myself popular among my fellow classmates because I had a sense of humor. However, good as I was, I seldom was given the honor of *sanhao xuesheng* (good student in three aspects), which meant being a good student in ideology, study, and health. It was the greatest honor, equivalent to being a good citizen here in the States. The reason I didn't get the honor, as I figured out later, was that I liked to freely express my judgment of others, but not without sarcasm, which I thought of as humor. So I would time and again offend my fellow students, who in turn would either report to the teachers or, worse still, not vote for me. The honor would go to SY nearly every year. Yeah, she was a good student and everything, but I thought I was much better. Actually the major difference between us was really that I was genuinely quick, while she sneakily calculated. For instance, when a teacher asked a question in class, I was quick to jump the gun, trying to be the first to give the answer—well, to show off in order to win some admiration. Naturally, the answer could not be perfect. SY would bring up the rear by giving a more thoughtful answer, one that would be right within the realm of the teacher's expectations and, as you can guess, mostly developed upon my premises.

When I was seven, my father took me to Beijing and we visited the Beijing Zoo, where I saw many animals, such as pandas, snakes, and zebras, for the first time in my life. Soon after we came back from Beijing, a teacher asked us to make sentences with the phrase "xiang . . . yiyang [look like]": "A zebra looks like a horse." I immediately put my newly acquired knowledge into language practice. But the teacher was hesitant to give me praise. Then SY

raised her hand. "A zebra looks like a horse, but it is not a horse."
"Good, very good," responded the teacher. But as far as I knew, SY
had never even been to Beijing, let alone seen a zebra.

So we used to be competitors, at least that was the case in my
mind. SY was the only child of a pair of philosopher parents; both
taught in the department of philosophy. Her mother, who was several years older than her father, was a target of gossip. Time and
again I overheard my mother talking to other women about how
her political straight face had been the asset that successfully lured
SY's father, a good looking, smart man, into marrying her. SY surely
had inherited the talents of her parents: she was smart and politically correct, and she had a very retentive memory. Above all, she
had a pair of big eyes and a head of thick, shiny black hair. In her
bedroom—she had her own bedroom, and I shared one with my
brother!—there was a big photo of her at the age of four. She already had two pigtails with green ribbons. But in my four-year-old
photo, I look like a boy dressed in a miniature navy uniform with
a hat. As my mother explained to me later, I did not have enough
hair to be dressed like a girl. In any case, I did not like her—that
was for sure. But my *intense* dislike for her started when she rede-
fined my name.

Nearly every Chinese name has a story, and the story of my
name is definitely a nice one. I have always been proud of my
name; it looks sophisticated in Chinese, and, best of all, it is not
gender specific. It always invites explanation, which I am always
ready to provide. People usually ask me, "Is it your pen name?"
Do you get a feel for its sophistication? In fact, till this day I have
never tired of explaining my name with the same wording: "*Bai* is
in the third tone and means 'cypress.' *Di* has a wood radical. The
other part, *li,* is the word for 'slave.' It is a kind of wood, not
eye catching, but resilient and very able to survive. Because I am
the firstborn, my parents hope that I will be that independent."
This is the story my father told me. I feel that my name stands for
me: not especially pretty, but independent and strong.

Once I was telling this proud story to some other kids in school
when SY cut in, "Bai Di means your parents want you to have *yi
bai ge didi* [one hundred brothers]. When you were born, they were

disappointed because you are a girl. My dad told me that. I checked the dictionary, 'di' is a tree, but it also meant brother in ancient times."

So said the dictionary, what could I say! From then on, I had a humiliating nickname: "One Hundred Brothers." I felt devalued.

We only became friends after the closing of school in the summer of 1966. After summer vacation, we were told that we should stay home for a while because the teachers and grownups were organizing a movement. As a boarding school pupil, going home equaled going to heaven.

Ordinarily, when school was in session we stayed in school from Monday morning till Saturday evening. The school bus would drive us home on Saturdays. The bus home was filled with euphoria; we sang songs at the top of our lungs and shrieked, "We are going home, we are going home!" Sundays were the only time for me not to be constricted: no strict time slots for different activities, just lying in bed, lazing around, going shopping or window shopping with Grandma, listening to some "adult conversations" between my mother, father, uncles, and aunts. On Monday mornings, it was a different story. The bus would come to pick us up in front of the gate of our courtyard. The usually quiet area turned virtually into a battlefield. The younger kids would cry and kick, trying not to get on the bus. The more seasoned ones like myself just passively accepted their fate. The bus with its sickening diesel smell would take me to those long weeknights during which, in bed, with tears of self-pity, I imagined killing myself to make my mother, who always pushed me onto the bus, feel sorry for sending me away from home.

Not going to school for me at that moment was a blessing, especially because I was a year away from the middle-school entrance examination. The (over)expectation of my parents was overwhelming. They were sure that I would defeat all the other kids in the examination. Our neighborhood was full of all kinds of professors and lecturers from one of the province's top universities. Each and every one thought that their own offspring were the smartest. My mother was very competitive in nature; she wanted the best of everything. I was the extension of her ego; I knew then I had to triumph in the competitive citywide exam so as to get into No. 3 Middle School, the key school in the city.

The imminent exam gave me insomnia that even today accompanies me whenever I am under pressure. The dark circles under my eyes caught the attention of my uncle one Sunday. In the hospital, the doctor tested me by asking me to close my eyes. My eyelids were shaking violently, which was taken to be a sure sign of a nervous disorder. The doctor said that it was a rare case for a ten-year-old. I do not know why nobody ever asked me the reason for my sleeping disorder. My parents, the teachers, everybody expected something I knew was too much for me to accomplish. The fear of failing others' expectations debilitated me.

Then came news too good to be true: I did not have to go to school! No more getting up early to line up and do exercises in the chilly Harbin morning, no more report cards I feared were not good enough to hand to my mother, no more pressure to be selected as "Good Student." And to hell with No. 3 Middle School! Our previously quiet courtyard was transformed into a bustle and rustle locus where I was to learn things beyond the confines of the boarding school and home. It was the first time in my life that I could play without being burdened by a sense of guilt. We played wholeheartedly despite the fact that nearly everybody's parents were getting into some form of trouble. In our neighborhood, Red Guards pasted *dazibao* (big character posters) all over the place, and some of them had my father's name on them with big scarlet crosses. They also framed nearly every door in the yard with revolutionary antithetical couplets and horizontal scrolls. The scroll over the door of my home read *goudong* (dog-hole). Our next door neighbor's read *yichou wannian* (leaving a stink for ten thousand years). There were, of course, many moments of uncertainty in my heart. But my father's optimism toward the movement shielded me from being disturbed emotionally. More importantly, fear was equally shared and disgrace was collectively, sometimes humorously, accepted.

Gao Bobo (Uncle Gao) was arguably the highest ranking official living in our courtyard. He worked in city government. Before the Cultural Revolution, he was really somebody. A black car with green silk curtains on the windows would pick up him and his wife to do their Sunday shopping. When they disappeared into the car, we would run after it, all the way to the gate. During the first few months of the Cultural Revolution, Gao Bobo would often appear in the yard, not waiting for his black car, but with a group of middle-aged Red Guards from his work unit. They put a tall paper dunce cap on him and paraded him around the yard to be humiliated.

One day, Gao Bobo walked back without the company of the Red Guards. Instead, a group of capitalist-roaders, all with paper hats on, paraded with him. We followed this strange group into the hallway where Gao Bobo lived. They moved out some chairs from Gao Bobo's apartment and started to re-paste the peeled-off antithetical couplets and the horizontal scroll around his door. I thought it funny because Gao Bobo was taking this seriously. He was actually supervising the re-pasting work: "The left end should be higher, higher . . . OK, perfect; put more glue on . . . Good." After completing the job, the group left. That night I shared this story with my parents. They laughed hard. "Lao Gao is super," my father commented. "He carries his revolutionary optimism through thick and thin."

My father was no less optimistic in dealing with the mass movement. Every evening, we waited anxiously for him to come home. When I heard the sound of his key in the lock, I rushed to the door to open it for him, and my blind brother had his slippers ready. Father brought with him a unique, warm smell that permeated the room with its vitality. While I busily arranged the table for the family dinner, my mother would always ask the same question: "How was your day?" My father never talked about the physical abuses he endured in those daily struggle meetings. Instead he usually had some jokes to share. "Your mom always complains that I am short. But being short is not always a shortcoming. In the struggle meetings, we have to bend over to acknowledge our guilt. I am always praised by the Red Guards for having the best attitude since I bend the lowest. Actually it's because I am the shortest in the gang." We laughed and enjoyed our dinner.

While the adults were busy with struggle meetings, self-examinations, and revolutionary activities, we girls spent most of our time molding ourselves: reciting Chairman Mao's quotations, singing revolutionary songs, and working on our gymnastics. We practiced splits and bending backward until our hands touched the ground—all the moves we had learned from the street performances of Red Guards. Boys usually were tumbling alongside us or watching us with very critical eyes. They would cheer at somebody's excellent performance. We were no longer classmates, we were playmates.

Our favorite playground was a big sand dune behind the east buildings. The sand had been left there by a failed construction project. A haven for gymnastic practice and an ideal hangout, the sand dune attracted not only kids free from school, but also all kinds of peddlers, whose presence was instrumental for our later power struggle at home. It was on that sand dune that SY, JH, and I became friends. If birds of a feather flock together, then I have to infer that our flock was made up of the best gymnasts—which was considered quite an achievement back then.

Every flock must have a leader, and SY was naturally the one. When I say that she was calculating, I really mean that she had a mental calmness unfitting to her age. To her, problems imply not worries but the need to search for solutions. It must have been her who suggested that we seize power at home to solve our thorny problem of lacking pocket money.

Up until the Cultural Revolution, we boarding school students were virtually locked up, separated from the real world, where *jingji jichu* (the economic base) was always vital. Money did not ring a bell with us because we were raised in an idealistic Communist-style boarding school. We ate what was provided, we wore what our parents sent. Once out of the "Communist" system, the power of money became clearer each and every day, and various desires began to creep into our minds. In 1966 one cent could buy two pieces of candy—and, since collecting candy wrappers was a fashion, we could easily make a friend by sharing a wrapper. Three cents would buy a Popsicle, and letting someone take a lick of it definitely showed goodwill. With ten cents, one would be treated as the king or queen of the dune, if nothing else. On that sand dune with the peddlers, I learned that money was the thing to have to be looked up to. Till this day, I am still not sure why my parents never bothered to put some pennies in my pocket. Either they were too involved in the revolutionary movement to pay attention to my materialistic and social needs, or they just consciously tried to prevent me from falling victim to what Marx called "commodity fetishism."

SY suggested that we should make revolution at home. If our parents were the targets of the Red Guards' revolution, why should they be immune from our struggle against their bourgeois ideas? After all, we were Little Red Guards! SY's wise suggestion was warmly received and positively responded to by me and JH. At that moment, both JH and I became instant admirers of SY's intensely trendy lexicon and its amazing appropriateness and adaptability when used in describing our desires and our lives. As I've said, I was a quick learner, and JH was not slow either. We had already made up our inner-circle language. For instance, when the three of us agreed to include a new girl into our circle, we would not say *gentahao* (let her in). It sounded naive. We preferred to say, "Chairman Mao teaches us: *Tuanjie qilai quzhengqu gengda de shengli* [Unite striving for greater victory]." If we started to dislike her, instead of saying *bugentahao* (we do not like her any more), we would say, "Chairman Mao says that *Geming bushi qingke chifan* [making revolution is not inviting people over for dinner]." From others' perspective, we perhaps mismatched and misinterpreted everything. But we were very comfortable with our choice of grand-sounding words to say what we wanted to say.

JH, another member of our gang of three, had a charm of her own. She was only a year older than SY and I, but in our eyes she represented maturity. Though her mother was the headmaster of our boarding school, JH did not attend our school because her family could not afford it. That was why she knew everything that SY and I wanted to know but never had a chance to know. Once she said, "When a girl is about twelve or thirteen, something will happen to her. Guess what that thing is."

"She'll get a big belly," I immediately responded without giving any thought, but correctly assuming that JH's questions were usually of a biological nature.

"Wrong," JH said, "you have to have blood first. Then if a man touches you, your belly will get big." Right then and there, I had my first lesson in human reproduction.

So you can see that SY and I accepted JH as our friend. Not only were we all good at gymnastics, but she brought a breath of fresh air into our lives. SY and I only went to the sand dune to play, but JH came to the dune with a pile of dirty cooking utensils to clean. From her I learned that sand could be used as cleanser, especially for oily smudges on cookware. In terms of gymnastics, she was much better than SY and I. She could do the splits the straightest. And her waist was undoubtedly the supplest of all, as soft as a noodle, which was really cool back then. When she arched backward, her head could touch her feet; she virtually became a circle. I was good at the splits, but I felt dizzy when I tried to arch over backward. Years later, when the mass production of model theater started, her talent was officially recognized. She acted as Xi'er and Wu Qinghua, the women protagonists in the revolutionary model ballets *The White-Haired Girl* and *Red Detachment of Women*, respectively, in her middle school performing troupe before she went to the countryside to join her sister in 1969.

Now it was the winter of 1967, and we were good friends in spite of the different social positions of our parents and our different upbringings, primarily because the three of us were keen on twisting our bodies into different postures and feeling beautiful when we did. We also needed each other to make it through our wandering years without much adult guidance or supervision. To quote SY's words, which were mostly quotes from Chairman Mao, *Women doshi laizi wuhusihai, weile yige gongtong de geming mubiao zoudao yiqi laile* (We came together from five lakes and four seas for one revolutionary purpose).

Another famous quote from Chairman Mao, which calls for unity in spite of differences, helped us sustain our friendship: *qiudatong, cunxiaoyi* (Seek common ground on major issues while reserving differences on minor ones). To translate it into contemporary lexicon, this means that people with different backgrounds should get along, as in a melting pot or a salad bowl. The purpose of this mutual tolerance advocated by Mao was to encourage the masses to revolutionize.

But my acceptance of JH was not really all that lofty in nature. Besides her amazing physical flexibility, she was the kind of

girl I was not, and the truth is that girls of my age adored difference. During that summer, she wore a shirt with two breast pockets that always seemed full of neat stuff. SY speculated that there
must be a handkerchief in each one to make them look so full. But
I had a different interpretation. I observed that when JH ran, those
two pockets shook. When we became friends, we asked her about
her pockets, which were now gone because we had all changed to
thicker fall clothes; she just said proudly, *"Shengli xianxiang* [physi-
ological phenomenon]." After that, SY and I sinisterly referred to
her as Physiological Phenomenon behind her back.

JH had a lot of other kinds of biological stuff to share with us.
She had two big brothers and one big sister. All of them were Red
Guards, one was in college, and the other two were in secondary
school. They were all serious-looking, especially her brothers, and
they were cocky. Her family's three-bedroom apartment was always
full of pretentious young men and women with red bands on their
arms. They were organizing a revolution, and some of them had
been to Beijing to see Chairman Mao. They never even cast us as
much as a glance when we were there. Their obvious lack of interest in us further aroused our curiosity and respect. But JH was pretty
good at stripping off their seriousness. From her we had learned
that they were also doing something not so revolutionary. JH would
tell us which man was paired with which woman, who was dating
whom. And the most exciting topic was always who had dumped
whom, the situation described as *wo shi jiao yang jun shi liu* (I lost
my proud Poplar and you your Willow) in our lexicon, which is a
line from one of Chairman Mao's poems. In that poem Chairman
Mao lamented the loss of his first wife, who was killed by the Nationalists. Once JH also told us that she saw her college-student
brother kissing one of his women comrades-in-arms in one of the
bedrooms. JH did not use the word *kiss* in her narration of the
event. She alluded to it as "they have really made a word *'lu'*," a
quote from a 1960s novel *Great Changes in a Mountain Village*
(Shanxiang Jubian) written by Zhou Libo. *Lu* is a Chinese character in the shape of two mouths linked together. So to "make the
word lu" means to kiss.

Our daily conversation was imbued not only with Mao's

quotations but also language from literary works. My family had a good collection of books in Russian and Chinese because my parents both majored in Russian literature in college. In the early fall of 1966, our house was searched by the Red Guards from my father's university. Ironically, most of his books, which were labeled "poisonous," were left on the bookshelves untouched. Instead, the Red Guards confiscated some of our family property, which, according to my mother, should not have been taken away; they took things like family photo albums and some of her clothes. My mother still holds a grudge that they took a valuable mahjong set made of animal bones. Most of the things taken were later returned to us, but the mahjong set is still at large. Just last summer my mother came to visit me from China, and she brought Mike a mahjong set.

"These are made of plastic. The feel is not good," she started again. "Do you remember the set that the Red Guards took away? Those were good, you cannot find anything of that quality any more."

I definitely don't have any memory of that mahjong set. What I do remember is that the Red Guards took away my favorite books. Among them were *A Thousand and One Nights*, *Grimm's Fairy Tales*, and *A Hundred Thousand Whys*, a children's encyclopedia on science. They were all birthday gifts from my father and his friends. Before the Cultural Revolution, I would spent my free time on Sundays reading and rereading these books, especially *A Hundred Thousand Whys*. I had learned from it why there are little holes in bread, why a zebra has stripes on its body, why hens lay more eggs in summer, and why I would have a different weight on Mars. I wanted to be a scientist or an astronaut so that I could ask more whys and publish the answers in books. My parents strongly encouraged my interest in science. "The humanities and the social sciences lead you nowhere; they only invite trouble," my Mother said whenever my future was discussed.

My favorite books were taken away and so were my mother's plans for my future. Summer passed. Soon the harsh Harbin winter set in, and we relocated our youthful activities indoors; we went from bending our bodies to enriching our minds. In the winter of

1967, I began freely reading *dashu* (big books), the novels my mother and father read. I could now read these books without my parents' restriction. Before the Cultural Revolution, I may have had a peek or two at those novels from time to time, but I felt guilty about doing so. Mother said to me many times that novels were for entertainment, for grownups' entertainment. As a child, I could not afford the time to be entertained; I had to spend my time studying, especially studying science. Besides, novels have some biological descriptions morally unfit for me to know, Mother insisted. Now studying science was no longer an obligation, and I had a lot of time at my disposal. What's more, I was free from my parents' surveillance, for they were occupied by the revolution. I, with my buddies, read novels of all kinds, and we shared our parents' collections.

In that period of reading literary works by both Russian and Chinese writers, I did not have the ability to explore their social significance or revolutionary themes. My unguided reading of these works now labeled propagandist did not strike me at the time as being different from other stories of moral conflict, or from fables, or from adventures. "Virtue/communism vs. evil/capitalism," "good/working people vs. bad/landlords"—these formed my imaginary world of human richness and dramatic complexity. My limited world was extended by words that became visually meaningful images indelibly printed on my mind. My own life experiences played an important part in my interpretation of those works. When Pavel Korchagin lost his eyesight in *How Steel Is Tempered,* I shed more than a few tears. He reminded me of my beloved younger brother Dalin, who was born blind, and I tried to encourage him to become a writer, as Paul did, by reading to him. The biography *Gulia's Road* contained photos of Little Hedgehog, Gulia's six-year-old son, who I thought looked very much like myself when I was four. The death of Gulia, a Russian woman revolutionary, bothered me deeply because I associated her with my own mother, a Russian teacher.

I have to admit that the most exciting aspect of novels was reading about the biological phenomena JH epitomized and Mother abhorred. A pre-teenager, I had already experienced an uneasy sensation, a wrenching of the heart, an unspeakable excitement when coming across written descriptions of those physiological phenomena.

With a new book in hand, I would consciously or unconsciously leaf through looking for words or phrases of romance. After I had exhausted all love scenes, I would officially start a serious reading, which meant following the story from cover to cover. Of course I was impressed with the revolutionary heroes and heroines, but it was only the romantic heroes who stayed on my mind. For instance, in *Great Changes in a Mountain Village,* the handsome young man who led the village militia refuses to accept the love of the most beautiful girl in the village because of her dubious family background. By twists and turns, he finally accepts her love and makes the word lu with her. I liked this novel because it was idealistically romantic. What is more satisfyingly romantic than a tall, handsome militia leader embracing a beautiful girl on a wild mountain? Class struggle may have been the novel's ostensible theme, but I did not grasp that aspect of it. To be sure, I was not the only one learning about romance in revolutionary novels. When JH told us her brother and a woman were making the word lu, SY and I immediately got the clue.

JH, SY, and I decided, most probably at my suggestion, that our next step should be to actually see what we had read in books and heard from JH. JH, who knew everything, told us she knew a place where people went to kiss. On a bitterly cold night, we sneaked out of our houses and went to a local park to see people actually making lu with our own eyes.

The park was two blocks away from our residential courtyard. It used to be a burial ground for the White Russians who fled to China after the October Revolution. Because the people in the northeast called Russians *lao maozi* (hairy people), the place was commonly called Maozifenr (hairy people's graveyard). After 1945, when the Communist Party took control of Harbin, the government leveled the ground and made it a public park. But even as a public park it still had a ghostly eeriness about it, with its white picket fence and pitch-black wooden gate. In summer, one could spot gardeners planting flowers around a lonely pavilion. In winter, it became a desolate place covered with snow. Not many people frequented the park, because of its notoriety for being haunted by foreign ghosts. My father's mother told me stories about those foreign ghosts, how they appeared at night, their bodies covered with long yellow hair, to prey on Chinese girls who stayed out at night when they should be home. The ghosts in Grandma's stories were as gender biased as she was. Her ghosts only came after us girls; boys were immune to their threat. "Boys are stronger and they are full of *yang*. They will drive the ghosts away." "But I am stronger than my brother," I protested. Grandma's gendered explanations never convinced me.

Young as I was, I knew that she and Mother never liked each other. They certainly had extremely different ways of looking at my future. While Mother pushed me tenaciously toward becoming her idea of a successful woman—a scientist, professor, or astronaut—Grandma seemed to prepare me for failure and disappointment to combat her emancipated, educated daughter-in-law. I had an ambiguous feeling toward Grandma. I loved her, and she was the only one in the family who comforted me when Mother became nasty. And she could afford the time to tell me stories. But sometimes I resisted her because of her different ways of treating my brother and me. For instance, she called me Xiaodir (little Di) and my brother, seven years my junior, Dalin (big Lin). By the way, the *r* she attached to my name doubles the belittling effect in Chinese. At the time, I thought she was too old to tell the difference between big and small. "I am big, my brother is small," I kept correcting her, but she wouldn't budge. She would continue to call me Xiaodir, which made her Shandong accent extremely annoying. I didn't like her renaming me, not because of the gender thing, but because my name is like a habit, and changing it is painful.

But back to the ghosts. I had been in Maozifenr park only once at night. It was before National Day on October 1, 1964. Some students from our school had been chosen to participate in the celebration of the fifteen-year anniversary of the founding of the People's Republic. I was one of the lucky few chosen to form words on the city square as the background for the big festival parade. But, because the school did not have enough money to provide colored bouquets for each participant, we had to make the bouquets ourselves. I spent the following weekend at home searching everywhere for a branchlike frame for my bouquet. I did not find anything. Then Maozifenr came to mind. There were a lot of bushes and shrubs in that park. If only I could break a branch, the problem would be solved. But I knew it was the wrong thing to do. A good student should not destroy state property, one of the basic principles I was taught in school and at home. And I took those principles quite seriously. In my heart, I never gave up trying to be a "Good Student in Three Aspects," never. But this time my need to participate in the celebration overrode my conscience. I went to the park after dark. When I was sure that nobody was around, I snapped off a twig or two and ran home.

Maozifenr was appropriately renamed Guijianchou Gongyuan (Frustrating the Ghosts Park) by the Red Guards at the very start of the Cultural Revolution. Indeed the raging tide of revolution had swept away all the evil ghosts. The ghostly white fence was repainted dark red and the black gate was nowhere to be found. The formerly quiet streets around the park became noisy with mass parades. The foreign ghosts must have surely been frustrated to see that during the day their holy burial ground was a revolutionary rallying place for Red Guards from the nearby middle-school and, at night, a comfortable shelter for the Red Guards' romantic rendezvous.

One bitter cold January night, SY, JH, and I waited behind the bushes for a couple to go into the pavilion, which according to JH was the love nest. I knew what we were doing was indecent. So did the two of them. Hadn't Chairman Mao asked us to be noble-minded and pure-hearted, to become persons of moral integrity above vulgar interests? Trying to ease my pounding heart and sense of guilt, I began making snowballs with my gloved hands as I lay there. It was so cold that night that the snow was not even sticky. I thought of what Grandma had told me: people could easily freeze to death when the snow became dusty. And, of course, I recalled her story about the ghosts underground trying to get to Chinese girls who stayed out late. Uneasy as I was, I did not feel scared. Chairman Mao said, "If the East Wind fails to prevail over the West Wind, then the West Wind prevails over the East Wind." Now I was virtually lying above those devils, and they did not dare come out to get me, so the East Wind prevailed over the West Wind.

Amidst all those rambling thoughts, what I felt was the north wind blowing across my face, bitterly cold and sharp as a knife. The three of us had waited a long, long time; it seemed like ages. Nothing happened, nobody came. When our feet became numb from the cold, we decided to abort the plan.

The Maozifenr event and our power-seizure struggle at home marked the pinnacle of our coming-of-age adventures before returning to school in the winter of 1968. We had tested the forbidden, contested parental authority, and in our own petty way, enacted the return of the formerly repressed.

THE 1990s

While writing this piece, I talked with my parents, who still live in Harbin and with whom I speak often by phone, about my memories of that year and a half. We talked specifically about my power seizure in the winter of 1967, which I think was instrumental in molding the person I am today. (By the way, they did not know my Maozifenr adventure.) Since that year, I have become a career woman with a feminist conviction in challenging authoritative establishments and in advocating women's rights. But neither of my parents recalled my rebellious action at all. They only remember me as being a nice, responsible daughter and a super sister. When I mentioned my powerful appropriation of political rhetoric for the purpose of satisfying my personal needs, my mother just laughed, "Everybody did that. You think it was just you? Think again."

What she remembers is what I have forgotten. Around 1967, she said, I bought a tiny lock, attached it to one of the desk drawers, and claimed the drawer as mine. "I noticed that and sensed that you had grown up. You wanted your own ground, and you started to keep us from knowing your secrets. That was the moment you split from us."

"Yeah," my father pitched in via speakerphone, "when you were a teenager, you wanted your own space, a room of your own [my father was very proud of my master's thesis on Virginia Woolf]. I guess that was the beginning of your feminism."

I did buy a lock. The three of us each bought one after we got our pocket money. It was cool to have one's own drawer and have it locked up. But was that cheap, poorly made, tiny lock the starting point of my independence?

"When you were born," Father continued, "your mother and I checked the largest dictionary we could find for an hour to choose your name. You may be destined to be an independent woman. Rectification of names, hahahaa." So essentialist, my father!

Now, I myself am the mother of a teenage son. By reflecting on my own childhood desires and dreams, I feel that I understand Mike more. Despite all the differences between us in terms of place, time, and especially language, the images of a teenage boy adorned in Nike sneakers and baggy khaki pants and that of a ten-year-old girl dressed in a faded army uniform have converged in my mind's eyes. Whether in English or in Maoist discourse, in 1990s America or in 1960s China, it is in this interplay between political discourse and personal needs that I see the resemblance between my son of today and the Bai Xiaodir of some thirty years ago.

Yes, we grew up against strikingly different socioeconomic backgrounds; mine with Maoist puritan utopian dream, and his with humanist commodity fantasies. But both of us have experienced growing pains, and both of us have employed trendy words to assert the omnipresent "self." Aren't nonconformist, rebellious acts, even for a short while, toward the authority of one's parents, family, and society, a rite of passage, a necessary step in growing up?

What are JH and SY doing now? I suddenly feel an urge to find them, to see what they have become. Do they remember what I remember of those eighteen months? My memory of the period is composed of selected images—SY's self-confidence, JH's care-free attitude, the sand dune, Father's swimming cap, dusty snow, juggling with Chairman Mao's quotations, the word lu. For me, those images are a thread linking me to my past. What do SY and JH remember as our common past? Do they remember our power-seizure struggle and that freezing night in the graveyard? And what about those tiny locks? Have they played any role in the formation of these women's political beliefs? Do they share my fond feelings toward our colorful daily lives during a historical period said to be

absolutely authoritarian? Most importantly, would they agree that
our idiosyncratic appropriation of a hegemonic discourse shows
that the power of a language lies in its everyday signifying practices rather than in its compulsory imposition of a fixed meaning?

I think they would.

JIANG JIN

"TIMES HAVE CHANGED; MEN AND WOMEN ARE THE SAME"

I grew up in a revolutionary era, an era marked by a loud, distinctive voice announcing, "Times have changed; men and women are the same." The Western reader may be skeptical about the idea that men and women are the same; but in the context of the newly established People's Republic of China, this slogan, in its simplistic way, conveyed a powerful message to millions of Chinese women that in this new era men and women were equal. The new constitution gave women the same rights as it gave men. The state called upon women to work outside the home and promised to reward them with equal pay. The new orthodoxy also held that men and women were equal in terms of intellectual competence, political consciousness, and even physical strength. The rhetoric of women's liberation and a state policy that fostered gender equality informed my growing-up experience in the Maoist era and, to a large extent, shaped my identity and the life path I have chosen.

My childhood was full of excitement and adventure, and I was not at all constrained by the fact that I was a girl. So I had numerous fights with boys. I still vividly remember my first grand victory in one such fight shortly after I entered kindergarten. Kindergarten was a place where Darwin's law that the strong survive applied whenever the teacher was away. Numerous fights forged a natural power-based hierarchy among the kindergartners. One day when I was playing with a foreign doll *(yang wawa)*, the "second king" in my class tried to take my doll from me. The second king feared no one but the grand king, and certainly not me. But sometimes the weaker was aided by a sense of justice. Although I was not a big child, I would not let him take my doll away. As I tried to get my toy back, we became entangled with each other. We wrestled and rolled on the floor of our classroom, scratching each other's faces and arms. In the end, I threw the boy on the floor, pressing him down on his back and sitting on his stomach. After a while our teacher came in and pulled me off the boy. Of course the teacher scolded me, but from then on no boy ever tried to bother me again. In another kindergarten class, I was the favorite girl of the grand king—the most powerful boy in the class. He was a big boy, and his head was disproportionately large. He had large eyes and thick eyebrows, like the revolutionary heroes in movies. He regarded me as the prettiest girl in the class and took me on as his protégée. Later, we both went to the same primary school and were in the same class. He became shy, no longer as bold. We didn't play together anymore, for I was just as naughty as before.

My primary school was one of the best in town, and admission was competitive. The school was experimenting with a five-year program instead of the standard six-year program, with English courses starting in the fourth grade (at that time very few primary schools offered foreign language courses). The physical plant of my school was the envy of neighboring schools, most of which had no campus but only small courtyards. My school had a lovely campus with ample open space for basketball courts, soccer fields, and running tracks. Moreover, we had a huge Ping-Pong room equipped with five tables, and I was on the school Ping-Pong team. On days when the team was not training, I found paradise in a special secluded area of the campus set off from the main fields. This area contained a sand dune, a small pond with a single-log bridge, an iron climber, a mini-hill, and gymnastic equipment. After school I spent hours exploring this miniature world, alone and with other kids. In the ten-minute breaks between classes I played games with the other kids. Several times I strayed too far from the classroom and could not get back in time when the bell rang, even though I ran my fastest. My Chinese teacher, Ms. Xu, was a strict disciplinarian who wouldn't tolerate my lack of punctuality. Once I ran right into her on the stairway while the bell was ringing. She stopped me and pulled my ear hard, scolding, "Didn't you hear the bell!"

At school, girls as well as boys were expected to excel in all three areas—academics, political consciousness, and sports. My position at school was determined not by my gender but by my good grades. Schoolwork was never difficult for me. I was easily among the top ones in my class in math and Chinese. In my second year, perhaps trying to "tame" me, my teacher made me leader of the class's academic and sports activities. I was proud of my new post. Every morning, as our teacher walked into the classroom, I shouted, "Stand up!" As the whole class stood up, we shouted together: "Good morning, teacher!" The good days did not last very long. I was soon as naughty as before. One day, I walked into the classroom and discovered that a soft-speaking, self-conscious boy was standing in my former position. That was it—my adventure into an "official" career was over.

At home, we kids turned the roof of our big four-story apartment building into a playground. We ran at top speed as we played hide-and-seek, the chimneys and water towers on the roof becoming obstacles that made the game more intriguing. Soon our running damaged the roof and caused several leaks in the top-story apartments. The roof was not meant to be a playground, and the authorities later closed it off to kids.

I fell many times while running. When I returned home with blood on my knees or cuts on my hands, my mother would hurry to clean the wounds and put red antiseptic liquid on them, scolding me at the same time: "You've surely become a wild child. You will certainly get your legs broken some day. Don't run again!" But she knew I would keep on running.

I knew Mother was proud of me, not because I hurt myself in these wild games but because of my good grades. My parents were both college-educated liberal intellectuals who believed in a well-balanced education for both daughters and sons, and this included outings with my father. A favorite place he often took my siblings and me was Peace Park, where, for a small fee, we could play Ping-Pong, roller-skate, or swim. Later, Father bought a pair of used roller skates, which became a treasure for us children. He loved these sports and enjoyed them as much as we did. We also had a family library filled with great classics, including *Records of the Grand Historian, Dream of the Red Chamber, The Complete Work of Lu Xun*, and *The Red Cliff*. Whenever I had time—after school and my wild games—I would sit quietly and immerse myself in these great books.

Although I enjoyed reading, my childhood dream was to become an astronomer and explore the sky. Summer nights during my childhood were always hot, and the stars were always bright and beyond number in the deep blue sky. Like other families in the neighborhood, we brought small folding beds, bed sheets, or bamboo mats to the roof, where we slept for the first few hours of the night, until the air cooled. On these summer nights my father and mother would point to the sky, naming different planets and stars in the Milky Way. They would say, "You'll grow up to become an astronomer, and you'll study all the fascinating secrets of the stars." Later, after the roof had been closed off, I sometimes slept on the balcony of our apartment on hot nights. Staring at the clear summer sky, I always thought of my parents' words about becoming a scientist and exploring the universe.

The Cultural Revolution (1966–1976) arrived at the end of my fourth year in primary school. At the time I did not realize that this meant my childhood dream would never materialize. Authorities such as teachers and parents were subjected to criticism, classes were canceled, and kids were set free to engage in all kinds of "revolutionary actions." My classmates and I were delighted when classes were canceled and we were called on to criticize our teachers. I wrote a big-character poster titled "Down with Big Fat Xu!" This was Ms. Xu, our Chinese teacher who had disciplined me by pulling my ears. My classmates had also suffered her discipline, and they signed their names on the poster. We put the poster in the classroom and stood on our desks, shouting, "Down with Big Fat Xu!" Ms. Xu, however, was not there that day. In fact, none of our teachers showed up. So we dispersed into the streets, watching older kids—the Red Guards—making their revolution.

The Red Guards, both male and female, painted revolutionary slogans on the streets using black and red paint. The characters that formed the slogans were larger than I. Leaflets condemning "the capitalist roaders" fell like snow from windows in the high-rise buildings. Red Guards shouted slogans through loud speakers and sang and danced revolutionary songs on makeshift stages: "We are Chairman Mao's Red Guards." It was great fun to watch. The girls in the Red Guards, who wore army uniforms and wide leather belts, particularly impressed my friends and me. Their activism and militant style inspired us. We too wanted to have some fun.

In the heat of that summer, Chairman Mao greeted the Red Guards in Tiananmen Square. From the balcony of the Gate of Heavenly Peace, Mao waved his huge hands at the sea of Red Guards. He invited the No. 1 guard to put a Red Guard band on his left arm, making Mao a Red Guard himself. At that, the Red Guards in the square all went crazy. They cried and shouted in their loudest voices: "Long live Chairman Mao! Long live Chairman Mao!" Some Red Guards fainted from excitement and exhaustion. Mao's audiences with the Red Guards were recorded in documentary films, which were instantly distributed throughout the country. The whole population of China, 800 million people, watched these events. Red Guards everywhere went crazy. They traveled to Beijing from all over the country to see Mao—"the brightest red sun in [their] heart," and everything was free of charge—trains, food, and lodging.

My big brother jumped into the action. He rebelled against my parents and demanded cash for his "revolutionary needs." He took the money and disappeared into the train station. He surely must have gone to Beijing, and then all over the country before coming home. My second brother followed suit. My older sister also tried to get on the train but was pushed off by the crowds. By the time she finally managed to get on a train bound to Beijing, she had missed Mao's audience.

At twelve I was too young to get on the overcrowded capital-bound train. But I took off with a classmate of mine and her sister, who was about two years our senior, on a "long march" toward the north. A local tailor shop made us, free of charge, a large red silk banner with gold characters that read, "The Long March Team of Mao Zedong Thought." The same gold characters were also printed on red arm bands. The "long march" was a legendary story about Chairman Mao and his revolution. In 1934 Mao led a retreat of the Red Army from the Jiangxi base area to escape the Nationalist army's destructive attacks. Mao and his army were on the road for a whole year, surviving not only the relentless pursuit of hostile armies but also incredible natural barriers such as the great snowy mountains and the vast grassy marshlands in the wild west. They started with eighty thousand men and thirty-five women. Only eight thousand made it to the Yanan area in Shaanxi Province. These men and women formed the core of Mao's revolution that swept China in the next fifteen years. Now Mao called on revolutionary youths to follow in the footsteps of the Red Army of the past to gain authentic revolutionary feelings. Many Red Guards indeed hiked the same route the Red Army traveled some thirty years before. Many others marched in the direction of Beijing. Our plan was to march to the ancient capital Nanjing, and from there we hoped to catch a train to Beijing.

Father sent us off one summer morning with encouraging words. (Mother was in the countryside at the time.) The first day, the three of us lined up and marched about twenty miles, carrying the red flag in front of us. That night we stayed in one of the many stations set up specifically to give free food and lodging to the pilgrim Red Guards. On the second day we reached Suzhou. The city's revolutionary history was rather obscure. It was, however, a scenic destination famous for its ancient gardens and historical sites. Instead of looking for revolutionary sites, we spent several days sightseeing, never mind that it had little to do with the life-and-death situation Mao and his Red Army had experienced in their long march. We then marched to Wuxi, our next scenic destination. There, fleas in the inn's bedding were enough to convince us to abandon our pilgrimage. We obtained free tickets and returned home by train, thus ending our little adventure.

The trip lasted only about a week. But it was the first time in my life that my friends and I initiated, planned, and carried out, albeit halfway, a travel plan by ourselves. On the trip, everywhere we went, lodging establishments, popular sightseeing sites, bus stations, small restaurants, we met middle school kids from all over the country. Some came by foot, most by train. We were the youngest among the traveling students, and we attracted a lot of attention from the older kids. They loved to tell us all kinds of things about themselves, their schools, the cities they came from, and what they understood of the Cultural Revolution. As it was, everyone had a little notebook and was ready to exchange addresses with new friends. I made friends with quite a few older kids, but, alas, my sincere wish to keep in touch was wiped aside by the relentless flow of life itself. But the memory of these transient friendships, more than anything else, made my first travel adventure a memorable experience.

My teenage years were full of adventures on the road. I was often alone at home during the middle of the Cultural Revolution period. Besides playing with my friends and the neighborhood kids I read a lot of books. My mind was filled with images of fascinating places: the Forbidden City, the emperors' tombs, the cave arts of Dunhuang, the Silk Road, the ancient Buddhist and Daoist temples in the great mountains, Paris, Rome, and the great Russian Plains. At night, in the quietness, I could hear the train rolling on the tracks: "chinklincha, chinklincha, chinklincha . . . ." My heart beat fast as I listened to the singing of the railway. One day, before my fifteenth birthday, I left home for Beijing by myself, without even asking for permission from my parents. They both were in the countryside, reforming their "bourgeois thinking" through labor. My brothers were God knows where, and my sister had gone to the countryside in remote Yunnan Province to "receive reeducation" from the peasants. I was alone at home and had read too much, so I decided I wanted to see the world. As the Chinese saying goes: "Read ten thousand books, and travel ten thousand miles [in order to obtain true knowledge]." Just to board the train was quite an adventure. The train was always crowded and moved slowly, stopping at every major city along the way. Peasants and vendors sold local delicacies and native products at the stations, speaking with local dialects. There was plenty of time on the train to eat, chat, and sleep. Unfamiliar places, strangers, and unexpected encounters constantly stretched my youthful mind. It was thrilling.

Looking back, I realize that I received, for the most part, a gender-neutral education from my family and school. I was taught that men and women were equal, that I was free to choose any professional career I aspired to, and that I would be successful. Young women like myself, educated in the Maoist rhetoric of women's liberation, considered themselves equal to men and expected to play an active role in the public realm. We young women, as Wang Zheng has pointed out in her essay, rejected the identity of housewife, wife, or even woman *(funü)* in favor of the gender-neutral identity of youth. In my youthful mind, prejudiced as it was, housewives and *funü* were synonymous with stodginess, ignorance, small mindedness, gossip, pettiness, and triviality, qualities related to the closed world of the family and neighborhood. Working women, in contrast, were part of the great revolution and were thus rational, public, and important. My mother, as an educated woman and a state cadre, embodied all of these positive qualities. I was proud of her. Few of my classmates' mothers, I thought, could surpass my mother if judged on these qualities. Very likely I was wrong, since I had met only a few of my classmates' mothers, but this was how I felt about my mother at the time.

I had taken my mother as my role model, albeit unconsciously. Mother was a liberated woman. She did not have bound feet and she was well educated. Moreover, she was a revolutionary woman. Mother was born in 1920 to a gentry family in Hebei Province, not far from Beijing. Two years before her birth the May Fourth patriotic movement erupted in Beijing and spread all over the country disseminating the idea of women's liberation and gender equality, among other revolutionary ideas, to almost every corner of the land. My grandfather, then a student in law school, was greatly influenced by the May Fourth movement. My grandmother was herself a pioneer professional woman who taught at the county primary school for many years until the birth of her second child. My grandparents sent all their children, three girls and three boys, to school.

Mother loved to tell us how well she did in school. She would say, "I was among the top ten in the very competitive entrance examination to the county teacher's school," or "my compositions were often read to the whole class as model essays." In the 1930s the Republican government supported teacher's schools nationwide to meet the nation's needs for qualified teachers. Students not only paid no tuition but also received a small monthly stipend. After the outbreak of the Sino-Japanese War (1937–1945), the government waived tuition for all the national universities in order not to lose the best students to the Communists, who were gaining increasing support among progressive, patriotic youths. Mother was admitted into National Northwestern United University in 1939. The university was formed jointly by six major national universities that retreated from Beijing in the face of the Japanese invasion and settled in Lanzhou, Gansu Province. In her high school and college years, my mother was active in the resisting-Japan movement and eventually became sympathetic to the Communist Party. She was convinced that the Guomindang government was corrupt and unable to lead the war against Japan. She joined a study group along with her best friends and became a supporter of the Communist Party, which she thought was the true leader of the national resistance to Japanese invasion. She majored in Russian because she believed the Soviet Union was the strongest fortress against fascism and the greatest country on earth. She dreamed that one day she could study in the Soviet Union. During these student activities my mother met my father, a senior student and an activist in the same study group. They got married after her graduation.

Mother worked all her life, after graduation from college and until retirement in her sixties, as a schoolteacher, school superintendent, journalist, and administrator. She wore short hair neatly cut at her ear and dressed in a simple blue suit. She looked natural that way, as if she had been born to be part of a revolution that pushed for women's liberation and overturned traditional gender-role ideas. She always went to work. The concept of my mother, in my young mind, was always related to the phrase *shang ban* (work on one's job). When I was young I spent most of the time in kindergartens and schools because my mother went out to *shang ban*. For two years, I lived in a boarding kindergarten because she was working in the countryside. I don't remember her ever taking sick leave or family leave, even when I was sick. Once I had surgery and stayed in the hospital for about a week. When I returned home, still in pain and weak, my mother went to work as usual, leaving my brother at home to heat lunch for me. I asked her to stay home with me, but she said she had to go and assured me that I would be all right. On another occasion, I had a high temperature and she was up all night taking care of me. In spite of her lack of sleep, she went to work the next morning. Before she left she came to my bed to kiss me good-bye. I was so angry with her for leaving me for work that I turned my face away and wouldn't let her kiss my lips. Other than these few occasions I really did not mind that she was away. I was used to the absence of my parents and enjoyed playing with my playmates. Usually the mothers of my playmates came home earlier than my mother did, and, to my dismay, they always took their children away from our games. Only then did I feel lonesome.

Mother loved reading poetry and literature. She read from the first-century poet Qu Yuan to Li Bo, Du Fu, Su Dongpo, and Li Qingzhao in the later dynasties. Her favorite was the Qing dynasty novel *Dream of the Red Chamber*. I have no idea how many times she has read it, but she can recite with ease the poems by Lin Daiyu, the novel's tragic beauty. At age eighty she still remembers these poems. Last autumn she went to see a flower exhibit at the Forest Park in the suburbs of Shanghai and was greatly impressed. She wrote me a letter including a poem she composed to record that experience; in it she alluded to Lin Daiyu's famous poem, *Interrogating the Chrysanthemum*.

I too loved reading. Ancient books, modern history, Chinese classics, or Western literature—I read whatever came into my hands. A family pastime was reading poems aloud. Mother and I enjoyed doing this most. We competed at family reunions during the Moon Festival and Chinese New Year celebrations. When my big brother's son was little, my mother taught him short classic poems. From time to time, she would test him by asking him to recite the poems. It was great fun to watch young and old enjoying this little intellectual game. It reminded me how my mother had taught me these poems when I was little.

Mother never pushed me to do "women's work," such as cooking, washing, grocery shopping, or needlework. Of course we had to do these chores, but Mother never attached special meaning to them. For her these were not specifically female tasks, but useful skills that children, both boys and girls, should learn and enjoy using in daily life. Mother herself did not always enjoy housekeeping, especially when she was tired from long hours of work and commuting. Watching her grudgingly shop and cook day in and day out, I also developed a distaste for excessive housekeeping. After I grew up I always managed to keep housekeeping at a minimal level.

The Cultural Revolution brought my childhood world of school and home to an abrupt end. Both my parents were sent down to the May Seventh cadres' school to proletarianize their thinking through agriculture work. May Seventh was the anniversary of Mao's instruction for intellectuals and state cadres to go to the countryside to receive reeducation from the peasants. Thus, all the farms established to accommodate cadres from cities were called May Seventh cadres schools. In the meantime, for about a year we did not have to go to school. Then school resumed and I found myself in a middle school that was not sure what to do with its students. It was not to teach "bourgeois knowledge," but it was not at all clear what "proletarian knowledge" was. So the students were sent to do manual work in the countryside and in factories, or they were kept on campus in classes no one was serious about. I soon lost interest in school. I began to explore the world on my own. Besides traveling and reading, I also discovered the world of our immediate neighborhood, which, I found, had values very different from those I had learned in my family and at my school.

It was ironic that the Cultural Revolution, the culmination of the Maoist revolution, not only opened a horizon beyond family and school for me but also exposed me to the traditional gender-role ideas previously hidden in our neighborhood. The Cultural Revolution did this by breaking down the walls of individual families in the neighborhood and thereby letting me see how other families lived their lives. It was this neighborhood world that showed me the traditional gender-role system still operating in families, despite the strident announcement by the state that "times have changed; men and women are the same."

The state ideology of women's liberation had a tremendous impact on children growing up during the Mao years. But for my mother's generation, the ideology of women's liberation was not very successful in breaking traditional gender-role ideas in the family. In the private domain, in homes across China, old gender norms and mores lingered. On the one hand, the state was moving to liberate the housewife from her subordinate position in the patriarchal family and elevate her to the status of a citizen with equal rights and equal social responsibilities. And yet, at home, the old patriarchal structure had not loosened its grip. Thus, the good woman—selfless and hard working—was torn between the state and the patriarchal family, both demanding her loyalty and service. The heroine of the socialist revolution represented in state propaganda was treated with suspicion and derision in the home, where old gender-role ideas still prevailed.

It is not to say that there was no interaction between the two worlds. People moving between these two spheres surely carried these conflicting ideas back and forth. Nor was it the case that gender equality had been achieved in the public domain, such as the workplace; and the patriarchal family was not entirely immune to the influence of state ideology. But during the early period of the People's Republic of China, by and large, the discrepancy of gender ideology between the public and private domains existed.

From the time I was two years old, my family lived in a former colonial high-rise apartment building in the Hongkou district. It is a four-story steel and concrete building erected by the Japanese in the 1920s. For more than half a century it was, until the 1990s, one of the few landmark buildings in the area. My father, a historian of modern China, liked to mention that Lu Xun and Feng Xuefeng, two prominent left-wing intellectuals, lived in this building in the late 1920s and early 1930s. From our family's fourth-floor apartment, I could see the skyscrapers along Nanjing Road in the former Anglo-American concession. Each year on National Day we could see fireworks in all directions.

The layout of the apartments in our building was identical. On each floor there were two large apartments, which were shared by two to three families. In one of these apartments our family occupied the larger room, originally designed as a living room, and shared the dining room, kitchen, and bathroom with another family. That family had two smaller rooms that were originally bedrooms. Three families shared the apartment next door. The front entry doors in our building were always locked carefully for security as well as privacy. At the back of each apartment was a kitchen, from where a backdoor led to a private stairway to which only the residents had access. Women working in the kitchen used the stairway to raise chickens and communicate with one another, and the kids used it as a playground.

Located in the former Japanese concession, this old colonial building housed people of moderate means. In the 1950s and 1960s, poorer city residents could not afford the relatively high rents of high-rise apartments and lived in low-rise buildings or shanties. The rich, on the other hand, settled in the former French and Anglo-American concessions at the center of the city.

In our building the nuclear family was the norm. The father was the head of the family in every way—he was the most educated, the main breadwinner, the main decision maker, and the "head of household" on the official residential registration. While many wives worked outside the home, they generally earned less and carried on the role of the traditional housewife at home.[1] My family was somewhat at variance with this neighborhood and its values. Except for the fact that my father was listed as the head of the family in government registers, I perceived my parents as totally equal partners. They both worked and contributed comparable amounts to support the family. In fact, my mother earned 10 percent more than my father after he became one of the early victims of the party's political campaigns in the 1950s. My parents always consulted each other in making decisions and did not treat their children differently because of their sex. For me, my family was truly a gender-equal household that conformed to what I learned at school and from the mass media. But the discrepancy between the two different value systems started immediately outside the door of our family room.

In the late 1950s the state extended its control over residential neighborhoods by establishing multilevel semiofficial residential committees. During the Cultural Revolution the state used these grassroots committees to enter the private space of the family. This mobilization forced open the doors of individual households to the prying eyes of neighbors as well as to state agencies. At the lowest level of these semiofficial residential committees was the liaison whose primary objective was to report on any antirevolutionary activities of his or her neighbors, but also to distribute food and clothing coupons, collect small fees, or deliver announcements from the street committee. The seven apartments in our building formed a unit with its own liaison. Our liaison was a housewife living one floor below our apartment. Everybody called her mother of the Liu family.[2] I feared and disliked her. She was not a woman like my mother, my teacher, or the revolutionary women I saw in the movies. She was petty and vicious and ruled the neighborhood with her powerful tongue. Once she stopped me in the stairway and said, "Your mother is a college graduate. She does not stoop to household chores, I suppose?" I ran away from her as quickly as I could.

Mother of the Liu family was fond of the Zheng family, who shared the apartment with my family. The Zhengs were typical of Shanghai's *xiao shimin,* the "petty urbanites," vividly described by the late novelist Zhang Ailing and historians Yeh Wen-hsin and Lu Hanchao.[3] Mr. and Mrs. Zheng were both from well-to-do families, but they were midlevel workers in a power plant. Mr. Zheng was a technician; Mrs. Zheng was the guardian of the storehouse. Mr. and Mrs. Zheng held themselves out as college graduates even though they had attended an unaccredited night college associated with the power plant. Mr. and Mrs. Zheng felt superior to their neighbors, most of whom had no college education. However, during the Cultural Revolution, the revolutionary rebels at the power plant accused Mr. Zheng of stalking young women, and they verbally attacked him in public by writing accusations on big-character posters. These tactics humiliated Mr. Zheng, and he was no longer held in any esteem by his neighbors. In fact, because of these attacks, Mr. Zheng kept a low profile, hardly saying a word in public. By contrast, Mrs. Zheng got through the Cultural Revolution relatively unscathed. Since the Zhengs did not have much to do during the Cultural Revolution, they concentrated instead on their family. By the middle of the Cultural Revolution the

Zhengs stood out as one of the better-managed households in the neighborhood. For this the whole family was held in high regard by the neighbors, despite the ongoing revolution meant to dissolve the private domain of the family.

Like my mother, Mrs. Zheng played dual roles: socialist worker and housewife. Unlike my mother, however, she was faithful to the traditional role of a housewife. She listened to her husband, never quarreling with him or directly challenging his decisions. While my parents encouraged freethinking and a free spirit in their children, Mrs. Zheng tried to control every aspect of her daughters' lives. She supervised their schoolwork, ordered them about while they did chores, and never allowed them to answer back. She and her daughters were quite an effective housekeeping team. Every morning they went to the market to buy meat and vegetables. Before going to work, she assigned her daughters household tasks for the day. When she came home in the evening, her daughters had already made preliminary preparations for supper, which was served as soon as Mr. Zheng came home. On weekends she prepared banquets to entertain relatives and her husband's important connections (*guanxi*).[4] This type of socializing helped the family obtain all kinds of benefits, material and otherwise. For instance, Mr. and Mrs. Zheng managed to put their eldest daughter in a professional school in the early 1970s, thus saving her from being sent to the countryside and assuring her a better education than most.

I watched this neighborhood drama with confusion. I did not quite understand how my neighbors could still be stuck in the old-fashioned gender inequalities in the midst of the revolution.

The Lais next door were from Guangdong Province. Mr. Lai seemed to me to be a decent man, not calculating and small-minded like Mr. Zheng. He was aloof from neighborhood gossip and always smiled at me. He allowed me to read books from his shelves, treasures that included Romain Roland's *Jean Christophe*; Dickens's *A Tale of Two Cities*; Ivan Turgenev's *Huntsman's Sketches, Fathers and Sons,* and *Nest of the Gentry*; Dostoyevsky's *Crime and Punishment* and *The Idiot*; and Tolstoy's *Anna Karenina, Resurrection,* and *War and Peace*. As a teenager, I spent hours at the Lais's reading. The Lais's eldest son also loved to read. So the two of us would sit reading quietly for hours when our parents were away at work.

Mr. Lai worked as a technician in a paint factory. Perhaps because he was a technician (not a political figure), Mr. Lai was not attacked during the Cultural Revolution. He went to work every day. When he came home, he would sit on the couch and his wife would instantly bring his slippers, a cup of hot tea, and the newspaper. He ate when dinner was served and, after eating, retired to their family room to continue reading while his wife cleaned up. He never seemed concerned with housekeeping matters. Of course not, his wife took care of everything!

Mother of the Lai family (or Mrs. Lai) was quite a figure. She was an elementary school teacher, but her main concern was her family. Unlike Mrs. Zheng, who had two daughters under her command, Mrs. Lai could not count much on her sons and had to do most of the housework. She was a tall, strong woman with a loud voice. Though submissive to her husband, serving him from head to toe, she was aggressive and domineering toward everyone else, including her two sons. She sometimes even quarreled with her husband. She certainly was not without power in her family—she earned it by working hard. I did not envy her. Later I learned that her aggressiveness had to do with her deep anger and frustration over her husband, who had a relationship with a woman right next door.

Compared to our neighbors, our household was disorganized. We ate dinner late because we didn't start to cook until we felt hungry. By the time we sat down to dinner, the Zhengs were finishing theirs. We often missed the best produce and ingredients at the market because no one in my family was willing to get up at four o'clock in the morning to rush to the market, as Mrs. Zheng and her daughters did routinely. When the Zheng women came back around seven with their basket full of fresh vegetables and meat, Mother would walk to the market to get whatever was still available. To her it was just food. But to Mrs. Zheng, putting a good meal on the table was the hallmark of a good household manager, an identity that my mother did not share.

Before my seventeenth birthday I went to Lianjiang Farm in Anhui Province. Mother came home to pack for me but had to hurry back to the countryside before she could send me off. On the day of departure the students gathered in the compound of a middle school, where six buses were waiting to carry us away. People around me were crying, but I shed no tears. A little adventurer like me was actually quite excited about this new journey. I had wanted to go even farther away from Shanghai, but my request to go to Yunnan Province was denied by the school authorities. They said they could not let me go so far away by myself and that I had to go with the group. My father, disappointed, sent me off. He had hoped that at least one daughter could have stayed in Shanghai, my sister already having gone to the countryside. I assured him that I would be all right and that I would come home as soon as I had a home leave.

Lianjiang Farm was located in the hilly country south of the Yangzi River. The landscape formed by rolling hills and clear rivers was breathtaking. Toward the north was the famous Yellow Mountain range; toward the south was the scenic Xin'an River. The area, historically the Huizhou prefecture, was also rich in cultural history, with well-preserved architecture from the Ming and Qing dynasties. In Shexian, ancient decorative arches commemorating chaste widows still loomed over the main street marketplace, silently witnessing women's ordeals, and perhaps their power, in the past. I seized every opportunity to explore this area. I went down the Xin'an River on the local commuter steamboat, hitched rides with truckers going to Wuhu, or took the bus to the Yellow Mountain and the ancient towns at its foothills. Everywhere I went I met interesting people—not traveling students but local folks. Peasants, vendors, and local merchants tried to sell me local products, from the historically famous ink cake and brush to sesame oil and crabs. During these transactions and chats on the road the local people and I asked many questions of one another: "What are you?" "Where are you from?" "What are you up to?" We were each curious about the other. I wanted to learn about their way of life in the hinterlands, and they wondered what I, an "educated youth" from Shanghai, was up to in a place so far away from home.

At the farm, however, I again encountered the practice of traditional gender roles of girls in my own generation. The company I belonged to had a two-story dormitory building. Girls lived upstairs and boys downstairs. There were four or five bunk beds in each room, accommodating eight to ten farmers. Three kinds of young farmers were held in high esteem: skilled and fast farmhands, good writers, and accomplished needleworkers. Most of the time we worked in the field, growing rice, maize, and vegetables. In the evenings, after a day of hard work in the field, we girls sat together in our dorm room and chatted while doing needlework such as embroidery and knitting. While the skilled farmhands led the work in the field, the most sophisticated needleworkers were the center of evening gatherings. There was a silent competition among the best: those who could produce the most sophisticated designs were highly esteemed.

My friends taught me how to do fancy needlework, and I enjoyed knitting and embroidering. I made quite a few decorative tablecloths and other furniture coverings, and I was very happy with my products. I began knitting a wool sweater for myself, starting with the body section. My friend Peimin used to say, "Gee! You are so slow. I wonder if you will ever finish the whole sweater." I ignored her comments and continued working. One day I returned to the dorm after work and found the whole sweater finished. Peimin had made the sleeves and attached them to the body I had just finished. I was upset and told her that I had wanted to do the whole thing myself. But she simply smiled and said, "I lost patience watching you going so slowly with it. I thought you would never finish." I am pretty sure I would have finished by myself, but to this day I have never started to knit another sweater.

To my friends I was a nerd, and they respected that. I served as the record keeper for my platoon, secretary for my company, and editor of the company's wall publications. I was the author of our farm song, which became very popular among the farmers. I still remember the last two lines of the lyrics: "In making the revolution we are not afraid of hardship; as Chairman Mao's soldiers we have broad minds."

Peimin was from a working-class family. Just as my skills in intellectual work reflected my upbringing, Peimin's skill in handcrafts revealed her upbringing and expectations of life. Needlework was a traditional means of income and a skill crucial to the good repair of a family's clothing. As gracefulness used to be the mark of a good upbringing in a daughter of the bourgeoisie, good needle-work represented good upbringing in a working-class daughter; hence it was crucial to her finding a good match. I knew that for my friend marriage was the most important thing to focus on and prepare for. And she knew that my dream was to go to college. Our different upbringings seem to have instilled in our minds different identities and expectations of life. My identity had little to do with my gender, while hers was influenced by traditional gender-role ideas.

At the end of the Cultural Revolution the young farmers all left the farm one after another and went on their different life paths. In February 1978 I entered a major university in Shanghai after I passed the first college entrance examination after the Cultural Revolution. Peimin and many others were assigned jobs in Shanghai's factories and got married within a few years. Since then, twenty-two years have gone by. I have earned a doctoral degree and teach at an American college. I often wonder what has become of Peimin. Has she had a happy marriage? Does she like her job? Has she retired early, just as many middle-aged female workers in China have been forced to do? She must have a child. How is her child? I know I will find her someday. And I am sure she has enjoyed and suffered life over the years, just as I have, but probably in very different ways.

During my college years, after the end of the Maoist era, the meaning of women's liberation and gender equality became open to debate. It was a frequently visited topic in our dorm room shared by eight classmates. Some emerging feminists questioned the slogan "Times have changed; men and women are the same." They argued that women were equal to but different from men. One girl declared: "Wanting to look beautiful is in a woman's nature [nüren tianxing aimei]. Of course women are equal to men in status. But it doesn't mean that I can't be a woman and look pretty. I don't like to dress like a man. I should have the right to wear make-up and nice clothes if I want." We giggled at these bold remarks. It was true that in the Mao years everyone wore the same clothes—dark-blue suits and green army uniforms. Another girl hesitated: "But, isn't it a form of gender inequality if women have to please men with their appearance while men only need to focus on their careers?" I said that we were first and foremost human beings and entitled to equal rights for all. Biological sex only came as a second trait. Therefore, I argued, one should first be a human being and then a woman. Despite the naïveté and simplicity in these arguments, it is obvious that my classmates and I all shared the same starting point—the principle of gender equality was to us a self-evident truth. This was perhaps the single most positive legacy the Maoist era had bestowed on us. From that base we could explore further the meaning of freedom from gender stereotypes.

NOTES

1. Susan Mann discusses in some detail the cult of domesticity in Ningbo immigrants in Republican Shanghai. One can also see this phenomenon of stay-at-home wives among the newly risen Shanghai middle-class families in immigrant groups from other regions such as Guangdong and Jiangsu. Susan Mann, "The Cult of Domesticity in Republican Shanghai's Middle Class," *Research on Women in Modern Chinese History* 3 (1994).
2. Mother of the Liu family is a local form of address. It would be equivalent to Mrs. Liu.
3. Zhang Ailing, "Alas, Shanghainese," and numerous other short stories and essays about Shanghai. See Zhang, "Daodi shi Shanghai ren" (Alas, Shanghainese), *Zazhi* 11, no. 4 (August 1943). The essay was later published in *Liuyan* (Gossip) in 1968, 1991, and 1995. Wen-hsin Yeh, "Progressive Journalism and Shanghai's Petty Urbanites: Zou Taofen and the *Shenghuo Weekly*, 1926–1945," in *Shanghai Sojourners*, ed. Frederic Wakeman Jr. and Wen-hsin Yeh (Berkeley: Institute of East Asian Studies, University of California, 1992). Lu Hanchao, *Beyond the Neon Lights: Everyday Shanghai in the Early Twentieth Century* (Berkeley: University of California Press).
4. *Guanxi* means people who have important connections.

LIHUA WANG

GENDER CONSCIOUSNESS IN MY TEEN YEARS

Wh002hile studying in America, I was surprised to find that youth as a gender-neutral idea was not as popular a concept here as it was in China. Instead, social perceptions of gender differences exist between girls and boys in early childhood. Even newborn babies are subjected to gender differentiation: pink and blue ribbons traditionally mark female and male infants. As a teenager in China in the 1970s, however, I was able to positively identify myself as a non-gendered youth with strengths, strengths that were won through constant struggles with the contradictions of being a youth and a woman.

TO BE A YOUTH

My high school graduation was the first time I was consciously introduced to the idea of youth. Our principal, a woman in her mid-thirties who wore a blue Mao jacket, gave a speech that drew a romantic picture of what it meant to be a youth. Two of the points she brought up made a great impression on me: the young people of China were the morning sun and the future of our society, and therefore we must discipline ourselves by working for the people.

The excitement in her voice filled me with encouragement and hope.

Several days after graduation, I was assigned a job at a hotel. This was exciting news. I brimmed with the idealism of youth and eagerness to make my own way in the world. The principal portrayed the workplace as an exciting arena in which we could employ the skills and knowledge we had learned in school. We would now do our part to help build a better China. Despite the principal's glowing words, I was nervous about my future at the hotel. All my life, I had imagined serving the country as a worker, peasant, and soldier; yet it had never occurred to me that I would actually be a worker, peasant, or soldier. Now it was about to happen.

When I was nine I learned to sing a song called "What My Dream Is." The lyrics expressed the revolutionary ideals I had embraced. Singing this song made me feel I could carry out the young people's mission of building our country, just like my father's generation had. But now I was uncertain as to which path to take. My parents wanted me to be a medical doctor. In their minds, this was a good occupation for a woman. Doctors made significant contributions to society by caring for the sick and were respected regardless of gender. However, I wanted to be a biologist and work with animals.

With these thoughts in mind, I began work at the Xin Qiao hotel. On my first day I was given a tour of the grand hotel. This building, constructed in 1954, rose in my mind almost like a palace. Containing more than one hundred guestrooms, three restaurants, several large function rooms, and a garden courtyard, the hotel was impressive. Its floors were covered with red carpet, and chandeliers hung from the lobby ceiling. In Beijing, the Xin Qiao Hotel was one of the few places open to foreigners during the seventies, most frequently accommodating Japanese businessmen. When President Nixon visited China in 1972, some of his staff stayed here.

I felt excited after the new staff orientation, but I was also uneasy about stepping into a totally new and strange world. My feet seemed to move awkwardly on the hotel's soft carpet, and I actually had to concentrate on not stumbling. But I was most troubled by the realization that my colleagues seemed entirely different from me. The hotel staff, in their uniform of white shirts and blue pants, reminded me of the women I had seen working in neighborhood hotels. They were absorbed in gossip and family business, oblivious to social issues or glorious ideas. I could have no respect for this type of woman.

I was startled to learn that I would be a manual worker. Serving food fulfilled neither my dreams of my place in the work world nor my image of the heroic peasant and factory worker. The prospect of life as a waitress horrified me. How would I interact with the people around me? Could such people ever become my comrades? Could I trust them as coworkers? I was overwhelmed by my initial disappointment, and it was with great reluctance that I changed into the same white shirt and blue pants the rest of the hotel staff wore. Unlike other young women in my group, I had no desire to see myself in the mirror. I must look like one of those restaurant women back home, I thought.

After several days of orientation at the restaurant, I began to feel more at ease and began to wonder who my *shi fu* (mentor) would be. Usually, an older person with good work experience and a "proper revolutionary" attitude would be asked to be shi fu for newcomers. My mentor was named Liu, a woman in her forties who seemed to have much experience. Her short hair was pulled up by two bands on either side. She had dark skin and several deep lines in her forehead, and she was short—the top of her head reached only to my chin. Her appearance did not fit my idea of a proper mentor. I always thought a mentor should be more like Sister Jiang, a highly cultured lead female character in a revolutionary opera. Jiang sister is tall with refined manners and wears a dark-blue Chinese qi pao dress and a red scarf draping her shoulders.

Thinking back, I can see this image of a heroine hid many levels of representations which shaped my gender consciousness. Recently, as I discussed with friends the meaning of Sister Jiang, I began to realize how much her image meant to me as a role model when I entered womanhood. On one level, Sister Jiang represented a revolutionary who had devoted her life to the cause of fighting for justice regardless of gender identity. At the same time, it was her red scarf and qi pao dress, which revealed her feminine beauty, that differentiated her from other types of revolutionary heroes. She was a strong woman with revolutionary qualities of devotion, endurance, and responsibility for the society whose life did not revolve around a man. The red in her scarf referred to both the traditional symbol of happiness and the revolutionary symbol of blood in the CCP's flag. The blue, a gender-neutral color in China, could be associated with both male and female. Thus, Sister Jiang stands out as an androgynous image and as a revolutionary hero.

Liu shi fu seemed far removed from the heroic image of Sister Jiang. Even her voice, which carried the strong accent of northeastern China, was vulgar. To me, only a Beijing accent denoted a person of intelligence and education. Everything Liu shi fu did confirmed my negative image of her, including smoking. In movies I had seen, only entertainers, Nationalist female spies, and prostitutes smoked. Although my father smoked a pack of cigarettes a day, it never occurred to me to question him or associate his smoking habit with a negative image. This was reserved for women, and Liu shi fu's smoking habit made me wonder if she could be trusted and if she was good enough to be my mentor.

It was only after working with Liu shi fu for some time that I was able to overcome my biased ideas. Our close interaction in the restaurant began after our teamwork on the Monday night shift. One night, after nine o'clock, the restaurant became very quiet. Soon, only two waitresses were left. "I am working in the dish washing room," I told Liu shi fu loudly. Although I did not particularly like to wash dishes, the washing room was separate from the restaurant and allowed me to work alone. I turned on the water and slowly washed one plate after another. My thoughts flowed with the water: What I should do with Liu shi fu after we finish our work? Should I talk to her alone in the restaurant? What should I tell her if she is curious about me and my family?

"Xiao Wang, it is time to take a break," Liu shi fu's voice called, interrupting my thoughts. "OK," I replied hesitantly. For me, there were family secrets to keep, and I did not want to share them with anyone in the hotel. My family's political troubles started in 1966, when both of my parents were identified as enemies of the Cultural Revolution. Father was denounced in part because he agreed with Liu Shao-qi's openness toward a market economy. He had been in charge of the long-term planning section of the government's Ministry of Electrical Machinery and was labeled a "running dog of capitalism." Mother, a leader of the worker's union in a battery factory in Beijing, was denounced as a counterrevolutionary leader who had attempted to poison the minds of the working class.

Not too long after the Cultural Revolution, my father and mother left Beijing and moved to a village in Jiangxi Province, in the southern part of China, for reeducation. At sixteen, my sister, who had joined the Red Guards in 1966, left home and became a zhi qing in Shanxi Province. Living alone in Beijing for three years, with help from my neighbors, I finally finished high school in 1971 and started working at the Xin Qiao Hotel.

To my surprise, Liu shi fu showed no interest in learning about me or my family. Instead she shared her own life stories with me. I learned that she was one of only a few party members in our restaurant, that she took pride in her life as a waitress and a party member, and that her devotion to her work won her acceptance by the party.

As a mentor, Liu shi fu taught me the value of adopting a good work attitude. On one occasion she told me in her down-to-earth manner: "All you high school students, including my daughter, grew up in the 'honey jar.' You were not like me and the people of my generation, who suffered a lot in our lives." As a result of their experiences they had learned the value of *chi ku*.

I was quite familiar with the idea of chi ku, which means bearing hardship or eating bitterness. I learned it at the age of nine, in school, where weekly and monthly school cleanings were a means for students to temper themselves, and our willingness to clean windows and toilets demonstrated our ability to bear hardship. At home, my parents also constantly taught us children the value of chi ku. They believed that if a child did not prepare herself, she would not know how to deal with hardships in the real world. The concept as I now understand it has multiple meanings. Among other things, it can refer to physical endurance or psychological strength, and it can hold the abstract implication of referring to one's spirit. Sister Jiang had chi ku.

And so did Liu shi fu. I realized Sister Jiang and Liu shi fu had much in common. Liu shi fu was right that my generation should learn the value of bearing hardship. Her words not only had meaning for political Chinese youth but also for me personally. If I could learn to bear hardship and suffering, then I could prove to my parents that I could make it in the real world. Liu shi fu's teaching and her willingness to give me attention opened my eyes to her true character. She was, after all, a good model to follow.

One evening the restaurant was particularly crowded, even past our regular dinner time. I walked so much that evening that my legs felt like wooden logs. As I prepared to leave for the night, I saw that Liu shi fu had voluntarily stayed to help the night shift. I pushed myself to take another order and walked toward the basement kitchen. On the way, Liu shi fu held a large tray piled high with dirty dishes. I reached out for the tray, but it was too heavy for my weary arms to support. Liu shi fu laughed and caught the tray before it dropped. At that moment, it dawned on me that people like Liu shi fu truly believe in the value of self-sacrifice. My willingness to stay at work late that day seemed to impress Liu shi fu. One day, as we took a walk together, she invited me to visit her family. I accepted and told her it would be my pleasure. I had never received a personal invitation from a coworker. I was excited and felt grown up.

Shortly after I began working with Liu shi fu, we were recognized by coworkers as an outstanding team. One afternoon our group leader praised us in a meeting. I was even more proud when I received additional recognition in the summer of 1971 when I was officially accepted as a member of the Youth League. This was a great honor. I was one of the first among my fellow high school graduates to join the organization. Even my sister was not yet a member. It was the first time I had surpassed her in achievement, which gave me great satisfaction.

I did not openly show my joy at work. Modesty was a sign of maturity and good manners for a young person. At home I was less careful. "I have good news to share," I told my parents. "Only three out of thirty high school graduates were accepted into the Youth League." They were less impressed than I had expected. Instead, they asked what I planned as my next step at work. Although I was disappointed by their reaction, it hardly dimmed my own excitement.

NOT TO BE A HOUSEWIFE

My Youth League membership allowed me to define myself as a young worker rather than a waitress. Intoxicated with my new sense of importance, I began to find fault with many of the women working at the hotel. I regarded them as classic examples of the housewife type. Looking back, I see how prejudiced and aloof my attitude was, but at the time it flowed naturally from what I thought was my "critical" point of view.

For me, the typical housewife aspired to nothing more than caring for her family and gossiping with neighbors. She had no social or political consciousness whatsoever. She lived only for her offspring and husband and protected her narrow world by a self-imposed ignorance. She contrasted sharply with Sister Jiang, who devoted her life to the cause of the revolution.

The heroic example of Sister Jiang made me critical of my group of high school graduates, especially Dan Li. One summer day when it was Dan Li's turn to wash dishes, the washroom was hot and filled with steam. Everyone preferred to stay away from the "steam pot." Unfortunately, Dan Li had no choice in the matter. During my lunch hour, I looked in on comrade Dan Li in the washroom. When I saw the mountain of dirty dishes that covered almost every inch of the table, I exploded in anger. "Dan Li," I shouted. She did not reply, and I heard only the sounds of steaming hot water. Dan Li was relaxing in the hotel garden. I soon sent her rushing back to complete her tasks.

I disliked Dan Li not only for her lack of stamina but also for the way she embraced the stereotypical image of the fragile female. The other workers nicknamed her Lin Daiyu, a fragile female character from an elite family in *Dream of Red Mansions*. I was repulsed by the character, but Dan Li reveled in the comparison. For me, feminine beauty was to be found only in the image of Sister Jiang.

Of course it never occurred to me that my prejudiced view of housewives was partly derived from sexist official ideology. The party line taught that only work performed outside of the home was to be respected. Women who remained as domestic workers were looked down upon. Influenced by this prevailing view of women's work, I wanted to disassociate myself from traditional women. I wanted to show everyone that I was a revolutionary female.

Reading at work seemed to me an excellent way of demonstrating my difference and challenging the housewife mentality that prevailed in the restaurant. Hotel officials did not prohibit reading on the job, but they did draw the line at "bourgeois literature" written by authors such as Shakespeare, Jules Verne, or Robert Louis Stevenson. From the beginning of the Cultural Revolution, foreign novels, love stories, and folk fiction were identified as feudalist, capitalist, and poisonous. Now I purposefully challenged the correct "reading code" I had learned during my high school years.

But to my surprise and disappointment, my coworkers only encouraged me. "It is good for your to read during breaks," a married waitress told me. "You can learn something rather than waste your time at the restaurant." Another advised me, "Don't be like one of us, spending all your spare time worrying about the family business. Reading is education that will bring you a better future." "We should call her 'little intellectual [*xia zhi shi fen zi*],'" someone else said. Laughter filled the room, and I did not know how to respond. I was moved by their encouragement. Their understanding and acceptance touched me and forced me to question my judgment of them. Even though my generalization of housewives did not change, I no longer used reading as a way to demonstrate the difference between us.

WE ARE THE WORLD

During the 1970s the hotel staff was organized to train in a military camp. In regard to revolutionary idealism, the training would provide city people—waitresses and waiters—with a chance to share in the experiences of peasants. Living outside Beijing would allow us to understand the outside world—that is, the rural parts of the society. More importantly, the training would illustrate for our young people the hardship of the heroic "Long March."

I was assigned to join the training for a month. About eighty hotel workers, ages seventeen to over fifty, formed my team. Like real soldiers, we all dressed in blue and green army jackets and hats, regardless of age and gender. Like real soldiers, we packed our blankets and put packs on our shoulders and marched forty to fifty miles a day. Like real soldiers, we sang revolutionary songs while we marched down the narrow dirt roads of the countryside. Loudly we repeated Mao's slogan: "Summon your determination, be not afraid to sacrifice oneself, remove a thousand obstacles, and strive for victory." Our voices reached toward the sky and bonded our spirits. Mao's saying, a source of strength for me throughout the training, connected me to the spirits of our fathers. Even today I remember how this experience made me feel proud to be a youth, a gender-neutral person, strong and independent.

Marching turned out to be a difficult task for me, especially in the beginning. Several blisters emerged on my feet after the first day of training. Even more alarming, I began menstruating, a reminder that I was now closer to being a woman—physically weak and lacking in endurance—than to being a youth. During our marching break, a young female friend whispered in my ear, "You look pale. Are you OK?" "Well," I replied, "my trouble [dao mei] is here." (Trouble was shorthand for menstruation, a euphemism we used to create a mysterious atmosphere while discussing our personal physical conditions in public without shame.) "March!" A loud voice bellowed, and I continued on the journey.

As a member of the Youth League, I volunteered to read aloud daily propaganda, written in a rhyming style, that described what had happened during the day's training. I told myself, "Don't show any weak symptom of menstruation during our march." According to conversations I had overheard, signs of menstruation included walking slowly, lacking physical energy, and looking pale. Although I could not control my skin color, I could control my energy level and walking speed. Cautious of being noticed, I stood outside the group and held bamboo clappers to accompany our rhythmic recitation of the day's propaganda. By the end of the day,

I wished the evening would come soon. By dinnertime, I lost my appetite and rushed to bed.

One day we did not march; instead we participated in the village's agricultural production, transplanting rice in a wet field. This job assignment made me very uneasy. I was not supposed to stand in cold water to transplant rice because of my menstruation. According to my mother's teachings, while menstruating I was to avoid cold things and heavy physical labor. However, I would not ask for a different work assignment. Not only would it be embarrassing, but it would be looked down upon because of my membership in the Youth League. Without hesitation, I joined the crowd in the rice field. My feet were shocked by the icy water and soon resembled red potatoes. I was singing songs in my heart to forget the stinging coldness when suddenly someone shouted, "Oh, look, there are leeches sucking on my leg!" We had already heard many terrible stories about working in wet rice fields, and I was afraid of this bloodsucking worm. Nevertheless, I ran over and helped the worker remove the leeches from his leg.

As the sun went down behind the hill, we finished our work and returned to the village. Several young people decided to explore the hillside nearby. "You young people just don't know how to save your energy," one elder team member commented. We hiked about half a mile, and our ears were filled with birds' songs and other sounds of nature. Shadows from the setting sun distinguished the surrounding hills with dark and light shades of green. I was intoxicated by the beauty and my closeness to Mother Earth. "Let me give you a hand," a young man said. Realizing that I was so close to a young and energetic man made my heart beat faster and faster. It was an exciting moment, something that had never happened to me before.

As we arrived at the top of the hill, one of us began to test for echoes. Soon we all followed suit, and shouts and laughter filled the air. I closed my eyes and paused for a while, letting the gentle winds pass by. Then, I opened my arms and slowly spun around, trying to embrace the world. A poetic voice whispered in my ears, "You young people look like the rising sun and the world belongs to you." I was not sure if I was listening to someone speaking Mao's words or if I was just imagining those feelings. During that moment it felt wonderful to be young and energetic, and to be responsible for the future of China.

Belonging to the training group enhanced my sense of connectedness. The hardship of training was made easier through our new, intimate relationships. By sharing our food, space, and work, we had experienced a special bonding.

GENDER CONSCIOUSNESS

In 1985 I crossed the Pacific Ocean to begin graduate school. I took my lessons in bearing hardship with me, and I have drawn strength from them during my years in America. The belief I had formed as a teenager that education would provide me with a good future motivated me to seek higher education. But the other part of my dream faded, that someday I, along with other Chinese young people, would be in charge of Chinese society. That dream, so clearly a reflection of Mao's era, was at one time a fountain from which I constantly drew strength, encouragement, and belief that through work I could become a useful person.

In my case, the idea of becoming a useful person in society guided me to learn, to bear hardships, and to temper myself in ways considered legitimate under Maoism. Being unfamiliar with Euro-American feminist ideas, I did not, however, develop a critical eye toward socialist ideology, and I was unaware of gender-related issues regarding work in the hotel. Gender hierarchy existed, but I did not see it. I did not realize I was assigned to a service job that reflected an extension of "traditional" women's work in the public sphere.

In 1998 I stood alone on Chong Wenmen Street, staring at a six-story brick building—the Xin Qiao Hotel. It seemed older and dwarfed by its more modern neighbors, several new skyscrapers. As I approached, I noticed the former front entrance was closed. It was replaced by a gold trim door that opened to the street in a new direction. I stood close by the building. The wind carried the dust of the street and memories past me. I felt an urge to follow that wind back to the days when I first entered this building, and my womanhood at age sixteen.

I realized I had come to this place to envision my past idealistic dreams, and I paused to wonder if they were now just as dated as this hotel. I could feel the wind begin to stir again, and I walked down the street, following the wind's direction, seeking to brave the world once again.

XUEPING ZHONG

BETWEEN "LIXIANG" AND CHILDHOOD DREAMS
Back from the Future to the Nearly Forgotten Yesteryears

Not long after I came to the United States in 1986, I was made aware of my childhood years.[1] Indeed, what was then old and uninteresting to me (about my past) was suddenly new and fascinating to others. Moreover, the past I thought I knew appeared to be imagined and understood very differently by the people I met and befriended. When a friend's friend met me at the airport, she could not guess I was the person she was to meet. She had assumed that I would be wearing a baggy Mao jacket. During many ensuing conversations with various people, I realized that my growing up without TV and other modern household appliances was often a source of conviction for many to feel lucky to be Americans. And my going to the countryside at the age of sixteen was yet another sad story of a Chinese youth. Some people thought I was putting on a brave face when I told them some of my early experiences in a matter-of-fact manner. Others decided we all had horrible stories to tell and encouraged me to write. Only one friend had a different take. He marveled at the young Chinese he had met who, seemingly out of the blue, were often both learned and interested in learning. "It's amazing," he said, "just think what you guys went through, and yet you all showed up normal and ready to do Ph.D. degrees." While I am not sure about the "normal" part, most of us did come for graduate school.[2]

Many of my fellow Chinese coming to this part of the world have encountered something similar. A few have already written memoirs that echo a sense of horror shared by many of my interlocutors. To me, however, having our past assumed and made aware of from a temporal distance and geographical dislocation has been rather uncanny: it creates a defamiliarization effect within the context in which I have been made to encounter "it" again. And it is through this "reencountering" that I have often experienced the sensation of suddenly finding myself turning invisible when "my/ our past" is being discussed. It is through such moments of sudden "disappearing" that I have come to realize that, in addition to the fact that most of us have ourselves lived the memory of the Mao era vicariously through other people's publicized memories, there is an "emptying effect" in how our past has been assumed. Indeed, the existing understanding (or the lack thereof) of our past tends to foreclose a need to look at the far more complex details of our lives during the Mao era; the life stories of generations of Chinese and their historical significance have been assumed, as it were, in a closed book. Perhaps it is time that we opened that "book" again.

As I began to think about my childhood years, what stood out in my mind the most (and what in turn became the topic of this piece) was my rather single-minded fixation on identifying with "being learned," which toward the latter years of the Mao era became my often unrealistic dream of going to college one day. It is a past mixed with many ironies of the time and place when and where I lived as a child, a teenager, and a young woman, in between the the teaching of "revolutionary ideals" *(geming lixiang)* and personal dreams. This essay ponders some of the moments when education, learning, and personal dreams were all entangled with both a familial context and the social and political contexts at large and how their mixed meanings are such that they cannot but complicate our understanding of that "past."

STARTING FROM AN END: A "TRIUMPHANT ESCAPE"
INTO COLLEGE

One day in early January 1978 I was chatting with friends in a room at the headquarters of the Donghai State Farm on the outskirts of Shanghai.[3] Suddenly, I heard someone yell out my name; I was wanted on the phone. Dashing into the operator's room, I picked up the receiver. The call was from Yao, a friend of mine. She was calling from the county seat of Nanhui County (one of the ten counties under the jurisdiction of Shanghai's municipal government), where she, as one of the clerks of the State Farm's ad hoc office for college admissions,[4] was picking up admission letters on behalf of the farm's authority. "There's a letter for you from Shanghai Normal University," she said in a calm voice. I started laughing and screaming, "Really? Really? You're not joking with me, are you?" "You know," she started laughing, "Xiao Zhang actually wanted me to play a practical joke on you. He suggested that I tell you we did not find anything for you. But I didn't think you'd have the stomach for it this time." At that moment, I was thankful that Yao did not joke with me.

Later that day she gave me the letter. Less than an hour had gone by, however, when she came to ask for it back. She had been criticized for having given the letter to me without going through the proper authority. Two days later, however, I received the letter without any explanation. Shortly after, I learned that, as its last attempt to stop me from going to college, the State Farm authority had sent someone to the university to persuade the latter to nullify my admission. The attempt failed.

Upon learning what had happened, some of my friends, still deeply accustomed to the Cultural Revolution way of doing things, urged me to write a big-character poster *(dazibao)* to denounce the farm's authority. "You're about to leave anyway. What's to be afraid of?" they asked. Though tempted, I decided my entrance into college was the best big-character poster.

On the eve of my departure, friends gathered at an informal farewell party at the headquarters of the State Farm where I worked. In the middle of the conversation, someone suddenly asked, as if having just discovered a new continent, "How come you've never had a boyfriend?" In spite of the impression some existing memoirs have given that all the young Chinese were sexually repressed during the Cultural Revolution, the truth of the matter was that by the time I was about to leave, most of the young people I worked with had years of romantic experiences. In fact, many coupled, generating occasional curiosity amongst colleagues and adding colorful content to our daily life. Indeed, at the moment of my departure, my lack of a boyfriend appeared rather unusual to many of them. "Who'd dare to approach her?" someone replied laughingly. "She always seems to be elsewhere. All she was concerned with was going to college someday." "Well, I always thought I was too young for that," I retorted, being the youngest among them. Still, they may have pegged me right: during my stay on the State Farm, I was quite wrapped up in my college dream, regardless of whether or not that dream was realistic.

What was incredible to me at that moment, however, was not that I did not have a boyfriend. Nor was it that I managed to pass the exams. Rather, it was that these dear friends of mine did not even so much as try to take the exams themselves. As they congratulated me, I was experiencing a sense of guilt and unease. "I'm sure that you could have passed those tests with flying colors if you had taken them, and I wouldn't even have had a chance to compete with you," I said, and I meant it. Indeed, most of these people belonged to the so-called *lao san jie* generation, who had been high-school students when the Cultural Revolution (1966–1976) started.[5] Even today, they are considered to have had a better secondary education than the seventies generation, to which I belong, which attended high school during the Cultural Revolution, when formal education was virtually nonexistent. No one in that room, however, said anything in response to my misplaced praise. Having gone through many difficulties in order to go to college, I understood the silence and did not continue that line of conversation.

Shortly after the gathering, I left the farm. While in college, I still felt from time to time that it was a fluke I had passed those exams. However, there was one thing I was quite certain of: my determination to take the exams came from something stubborn deep within. Only years later, when I looked back, did I wonder where I got the courage and why I did not hesitate to be defiant. Even though I am sure much was due to the fact that I was young and as a result did not know any better, I can say that accompanying this youthful rebellious streak was a child encouraged to dream. My triumphant escape into college was merely the end result of the zigzagging journey of the fate of many of my dreams. Some had long become history while others persisted.

DON'T BE A "XIUHUA ZHENTOU"

I was born in the heyday of the CCP's socialist revolution and socialist construction to two parents from very different backgrounds. My mother grew up in Shanghai, where her father squandered his business on his habit of opium smoking, while my father came from a once well-off Manchurian family in Beijing. In post-1949 Shanghai, they spent most of their waking hours at work, but they shared a love of learning, something that would affect their children's upbringing during the Mao era.

When I was born, my parents already had three boys. So, in my earliest memories, neighbors were telling me how pleased my father was when I came home from the hospital. "Oh, we could hear your father laughing and laughing. He was so happy," they said. However, in spite of their being somewhat protective of me (and of my younger sister, who was born two years later), my parents demonstrated little favoritism. My oldest brother was expected to set a good example. He was expected to do well in school, and he did. The rest of us were to follow in his footsteps. In many ways, I grew up with brothers as role models and did many things they did, such as learning to study hard, play sports, and yes, cook.[6] There was little gender division in my parents' demands for my brothers and for me and my sister. In this sense, mine was seemingly a genderless family. Only, of course, it wasn't.

Indeed, even though most of my memories of the early years consist of images, smells, and sounds, and days, months, and years of events are now mostly fragmented moments blurred together without beginning and end, some of my mother's *xiuli* (pruning) stands out in my memory, especially her teachings and warnings to her daughters.

As a somewhat absentminded child, I tended to lose things. Matters worsened when I was told to pick up my sister from her daycare on my way home from kindergarten (it was not unusual for busy parents to expect their children to be independent from an early age on). Many times I was distracted on the way home; things like an umbrella, a handkerchief, a glove, and even a shoe or two would disappear for no apparent reason. Every time when I had to face the music, Mother would scold me in gender-specific terms: "How can a girl be so careless [*cuxin*]?" As time went on, she was increasingly horrified by my carelessness. Every new thing I touched, I would damage: a new washbasin would fly out of my hands, a new jacket would be torn, and new pencils or pens would simply disappear from my pencil box. Once I even carelessly tripped over a hot stove and cracked open my forehead. *Mei tounao* (literally, no head or brain), a cartoon character in a children's film and magazine, *Xiaopengyou (Little Friends)*, well known for his absent-mindedness (in one story he forgot to put elevators in a 100–story building he designed), was Mother's nickname for me. And she would add, "But you're a *nü xiaoren*" (a Shanghai dialect term for young girls), apparently suggesting that girls were supposed to be neater and more careful than boys.

My mother was most concerned, however, that I not become a *xiuhua zhentou yibao cao* (an embroidered pillow stuffed with dried rice-straws) or a *congming miankong ben duchang* (smart face with stupid insides). When I started elementary school before the Cultural Revolution, these became my mother's standard warnings. During the first semester, when the newness of school wore out in no time, I quickly realized that school meant business, especially after my mother set me straight. One day when I was playing with a classmate in her home, Mother found me there. She told me to go home right away. Because she had come to get me, I knew something had gone very wrong. I was right. My math teacher had visited my home and told my mother I had not done my homework for a week. My mother was furious. She made me stand in the middle of our front room while she proceeded with a serious lecture

accompanied by a spanking. I was terribly scared, and the only hope
I had was that my father, who was an extremely kind but very busy
parent, would come home. She kept saying, "Do you want to
be a xiuhua zhentou?" "What's good about just having a smart
face?" After this little incident I realized that, to Mother, few things
were worse than not doing well in school and not taking learning seriously. As a girl, especially, it was no good to be just a smart
face.

When I was about seven, a new fad suddenly captured the
fancy of many girls in the neighborhood: they started wearing colorful and shiny hair ornaments. I went to Mother and told her that
I would like to have one as well. "All the girls in the neighborhood
have one," I told her excitedly. "You mean that it must be good
just because they all have one?" Mother asked. Sensing her reluctance, I said earnestly, "Yes. It's really pretty." "OK," she said, "let's
go and take a look." When we got to the store, I excitedly pointed
at my object of desire, "That's the one!" After finally figuring out
which one I meant, Mother turned to me and said, "Well, I don't
think you should wear it." "Why?" I couldn't believe what was happening and was on the verge of crying. "Well, for one thing, it's
rather ugly. There're too many colors, so it's too *xiangqi* [tacky].
Besides, I don't like it when you blindly follow other girls' fancy
and like what they like. Finally, it's not important whether a girl
is pretty or not, but it's important that she does well in school and
has *zhenbenshi* [real ability]." It goes without saying that I did not
get to wear that hair ornament.

After reading an earlier draft of this essay, a friend commented
that this little episode indicated my mother's elitist attitude toward
taste and ordinary people. My mother an elitist? At first I found this
reading somewhat far-fetched, because to me my mother couldn't
have been more ordinary in terms of social and political status. Then,
it dawned on me that this story may well help indicate the complex cultural dimensions of the environment in which I grew up.
In our upbringing, my mother, together with her own desire and
dreams, did play a complex role carrying with her many different
legacies both from her own and China's past. In this sense, one
can say that my mother's "pruning" of her daughters echoes a

deeply entrenched cultural attitude toward learning and an unquestioned acceptance of its superiority. Given specific historical and political contexts, however, such cultural legacy can carry varied meanings and produce necessary resistance values, especially for women.

To Mother, certainly, there was nothing inconsistent between telling me that as a girl I must be neat and careful (and should have taste) and saying that I should not be defined by just a feminine appearance. As someone who grew up in Shanghai and who used to be a fan of Hollywood films, my mother was curiously unaffected by the pursuit of femininity, which used to define Shanghai culture. If anything, she seemed to believe just the opposite: a woman should not rely on her feminine appearance for success in life. Although, incidentally, her conviction appeared to coincide with the alleged post-1949 defeminization practices and even with the famous lines from a poem of Mao's that "Chinese daughters have high aspiring minds/They love their battle array, not silks and satins," my mother's warnings to me (and my sister) did not seem to stem from their underlying political message.

Additionally, Mother was never particularly clear about what constituted zhenbenshi (real ability); but as long as I can remember, she used all kinds of people as possible role models to indicate what she meant. They included Cao Xueqin (the author of *Hong Lou Meng,* or *Dream of Red Mansions*) and other ancient Chinese men of letters; Balzac, Gogol, and other foreign writers or thinkers; and even the child of one of her colleagues. They were worthy of Mother's praise for one reason: they were all great (or potentially great) achievers (in a learned sense). Even though it never occurred to me, until now, that almost all of her good people were men, her role models nevertheless enhanced her warnings against a girl being just a smart face. Apparently, my earliest gender education in many ways contradicted today's visually oriented popular culture and the commercial culture in which women are encouraged to pursue a desirable feminine appearance (either in China or elsewhere in the world). And, as I have just mentioned, it was not carried out in the "iron girl" *(tie guniang)* model. If anything, it was, I believe, intelligence that my mother was drawn to and wanted her daughters to define themselves with (and hence her possible allegiance to traditional Chinese elitism).

Without being consciously aware of any of this at the time, I began to associate matters of appearance with intellectual inferiority. And it seemed only natural, therefore, that the first major decision I made for myself upon entering elementary school was to quit dance. Dancing, I was convinced, was only for *xiao guniang* (little girls). I decided to join extracurricular activities that were not just for girls: the International Affairs Group (Guoji Xingqu Xiaozu), the table-tennis team, and the writing competition. I believed that if I chose to do these things it would mean I was growing up. I wanted to learn to do something intelligent and sophisticated (even though what that constituted was a matter almost entirely subject to my childish whims). Quietly but surely, my mother's pruning began to slowly translate into my own ways of relating to the world and dreaming about the future.

"ZHENBENSHI", PRE–CULTURAL REVOLUTION EDUCATION, AND DAYDREAMS

The post-1949 modernizing agenda employed by the CCP was translated into concrete practices in various arenas, including education. Along with the "revolutionary ideal" (lixiang) ideology that taught youngsters to prepare themselves to be "revolutionary successors," children were also encouraged to study well. Such encouragement was emblematized by the ubiquitous presence of a famous slogan by Mao found on top of the front wall of almost every (urban) classroom: "haohao xuexi, tiantian xiangshang [study well and improve everyday]." Prior to the Cultural Revolution, youngsters were taught to take learning seriously as part of their duty to realize "revolutionary ideals" when they grew up. In concrete and more mundane terms, however, for children in urban China, and especially in big cities, the slogan was often translated into studying well so as to be able to attend a key high school. Two of my older brothers went to the same key high school and made my parents very proud. I am sure my mother's respect for "intelligence," mixed with the traditional belief of *xue er you ze shi* (study well in order

to become an official), was deeply embedded in my parents' expectations for their children to study well and in their pride when
we did. It was against such expectations and toward the latter part
of the first seventeen years, in which youngsters had been put into
the "pipeline" of regular education, when I began my schooling.

Education was a serious business at school. We had classes from
morning to afternoon, after which there were extracurricular activities. Every morning before classes, there was half an hour of pre-
class period in which we did arithmetic and practiced Chinese
characters. Almost everyday we were given a rectangle piece of pink
paper. On it was a list of arithmetic problems, and we would write
the answers to the problems in an exercise book. Before long, however, I became bored with the routine and had to go through an
"initiation," which I mentioned earlier, when my mother set me
straight. By the end of the first year, much to my chagrin, the first-
grade kids became the victims of an experimental project: we were
to graduate from elementary school in five years instead of the normal six. As a result, we were made to give up our summer break so
that we would become third graders when school started again. Everyday when I saw my neighborhood friends playing outside while
I was on my way to school, I felt most unlucky.[7] In contrast, needless to say, my parents were very pleased that I was given a chance
to learn more at an earlier age, so they told me I must feel proud
to have been given this opportunity.

Obviously, I was not born to like studying right away. In fact,
in face of the central concern of doing well in school so as to go
to a key high school, I became attracted to extracurricular activities. They provided me with something to fantasize about other
than just studying. Today my memory of this short period of "normal" schooling consists mainly of the after-school activities I was
involved in and of the daydreams I had during our mandatory nap
time every afternoon, when we buried our heads in our folded arms
on top of our desks. The daily nap time offered me half an hour to
dream about what I wanted to do other than schoolwork.

I spent my nap time daydreaming about becoming a musician,
convinced that musical ability must be counted as some kind of
"real ability." At one point I was more anxious about whether or

not I had been accepted by the attached elementary school of Shanghai Conservatory of Music than I was about my examination results. The lure of Western music instruments was, of course, not just a child's fantasy. It was also symptomatic of the irony of the time in which we grew up. While the CCP's party-state cut off many links with the West, it still promoted certain Western things. Western classical music was one of them. Additionally, because the state supported symphony troupes both nationally and locally, I naturally imagined that the respect musicians commanded meant my dream of having this kind of "real ability" could someday earn me a lot of respect.

When a boy with a well-connected mother was given the opportunity to go to the Music Conservatory's attached elementary school, I was crestfallen. My music teacher, bless her heart, offered me an opportunity to learn to play the violin. So, after I was admitted to the "violin group" of the district's Children's Palace, where I went once a week on Sundays for lessons, I began to dream about becoming a violinist. But it was my first trip to the Children's Palace that I remember most vividly and consider symbolic of the times in which children like me lived, full of idealism and silly, banal, and yet meaningful details.

When I finally received a Sunday pass for the Children's Palace, I was thrilled despite misgivings about learning to play the violin. I felt I was on my way to learning another zhenbenshi. I so treasured that thin paper pass that, before going to the first day of my lessons, I put it in my right shoe, just like underground Communists did in movies, thinking it was the safest place. By the time I got to the palace, the pass was nowhere to be found in the shoe (it was reduced to little pink shreds). I did not realize it was not directly under one's foot that those movie characters put their secret notes. I was completely mortified upon discovering the consequence of my silly imitation. Daydreaming apparently was not going to get me out of this situation—I could not just go home, nor did I know how to get in without the pass. I stood at the gate, looking rather lost. One of the guards asked what I was doing there. After a moment of uncertainty, I told him I had come for my violin lessons but had lost my pass. I left out the detail of my foolishness. Apparently, the teaching that we should all be *chengshi de haizi* (honest children) in order to be qualified successors of the revolution was not enough to make me tell the whole truth. The old man let me enter, and from then on I went to the Children's Palace without the piece of paper that had vanished beneath my foot.

My dream to become a violinist, however, did not vanish accordingly. Although I had not set my heart on learning to play the violin, I had nevertheless continued to daydream about becoming a professional violinist, and did so in spite of the fact that we could not learn much, for our violin teacher often failed to show up. One day when she was absent, a group of foreign visitors were being shown to different instrument groups. The older kids in our group decided to close the door to our practicing room. For fear that someone might find out that we were in the room, they ordered us little kids to stand against the wall and not make noise. As we stood there without a sound, I began to daydream about never having to come again. I felt foolish having been made to hide like that. But when I put my head on top of the desk at school, being a violinist was still something I enjoyed daydreaming about.

During the short-lived years of a structured life in the elementary school, this everyday dreaming took me to worlds beyond the boundaries of my desk, the classroom, the fences surrounding the school, and the streets outside. When the Cultural Revolution broke out, however, my daydreaming quickly came to an end (and so did many of my dreams) when the schools were closed.

CULTURAL REVOLUTION AND "WO YAO DU SHU"

In the summer of 1997 I had my first post–Cultural Revolution reunion with my old neighborhood pals. I had not seen most of them for about twenty years, and all of them had become mothers and were working at different jobs. As different as our lives had become, what connected the twelve of us was our shared past. The conversation was mainly about the mischievous deeds these once-preteen girls did during the Cultural Revolution (such as the tricks played on neighborhood boys, songs we made up about neighborhood rival groups, etc.). As I listened and laughed with them over one story after another, I wondered aloud why I did not remember many of these things. Immediately they retorted: it was because I was often not there with them. "You did not come out as often as we did. Your mother did not like it when you and your sister were *ye zai waitou* [running wild outside]," one of them said.

Ironically, the outbreak of the Cultural Revolution had been the start of my new relationship with learning and my parents', especially my mother's, nagging about the need to continue studying. When the Cultural Revolution broke out, my mother became upset that her children did not have to go to school due to *tingke nao geming* (make revolution by stopping classes); what used to structure children's lives had ceased to function, leaving us with a greater degree of freedom. To me, the newfound freedom was refreshing, and I was secretly glad we did not have to go to school. I had more time than before to play with the neighborhood children. With that freedom, I occasionally found myself in the midst of some mindless behavior (such as joining other kids in taunting the "bad" people in our neighborhood) until my parents stopped me. I also actively joined the neighborhood children learning to sing revolutionary songs and doing what we thought were revolutionary deeds. One day, I joined them in making some revolutionary paper cuttings and putting them up on the walls at home. When Mother came home, I enthusiastically showed her the red-colored paper cuttings pasted on the walls and said proudly, "I made them myself." "It's so ugly," Mother said, paying no attention to my enthusiasm and pride. "Take them off." "But, but, but . . . ." I did not know what to say. "We're not going to have this kind of stuff at home. Did you hear me?" Mother said in a stern manner, giving no time for my unfinished buts. "If you have time, I'd rather you study. Time is precious. I don't like to see you waste it like this," Mother continued. "Here she goes again," I thought to myself as I reluctantly removed the paper cuttings. I had assumed that with the beginning of the Cultural Revolution and the closing of schools, Mother would not make us study anymore. But that was just wishful thinking on my part.

Not long after that, Mother gave a few elementary and middle-school textbooks to me and my sister. She had found them in our neighborhood recycling station, where all these books had ended up (and where Mao's red book and other Cultural Revolution materials would end up when all this was over). "But they are *feng, zi, xiu* [feudal, bourgeois, and revisionist] stuff and we're not supposed to read them anymore," I said to her. "It's never bad to know things. At least you'll know what feng, zi, xiu are when people say them," Mother said. "Besides," she continued, "what are you going to do if you don't know much when you grow up? Today people don't believe in study, but who knows what will happen later on. Whatever you learn, it will be yours. No one can take it away." Today I sometimes marvel at my mother's unwavering conviction in learning, although I did not appreciate it at the time. Indeed, I often found my parents too different from others, who seldom insisted their children should still study. To me, my parents' refrain *yicun guangyin yicun jin* (time is precious) was such a cliché that I did not want to register its meaning in my mind. Even though I took to heart that as a girl I must not be a xiuhua zhentou, or just a smart face, I did not always take my mother's teaching seriously. In fact, I sometimes silently rebelled by refusing to memorize the Tang poems she so eagerly made us recite. I had my own ideas about things, and it was because of them that I sometimes let Mother's words fall by the wayside.

Today I realize my parents' dreams for us were in many ways extensions of their own dreams. As a child, I was always proud my mother worked. My siblings and I were all latchkey kids, and I often secretly felt superior to children with stay-at-home mothers (although my pride did not prevent me from wishing my mother could come home earlier). Busy as she was, however, one of my mother's first priorities was to make sure we knew how she felt about the importance of studying and learning. She did not want us to lose out on what she did when she was young. Her memory of her own childhood dreams played a significant role in our upbringing.

Indeed, I grew up hearing from my aunts and uncle that when my mother was a child and teenager in the 1930s and 1940s in Shanghai, she wanted desperately to learn and took every opportunity to do so; they jokingly recalled various mishaps due to her tendency to forget things while reading. It so happened that when she passed her exams and was admitted to Gezhi Middle School (a high school famous both in pre- and post-1949 Shanghai), her father would not let her go and insisted she stay home and take care of her younger siblings because her mother had just died. Mother was in total despair. For two days her family could not find her—she had to weep her sorrow away and did so in a park.

This turn of events deeply affected and altered my mother's life's course, and she was determined her children would appreciate the opportunity to study. Even though she seldom resorted to the official language when talking to us, she was fond of telling us the story "Woyao Dushu" (I Want to Go to School) by Gao Yubao, a PLA-soldier-turned-writer who recounted his lack of education until he joined the Chinese Communist Party's army. My mother's own childhood story juxtaposed with Gao's "Wo Yao Du Shu" served as a constant reminder of why we all had to take learning *(xuexi)* seriously. So when the Cultural Revolution broke out it was, among other things, the denouncing of learning and the discontinuation of her children's education that made my mother upset with the Cultural Revolution.[8]

A few years into the Cultural Revolution I went to middle school. Education at school was minimal and could be interrupted at any moment. All the subjects had been renamed. Instead of mathematics, chemistry, and physics, for example, we took classes with titles like Foundational Knowledge of Industry *(gong ye ji chu zhi shi)*, or Foundational Knowledge of Agriculture *(nong ye ji chu zhi shi)*, and so forth. At the end of the first semester, however, there were still final exams. After taking the Foundational Knowledge of Industry exam, I walked home with some of my classmates. "It was so easy," one of them said. "Yes," I echoed, "all you need to do is memorize everything the night before the test." "Gosh, you really did the test?" one of the girls asked. "I didn't," she continued, "I just wrote, 'Chairman Mao teaches us don't pretend to know if you don't.' They'd for sure give me a passing grade," she said, apparently very impressed by her own rebellious deed. She was right; she (and many others in class) were able to get passing grades by using this famous quotation by Mao: "bu dong bu yao zhuang dong."

As a typical teenager, I was part of a group of girl classmates who always had something to say about boys and teachers, usually about how "uncool" they were. But I did not feel obliged to follow their example by neglecting my studies. As a result, I was not particularly "cool" either. Starting in the second semester, I decided to sit in the front row of the class of fifty students (teachers were not able to maintain order in class, so whoever wanted to learn chose to sit in the front row, where the teacher would teach whomever wanted to learn). I studied what was taught, including English lessons that began with the slogan "Long Live Chairman Mao" and continued with other slogans like "Long Live the Great Proletariat Dictatorship." And I took all the exams.

By then, apparently, my parents', especially Mother's, urge for us to learn had finally kicked in, and I followed the ethos of the time—being rebellious—by going against the grain. Instead of giving up studying, I decided that was the thing to do. Although I cannot fully explain why I chose to do that, I am sure it must have had something to do with my desire to compete with "popular kids," whose popularity was based on their open rebelliousness toward teachers and who were able to stop classes whenever they felt like it. When there seemed no other way available for me, my parents' nagging became a useful compensation: if you have learned something, it will forever be yours; no one can take it way. Even though Mother's zhenbenshi teaching appeared no longer realistic, she and my father's repeated expressions that learning was in and of itself a good thing might have quietly been transformed into my sense of who I wanted to be. Having "real ability" became less of a goal-oriented desire and more of a way to seek and maintain an equilibrium or, indeed, a sense of myself (or, in today's terminology, my "self-identity") in a rather confusing time. Incidentally, the fact that my parents did not encourage us to settle for being "ordinary," or, in the then politically correct language, to learn from workers, peasants, and soldiers and to become one of them, is yet another indication of the complexity of who they were (and are) as subjects of socialist China.

As for me, my decision meant that I would have various kinds of encounters with people who reacted to my "studying" act. One early summer evening during my middle-school years, for example, I was reading a Chinese equivalent of *Who's Who,* which included many people who had been *dadao* (ousted) and publicly denounced, including Liu Shaoqi, the president of the state, and Deng Xiaoping, the second biggest "capitalist roader" next to Liu. I was sitting in front of our apartment building where people gathered to sit during summertime. Seeing me sitting there with a book, a downstairs neighbor asked me, in a joking manner, if I could explain the meaning of *luo ji* (logic) to her. Although it was not an unfamiliar word— I had seen it in big-character posters and in newspapers and had heard it on the radio—I had no idea how to explain what it meant. I knew she was making fun of me for reading (when few people seemed to think it was the thing to do). Immediately, I found my classmates' use of Mao's quotation in their tests handy, so I replied: "I don't know. And Chairman Mao teaches us 'don't pretend to know if you don't.'" We both laughed.

Because I was doing something few people were doing and because my studying was not structured by adults and was therefore not imposed on me (in a routine manner), I felt a sense of power. I was the one who chose to study. With a twist of irony, my parents' nagging not only became my secret mental competition against some of my classmates, but also nourished my own desire (and dream) to learn. And this version of my own *wo yao du shu* was to remain a form of (albeit naive) defiance and resistance as I went into an unknown future. Today I wonder how I would have reacted to Mother's desire for us to learn if not for that unusual time. Perhaps I would have ended up resenting her pressure and demands and would not have taken learning seriously. Or perhaps education would have been too closely related to competition and practical goals to make me as motivated as I was during the Cultural Revolution.

"WO YAO DU SHU" AND THE STATE FARM

When I graduated from middle school, the Cultural Revolution had entered its later years. All graduates were "assigned a job." The nature of the job depended on where our older siblings were. It so happened that by the time I graduated, two of my older brothers were working in Shanghai and one in the countryside. To balance the ratio, I was to go to the countryside. By the time I graduated, Shanghai had stopped sending its graduates to other provinces, so going to the countryside meant going to the state farms scattered around the outskirts of Shanghai. I was assigned to Donghai State Farm in Nanhui County, where the real struggle to continue studying took place.

One week after we arrived at the brigade (one of the thirty-plus on this State Farm), manual labor began. To an urban teenager like me, it was no small challenge. Meanwhile, I tried to keep up with the study of various subjects, including geometry and other types of math, but fatigue from manual labor made it hard to keep up. As I listened to the English lessons on the radio, I could hardly keep awake.[9] According to my amused roommates, I would fall asleep while the lessons were broadcast, sitting on a stool with my head resting on my bed.

It was hard for me to learn much that way, but it was quickly known in the brigade that studying was important to me. Nevertheless, few appreciated my effort. During the time when "iron girls" were the models for young women, my desire to continue with my studies seemed to contradict the revolutionary ideals and norms of the time. One day, while I walked past the men's barracks, someone whistled at me. When I refused to turn around to look, I heard the taunting voice of a group of men saying, "Hey, look at this one. She's studying something called English. How weird. She is just afraid of doing the work in the fields." This was not the first time I encountered such taunts, but, curiously, it failed to affect me. My defense was my refusal to respond to them. Soon these guys turned their attention to other women, but from time to time they let me know their disapproval by refusing to help me in the fields.

The essence of what I was trying to do, which was considered odd and disagreeable to some of my fellow workers, may very well have been part of an implicit struggle in which some (young) people tried to define who they were. I unavoidably projected a different attitude toward working in the fields. Even though I have always looked upon my interests in education as implicitly politically oppositional to Cultural Revolution politics, it may also be true that my struggle was entangled with an elitist desire to escape the fields and become "learned."

One day my dream of going to college was seriously stirred when I learned that someone else had been chosen to go. Starting in 1971, some colleges and universities resumed recruiting students, mostly through recommendations. These students are known as WPS (worker, peasant, and soldier) students. A young cadre from our brigade was chosen as a WPS student to study Arabic at Beijing University. After being notified, he said to me, "It should have been you to study this subject [a foreign language]." "I could never be picked," I replied. Even though I was highly envious of him, I knew very well it was not likely I would ever be selected. Meanwhile, I had no idea that one day the Cultural Revolution would end and college entrance exams would be reinstated. Nevertheless, I was not going to give up studying. If anything, I became even more determined to continue.

I carried my college dream with me when I went to work at the headquarters of the State Farm. Working immediately below the big shots of the farm, I quickly encountered difficulties with them. They were bothered that I was learning English. One day, two party committee members (of the Red Guards generation) came to have a *tan hua* (talk) with me. "We want to send you to study in Shanghai," one of them began. I was pleasantly surprised, knowing that would be a good opportunity both to be away from the farm and to be able to do a lot of reading. Before I could say anything, the other continued, "But we have a condition. You must agree to give up learning English." Young and defiant as I was, I nevertheless knew that I should not be openly confrontational. "But it is just something I'm interested in doing. It is not for any specific purpose," I said. "Well," one of them said, sounding somewhat displeased, "you're now working on a state farm. Your job has nothing to do with English. What do you study it for?" They jabbered on. As they were talking, it dawned on me that I should say yes to them, because they would not know whether or not I continued with it in Shanghai. So without further ado, I told them that I'd give up learning English.

The following nine months in Shanghai turned out to be one

of the most eventful parts of recent Chinese history: the Cultural Revolution came to a dramatic end (with the death of Mao and the arrest of the Gang of Four). But when I returned to the farm, the familiar pattern of thinking and doing things had not changed so quickly. One day a friend of mine, looking serious, whispered to me that the secretary of the Party Committee of the Farm was not happy I was reading *Romance of the Three Kingdoms* (a fourteenth-century Chinese novel). It so happened that I roomed with three women who occupied ranking positions at the headquarters. One day, the party secretary wandered into our room—where I hardly spent any time except when I slept—and sat on my bed to talk with those important roommates of mine. Since privacy was not part of anybody's consciousness, his sitting on my bed, the only place I might leave some personal things, would not have been considered unusual. Without thinking, he picked up the book on the pillow. It was the *Three Kingdoms* novel I had been reading at night before going to bed. He said, "Where did she get the book? Why does she like to read such books?" Indeed, because as the Chinese saying goes, *shao bu kan san guo* (youngsters are not supposed to read the *Three Kingdoms*), this man must have found it troubling that I was reading the novel, supposedly unfit even for young men! Ironically, it was perhaps because I was young and female that he did not take my not-so-revolutionary behavior seriously. His annoyance with me did not become full-fledged until I refused to follow his instruction to give up sitting for college entrance exams.

In 1977 the central government issued a notice announcing the reinstatement of the college entrance examination. This meant heaven and earth to me. My main worry at that time was whether or not I would be able to pass the exams. However, one day I was told to see the party secretary. It was my first and last talk with him in his office. Very simply, he told me not to take the exams. I told him that I had already paid my registration fee, so I wanted to take the exams. Besides, I added, partly wanting to appease him, I may not be able to pass the exams. "If I fail, I will continue to stay on the farm," I said, knowing it was a perfectly useless thing to say (given the political situation then, where else could I go?). The old man did not succeed in stopping me from taking the exams. A few days later, I got on one of the trucks taking test takers from the farm to the county seat for the three-day examinations, an action that would lead to my last round of conflict with the farm's authority, and, of course, my ultimate triumphant escape into college.

Mother's *zhenbenshi* teaching soon ceased to be the primary source of my sense of myself when similar teaching stopped being marginal and became mainstream, but those yesteryears of mine were powerfully connected with a series of dreams spurred by the lure of possessing "real ability."

IRONY, OR ENTANGLEMENT, OF DREAMS

My mother told me that the day she learned about my admission to college she was so excited that she was unable to sleep all night. Even though my oldest brother was admitted to one of the best universities in Shanghai, Mother did not lose as much sleep over his success. She did not tell me what she was thinking about that night lying in bed awake, but I am certain she must have remembered her own dream decades earlier. In some ways we can say that while I was still on the State Farm wrapped up in the excitement of the realization of my own dreams, my mother's sleepless night signified a silent but meaningful moment when personal and generational dreams converged.

Even though my parents differed strongly in their reactions toward the Cultural Revolution, they never differed in their conviction that we, their children, must continue with our education even after the schools were closed. To them, the revolutionary ideals that children should all become the "successors of communism" did not (and should not) contradict their desire for their own children to become educated. To my parents, especially my father, the revolutionary causes he had struggled for as an underground party member always included the importance of learning. So, even though he often blindly bought into the party's doctrine, he failed to comply on at least one issue: the importance of education (or his deeply entrenched culturally conditioned conviction in the Confucian doctrine *xue er you ze shi* [a good scholar will make an official]).

Father never relented in his nagging that we must take learning seriously. Perhaps precisely because of that, he did not forbid my brothers from trying to find "taboo" books to read. Even though most of the time he was not home, I do not remember him saying much in terms of what we should and should not read.

In doing what they did, my parents were not intentionally resisting the official ideology. And yet neither were they ready to give up their own convictions and dreams when it came to their children's lives. They fostered a belief in us that learning was in and of itself a good thing. The irony, of course, was that for my father this teaching was good for the revolution (even though such an idea was considered counterrevolutionary during the Cultural Revolution), while for my mother it was almost strictly within the realm of her personal interests, her unfinished dreams, and her hopes for her children in what appeared to be a hopeless time for our education.

It goes without saying that many children's "revolutionary" songs of the Mao era, which taught youngsters to become "revolutionary successors," speak mainly to the ideals of the adults—those who had fought for them—and that when it came to our generation, the "ideals" inevitably became entangled with many other matters and issues. While those ideals continued to be upheld and profoundly influenced us (albeit to different degrees and even when we were resisting them), many, like my parents, were also (unselfconsciously) translating them into concrete hopes for the future of their own children. This translation was complicated—it came with the changes that occurred after the 1949 revolution and broadened our lives beyond slogans and "revolutionary ideals." Although many personal dreams died prematurely, the fact that children like me grew up with them tells a lot about the people who lived through the Mao era.

In this sense, I must say that between the lixiang teaching and childhood dreams was not just my personal or individual struggle to keep my own dreams alive. There were the entangled collective ideals, personal dreams, nightmarish experiences, and endless ironies and paradoxes. Mixed together, they encouraged both the beliefs in and practices of grandiose utopian ideals as well as hotbeds where individual dreams were nurtured and realized. As such, they constitute the complexity of our memories and our past.

NOTES

1. *Lixiang* means "ideals." Within the context of the Mao era, it specifically referred to "revolutionary ideals" *(geming lixiang)*, functioning as a political discourse for children and young people. Through songs, popular cultures, and education, children were taught to make the revolutionary ideals their own dreams and to become successors *(jiebanren)* of communism. As such, lixiang was ubiquitous in the public domains of children's lives.
2. Although I came to this country with a college degree and a valid visa, many other Chinese have had to come through illegal means. My friend's remarks, therefore, must be understood within this context. Not all Chinese were "lucky" enough to make it to urban and socially privileged groups.
3. There were eighteen state farms under the jurisdiction of the Shanghai municipal government. Sixteen of them were located in a number of counties on the outskirts of Shanghai. Two of them were in Jiangsu and Anhui Provinces. They "housed" 150,000 youngsters from Shanghai in the 1960s and 1970s. I was assigned to Donghai State Farm in Nanhui Province in 1973.
4. Because all the youngsters on the farm were no longer associated with their high schools. The only official channel for entering the exams and other related business was the farm authority, hence, the ad hoc office.
5. *Lao san jie* literally means "old three classes of graduates," specifically referring to the junior and high school students who, under normal circumstances, should have graduated in 1966, 1967, and 1968 respectively. Sometimes they are referred to as the Red Guards generation.
6. All of these, including cooking, were taught to us according to our order of birth, without any gender relevance. The emphasis was that good children helped out, and it was quite natural at that time that children were expected to help. In our household, learning to cook was necessary when both parents were busy, when we did not have grandparents living with us, and when we did not have a regular nanny to help. From time to time, when it was time for one of us to learn to cook, the whole family would have to endure a period of burnt rice or badly cooked vegetables (although we would not be given the honor of cooking "complicated" dishes until we grasped the basic skills). Fortunately, even though the siblings would complain, my parents always praised us for helping out. In fact, Mother was so good at it that she made us (at least me) feel cooking was like doing lab work—you can only succeed by repeatedly trying and paying attention.
7. I did not go to the same elementary school as most children in the neighborhood.
8. There was a constant sense of danger on my part every time I heard my mother's angry words about the Cultural Revolution, for fear other people might hear them. She must have known well enough not to express her real thoughts in public, and so did her children for not giving her away.
9. Starting in 1971 Shanghai People's Radio Station began to broadcast English lessons on a daily basis. Accompanying the lessons were textbooks available in bookstores. I started following the radio lessons before "graduating" from middle school.

ZHANG ZHEN

THE PRODUCTION OF SENSES IN AND OUT OF THE "EVERLASTING AUSPICIOUS LANE"
Shanghai, 1966–1976

WALKING ON A RUINED MAP

When I visited Shanghai in the fall of 1996, partly to conduct further research for my dissertation on the Shanghai cinema that flourished in the early decades of the twentieth century, I found myself at one point wandering around in my old neighborhood in the heart of the city. It is an area where old movie theaters are concentrated; some of them are still fully functional today, while a few have been converted to other uses over time. As a girl, I spent a lot of time in the old movie theaters watching a plethora of shows, voluntarily or involuntarily. The movies and performances I remember watching included "model operas" masterminded by Jiang Qing (Mao's wife, a former Old Shanghai actress); Albanian or North Korean melodrama films; stage performances by local schools; and newsreels about the independence movements in Africa. I know the streets, the stores, and the theaters in that area inside out. Not merely a spectator or witness, I had performed Mao's thought as a member of our neighborhood propaganda troupe either in the street or on these theater stages during the Cult Rev (the Great Proletarian Cultural Revolution was often abbreviated as *wenge,* thus Cult Rev). I was only a little girl in those days.

More than two decades have passed since I left home to attend Fu Dan university in the northern suburbs of the city and then on to a much longer and erratic journey in the world beyond. My memories of those venues, the events, and the people associated with that neighborhood have receded to the furthest background of my mind, behind layers of more recent pasts, or mingled with the latter in a disorderly fashion. Over the years, I have been so busy organizing my new lives in other parts of the world that those girlhood memories have been lodged in a dark corner of the past, and only a few fragments escape to my dreams and writings. But they have always been a specter with an undefinable shape.

My parents moved away from that area quite some years ago. I had not revisited that neighborhood for a few years, especially the Everlasting Auspicious Lane (Changjili), where I was born and grew up in the tumultuous sixties and seventies before China officially "opened its doors" to the outside world. This time I was shocked to learn that my old neighborhood was soon to be wiped out, just as the adjacent lanes that had already been pulverized by bulldozers. In place of this part of Old Shanghai, built in the twenties and thirties, which is situated in the so-called golden zone *(huangjing diduan)*, skyscrapers were to be erected to house shopping centers and offices. The residents, many of whom have lived here for generations, were being evacuated to brand-new residential compounds in the suburbs, which lack the warmth of an old community and the convenience of living in the center of the city.

I hurried to take a last look at the neighborhood and visit the remaining neighbors, taking along a camera. While having a photograph of myself taken at the entrance of the lane, which faces the hustling and bustling Tibet Road full of cars, people, and noises, I was overcome by a profound sense of loss triggered by the imminent disappearance of my place of origin. But I was even more struck by the rapid destruction of the past, a past I used to perceive as an everlasting present.

What has happened to that numbing sense of permanence or, rather, inertia that I experienced as a girl? I may have forgotten many details and messed up the order of things in my memory. That heaviness of an unchanging present, which always weighed on me while growing up in the years before Mao's death and the demise of the so-called Gang of Four in 1976, however, is something that has deeply settled in me. Chronology is less important; we were wrapped in a different consciousness of time—a time that was at once linear and monumental. Whenever images of that past flash in my mind, I feel a shudder, a sense of mixed terror and excitement. This feeling is not merely psychological; it flows through my limbs and up my spine. Where does this sensation come from? Why are the images from those times and places awash in heavy bright light instead of the darkness habitually associated with the "ten-year calamity" (*shinian haojie*; that is, the Cult Rev), which is seen, after the fact, by many Chinese and Westerners alike as a modern-day "dark age" in Chinese history? How should I account for my coming of age in the heart of a Chinese metropolis—the home base of the Gang of Four in that era? Why has there always been a sense of unease, or even disappointment, whenever I tell non-Chinese friends in America or elsewhere that my parents and I were not victimized in any dramatic or visible way, as so often described in standard narratives about the Cult Rev? Where do answers to these questions lie?

I entered the Everlasting Auspicious Lane as if entering the tunnel of memory. I wandered aimlessly along the meandering lane. The building where I spent my childhood was still standing, only it looked much more worn out. The black paint on the big gate had chipped off, but the address plate was firmly in the same old place. It was familiar yet strange. The family that occupied the back unit of the house where my family used to live had moved to newly assigned housing in the suburbs. The door and the windows were tightly shut. But I had no desire to peep into my childhood home, for there was nothing to be seen. Everything had been emptied out. Yet somehow something seemed to be lurking behind that closed door, those sealed windows. It now may be inhabited by ghosts from the past, and the girl that was me must be among them.

The rest of the lane was already half empty. Most black wooden gates were shut, so it was hard to make out whether or not people were still living behind them. The chill of the Chinese poetic idiom *renqu loukong* (the house is desolate when the inhabitants are gone) floated in the air while I walked gingerly down the lane, afraid that I might accidentally step on time bombs of memory long buried.

A sense of desolation pervaded the place. I did not meet any girl-hood friends of mine, who also participated in the girls' performing troupe. Some had dispersed long ago, gone as far as Japan or Canada. Others might be feeding their babies or taking a nap in the deep recesses of those dilapidated old row houses. But I did not feel like disturbing them. It had been too long, and we had become strangers.

Quickly I reached the end of the lane. Much more so than at the bustling street where the main entrance of the lane stood—the little back street at the end of the lane was the real extension of the communal life of ours and the neighboring lanes. It was part of a market where we did our daily grocery shopping and the necessary path that led to our schools. But the street market was nowhere to be found, gone also were the strong smells coming from fish stalls and various dinsum booths that permeated my childhood. A multistory, fluorescent-lit supermarket had been erected on the old premises.

I then looked for the kindergarten my siblings and I attended. Located just a couple of minutes away from our lane, it is housed in a row of townhouses at the end of the neighboring two lanes, with some of its windows facing the bygone market. Like the apartment where we lived, the kindergarten was already sealed off, waiting to be torn down. The archway of the lane leading to the kindergarten's front gate was barely standing, and the houses next to it were all gone, leaving only a huge area of rubble. It looked like a war-ravaged landscape. On that ruin once lived several of my close classmates from primary school. There used to be a sort of plaza in front of their dwellings. On summer evenings people cooled themselves with dried palm-leaf fans, ate watermelon, and played poker or chess under the dim yellow streetlights. I wondered where my old classmates had gone, especially that bad boy who shared the same desk with me and that girl who wore a big green ribbon in her hair and was the "flower" of our class.

SCENARIOS OF EVERYDAY LIFE

Old movie theaters, usually standing at key crossroads, have always been regarded fondly by Shanghai residents as landmarks and repositories of urban memory. There are numerous old movie theaters surrounding our neighborhood, such as the famous Da Shanghai Cinema (Great Shanghai, literally; known in old Shanghai as Metropole), which is only one block away from our lane and the kindergarten. Other first- or second-rate cinemas such as Da Guangming, Xinguang, Hongqi, Huangpu were within a short walk as well. I learned so much about life and the world in those theaters, even in the era of China's alienation from a large part of the world. In a society dominated by a puritanical sexual ideology, we felt that films from socialist countries like Romania, Yugoslavia, and North Korea provided us with glimpses of romantic love and lifestyles for us to emulate. The exotic mores and body language of the people portrayed in those foreign films stimulated our desires for the faraway lands beyond China's closed doors. They were phantom rides for us, and we traveled far by making a mere trip to a neighborhood cinema.

Indeed, many aspects of everyday life in residential lanes like ours were interconnected with neighborhood theaters. Cheap tickets basically turned these former luxurious movie houses into socialist nickelodeons. There was not much to see, but everyone could go to the theater to kill time or take advantage of the warmth generated by the crowd in winter or the air-conditioning or electric fans in the summer. Children and students received generous discounts. People thronged to the theaters not only because the crowded living space made it imperative for people, particularly the restless youth, to seek space for private reverie and romantic rendezvous, but also because they were a peculiar public space that allowed for forms of more flexible socialization other than those practiced in the official domain. It was in the dark theater, during the showings of the "model operas," that I first learned about the art of dating from seeing how young lovers engaged in touching, necking, and kissing. They often chose seats at the end of the auditorium or near the outside aisles. Heedless of what was happening on the screen, they indulged in their intimate world protected by darkness and urban anonymity.

For young women and girls, cinema was also a great school for learning about international fashion and feminine beauty. In a time when the blue or green Mao jacket, plain white shirt, and baggy trousers constituted standard dress code, the more attractive clothes worn by our socialist "brothers" and "sisters" in the movies brought hints of latest fashion "out there." Shanghai residents, especially those living in the central city, are known for their love and taste for fashion. Even when the rest of China was wearing the same clothes and hairstyles, we incessantly experimented with different cuts, adding a detail here or there. From watching North Korean movies, we were inspired to make the folds wider and deeper in our indigo rayon skirt (a standard piece to go with a white shirt and red scarf for Little Pioneers). When we danced to the revolutionary songs, fast swivels made our skirts flare like opened umbrellas, making us feel prettier, if not more feminine. From the Romanians, our mothers learned to adorn our uniform Louise Brook haircuts with nylon chiffon ribbons. Wide, colorful, and transparent, they accentuated the fragility and innocence of girlhood.

While middle-aged or older women preferred the Korean melodramas that inevitably involved the sacrifice of women, the appeal of films from Europe (the Europe of the eastern block, to be sure) was considerably greater to young people. Once an Albanian film (I have forgotten the title and the plot) was shown in town. The film was extremely popular, not so much for its political or aesthetic merits as for the hairstyle and wardrobe of the female protagonist. Some of the young women in our lane were so crazy about the heroine's hip-length coat with a wide collar that they went to see the movie over and over again, just to figure out how the coat was cut.

Sometimes it was hard to know whether the exotic looks cultivated by some young people were a result of the influence of the limited foreign movies available to us back then or if they also stemmed from an unconscious memory of Shanghai's "semicolonial" past. In Old Shanghai, Hollywood, UFA, and locally made Chinese cinema, among other things, supplied the Shanghai residents with competing versions of the dream of modern life. The complex social backgrounds of the people living in our lane inclined me to think a combination of the two might be the case.

The family that lived upstairs in our townhouse always intrigued me. There were four sons in that family. They stood out in the lane because they cultivated a certain "occidental style" (*yangqi*, a foreign and exotic flair). The two younger sons didn't want to go to the countryside for reeducation; instead, they stayed in the city as so-called social youth *(shehui qingnian)*, as opposed to the "revolutionary youth" *(geming qingnian)*, and taught themselves to be excellent tailors. Tall, handsome, and always impeccably dressed, they became the fashion leaders in the lane. Just as the women learned how to make a winter coat from an Albanian movie, they copied and re-created a hunting jacket and bell-bottoms they saw in Yugoslavian movies.

Of course, these things could not have happened at all during the first and most intense years of the Cult Rev, when Red Guards cut off girls' braids and tore up dandies' bell-bottoms in the street. In the beginning of the Cult Rev, that very family became the target of class struggle because they used to own a small factory assembling electric equipment, located in our building. According to the social classification of the time, they were petty capitalists. The former workshop area was converted into residences after the factory was confiscated, but the family was able to retain the upstairs as their living space.

I remember seeing their father wearing a dunce hat among the "bad elements" being purged in neighborhood political meetings. Later, the purge took on the more benign form of "reform through labor." He and other "bad elements" of our lane, including some former shop owners, hustlers, and foreign-educated intellectuals, were assigned to cleaning the lane and public latrines and other menial work. Because our small apartment had a wall situated in a strategic location in the lane, it was used by the neighborhood revolutionary committee as a kind of shrine of Mao's thought. "Never Forget Class Struggle," a famous quote by Mao, was painted in big red characters on the outer wall of our apartment; the "bad elements" had to report to the wall twice a day, before and after their sessions of forced labor. They would bow to the wall while reciting other quotations from Mao's little red book, followed by a daily self-criticism.

The petty capitalist from upstairs was among this group. I often climbed up the window and watched their daily rituals. I thought it was funny for them to bow to our apartment, and to me. Looking into their faces, I did not see any visible signs of evil or threat. Some of these people were usually very kind to me, praising me as a big little girl whenever they saw me doing homework or chores outside the house. Sitting on the window, I thought to myself, if I were Chairman Mao, I would forgive their past and let them go home to be with their children or grandchildren, who were, after all, my playmates. I felt somehow relieved to discover that one day the "bad elements" did not show up for the daily rituals of confession. Their performance had been deemed acceptable, and thus it was no longer necessary for them to recite Mao quotes in public. They were allowed to study at home from then on.

I had some inkling that my parents themselves might have come from "problematic" backgrounds, but I never dared to ask, afraid that the surfacing of truth might destroy the innocent background I had constructed in my mind. Because my mother lost her parents very early and seemed open and ready for social and individual change during the early phase of the Cult Rev, I identified with her more. But Mom's passion for politics receded quickly. She became irritable and dreaded going to work. I remember she often uttered the word *meaningless (meiyisi)* whenever politics was mentioned at home, which added to my confusion.

Many years later, I finally learned one of the reasons for my parents' depression and marginalization in their workplaces. My grandfather, a country doctor (mis)identified as a landlord (the village had to fill the quota), was subjected to some severe forms of class struggle. He was deprived of the right to practice medicine, and his collection of books and paintings were confiscated and vanished forever. He died in the early 1970s, when I had just become a class leader and a Little Red Pioneer. My mother's stepfather turned out to be a theater owner. Though his theater catered to the working class, he could not be considered a member of the proletarian class because he had been associated with the entertainment industry of Old Shanghai. The new establishment considered this industry to be sleazy and counterrevolutionary. But my parents protected us from knowing about these histories. As with many parents in that era, they did not want us to inherit their "complicated" *(fuza)* backgrounds.

To be sure, regardless of age, we were all armed with varying degrees of class consciousness and aware of the violence associated with it. I heard hair-raising tales, such as how a girl from the attached section (we called it Sanjiaodi—the Triangle) of our lane cut her throat with a kitchen chopper and filled a washbasin with her blood. She was later revived but went insane. There were mixed rumors about what was behind her sudden nervous breakdown. It was either because of her problematic family background or her sexual conduct, or both. Besides political problems, anything related to sex conjured up images of moral corruption and political downfall. Many cases of premarital sex or extramarital relationships were exposed. Though not considered a crime in the category of "people versus enemy" opposition, and largely seen as a redeemable error, the offenders were usually obliged to confess their wrongdoing and denounce themselves at the meetings. (Yes, there were lots of meetings.) But those incidents were rare and far between; for the most part, the humdrum of everyday life went on.

On the whole, it was quite impossible to draw crystal clear lines between classes in our lane. The old center of the city was known in new China for its complicated social composition. Landowners, ex-prostitutes, ex-capitalists, shopkeepers, barbers, bank clerks, teachers, engineers, and doctors lived in this lane. We went to the same market for groceries, shared the same public latrines, and dried our laundry on bamboo poles in the same air. There were frictions, but there was also constant, mutual help. The elders watched over kids of working couples; the youngsters ran errands for the elders in return. When it rained, people took in the laundry of the neighbors. Perhaps because every family had some "blemishes" on their class background and had probably enough political drama going on at their workplaces, people seemed to want to keep their home environment a place for rest and, as much as possible, for "normal" life.

PLAYING AND PERFORMING REVOLUTION

During the time when all schools were still closed for the Cult Rev, most students stayed at home and the neighborhood committee became their main political and social caretaker. It was a never-ending fun time. I was not school age yet, but I was old enough to want to hang around the older kids, even the teenagers. We played the usual hide-and-seek games a lot. The winding lane, its several irregular extensions (such as the Triangle), and the unlit doorways of many houses were an ideal labyrinth. In the era before television, the only way to spend the evening and burn calories was to play with other children. After supper, the dimly lit lane was full of kids, running, screaming, and laughing. We modeled our games after the guerrilla warfare we saw in revolutionary movies, especially *The Warfare in Air Shelters (Didaozhan)* and *The Railroad Guerrilla Platoon (Tiedao Youjidui)*, both made before the outbreak of the Cult Rev. Having exhausted the potential of the ground space in the lane, we also explored the rooftops, which proved to be far more suitable for adventurous chases.

Another favorite venue for our nighttime play was the No. 1 department store a few blocks away. When there were too few of us to play hide-and-seek games, some of us would band together to go there. We knew the layout of the store by heart. Evening was best time because the store was virtually empty. We could ride escalators freely and slide on the smooth marble floor in the basement. Like Charlie Chaplin and Paulette Goddard in *Modern Times*, we turned the entire store into our fantasy world. A few times, however, the guards caught us running wild and "deported" us from the premises. But we knew how to sneak back and find new territories free of their surveillance.

Such games were largely gender neutral. In those days, we hardly had any real toys. My sister and I shared a baby doll, and I sewed skirts and knit socks for her with leftover material from my mom's sewing basket. We also had a set of colored miniature kitchenware with which we played house. But we tired of them quickly. We wanted to mingle and play with the boys. Despite the official gender equality policy, it was obvious that most people still preferred boys. There was a boy of my age in the house, and he was treated like a little prince in his extended family. His grandmother, a housewife who gave birth to six children, doted on this only grandson, especially after his father was sent to an inland city to work. I always longed for a brother to look up to, a brother who would protect me and my sister and show us the masculine way of dealing with a tough life. But this boy was no such figure. He was shorter than I and had a perpetual runny nose; the thick yellow column between his nose and his upper lip was rather disgusting. I had to be content playing his games: chess, paper scrapers, spinning tops, and Ping-Pong. He was arrogant and short-tempered, but I enjoyed the games nevertheless. Somehow the idea of being an equal player with a fierce boy like him empowered me. I practiced hard, with both my mind and my arms, and I won frequently, which made him cry and throw tantrums. What a weepie, I thought to myself. After such incidents, his grandmother had to spend a lot of time pampering him and warning him not to play with me anymore. But he always came back the next day, challenging me with a new game or a new rule.

No matter how much I wanted to be like a boy, I knew I would never become one. But how did it feel to be a girl exactly? The abusive manners of some of the boys I played with made me yearn for the company of likeminded girls. Soon the occasion arose and we found ourselves forming a performing troupe under the leadership of a teenage girl from the townhouse next door. She had a funny nickname, the "Rotten Apple." She was among those students whose schools ceased operation during the Cult Rev. It was partly an assignment from the neighborhood committee that was supposed to make use of her artistic and organizational skills. At the same time, it would engage younger kids like us in something more meaningful than the anarchic hide-and-seek games that irritated some adults who preferred order and quietness. At the time, people all over China were forming propaganda troupes. Most of these were semiofficial and semiautonomous organizations. Their declared mission was to use singing and dancing to disseminate Mao's thought and the messages of the Cult Rev. In hindsight, it was like a kind of political evangelism in the form of a socialist vaudeville. We had seen some professional troupes performing in theaters nearby and were impressed by the costumes and makeup the actors wore. Cosmetics and perms were outlawed in those days; they were associated with the "decadent" lifestyle of Old Shanghai. But they were allowed on stage, thanks to artistic license!

When our troupe began to create its own repertoire and rehearsed diligently almost daily, we girls also began to long for the day when we could paint our faces and put on real theatrical costumes. Our enthusiasm was boundless. We practiced in an empty room in the Triangle that was at the disposal of the neighborhood committee. (It later became a garbage recycling station.) Rotten Apple was a rigorous producer, director, and choreographer. She made us start with the basics, training our suppleness and endurance. The revolutionary modern ballet was in vogue, thanks to the popularity of film versions of ballet plays such as *The White Haired Girl (Baimaonü)* and *The Red Detachment of Women (Hongse Niangzijun)*. Of course, our troupe had to have a couple of ballet skits taken from these and other model plays. We did not have the means to buy professional ballet shoes, so we tiptoed around the townhouse in our cloth-made Mary Jane's, humming the tunes from those movies. All of a sudden, the whole lane seemed to be taken over by our little "detachment." Our parents thought we were going crazy. My mother was dismayed that I wore out shoes so fast, and she did not have the time or the money to have new ones made.

I was particularly fond of one dance choreographed by Rotten Apple. It was based on a popular song called the "Goose Flies South." It was an exotic melody from Xinjiang, the lyrics were probably in Uighur. We sang it loudly, enchanted by the sounds of a language we did not understand (though it was obviously a hymn to Mao). I loved doing 360 degree turns, my arms stretched out like wings. I would close my eyes, imaging myself in a white flowing chiffon dress, flying out of the window, out of our lane, out of Shanghai, gliding and tumbling over mountains and rivers, toward the source of the song. Dancing made me feel light, happy, and beautiful. I discovered the girl in me—not a timid girl with coy manners, but a girl with the spirit and body of the legendary Monkey King, a master of metamorphosis. I was not much of a singer, but I did not care for those hyperbolic songs idolizing Mao and the party anyway. They gave me goose bumps. Dancing, however, transformed my mind and body; I could slip into many roles and felt at home in the expressive movement. Rotten Apple always encouraged me and praised my improvisation while relentlessly criticizing my partner—her cousin Little Spring—for being lazy and stiff. As a preschool girl, the unreserved praise from a seasoned teenager greatly amplified my sense of self-worth.

I also liked the grand finale in our repertoire, which we called "The Whole World Is a Big Family." It was nothing original. We copied it from professional troupes. I usually played the Red Guard, who was actually nothing more than a tour guide. First I gave a speech about the future utopia in which all the nations of the world would become brothers and sisters; then I introduced delegates from each nation to the audience. Dressed in distinct national costumes, each delegate would either sing a song or do a dance number. In the end, we held each other's hands and danced in a circle, symbolizing our friendship and the unity of the global family.

After several weeks of intensive rehearsals, Rotten Apple decided it was time for us to go public. Our dream came true: We got to paint our face and lips red and our eyebrows thick and dark. I had no idea how and where Rotten Apple managed to get those rare cosmetics. We also had real costumes. Most were on loan from local schools or the propaganda troupe of the district. One spring evening we marched to the No. 1 department store and installed ourselves at the best spot on the corner of Nanjing Road and Tibet Road, right in front of the huge display windows. To our own surprise, none of us suffered from stage fright. Perhaps it was because we were not really standing on an elevated stage. The street was but an extension of our lane. Besides, the store had long since been incorporated into our playing field. Our performance drew a big crowd, who cheered us all the way through. Nearby, there were a few other troupes performing as well. It was almost like a soccer match. We all felt very competitive. Rotten Apple screamed and stomped like a panicking coach. But later she told us that we were all super.

That was an unforgettable evening. In retrospect, I see that performance as a rite of passage. We faced the world and proved that we were fearless. We were now one step closer to the heroines in *The Red Detachment of Women*, except for the fact that we were led by a capable teenage girl instead of a repressed male party leader. Although the content of our program was mostly propaganda stuff, we were too young to understand the meaning of the messages we carried. We could not even pronounce certain words correctly. Likewise, our audience was amused by our childish and playful rendering of such weighty political rhetoric rather than the messages we were supposed to deliver. The whole show must have had a defamiliarizing effect. The songs and slogans were grandiose and hyperbolic, but our performance was endearing and even entertaining.

We repeated our performance in front of the department store several times. Afterward, we moved on to other venues such as neighborhood headquarters and school auditoriums. We became quite famous in the area. The performances also solidified the bonds between us. Some of the girls continued to be my best friends for a long time after the troupe disbanded. In a chaotic time, our troupe produced a sense of community and a measure of gender awareness for us. The boys in the lane had laughed at us when we were rehearsing, but now they were envious of our accomplishment, solidarity, and, unlikely as it may sound, glamour. That glamour, however, did not last long. Suddenly, Rotten Apple told us that she could no longer direct us. The revolution entered a new stage; schools resumed classes and all students had to return to their classrooms.

THE SENTIMENTAL EDUCATION OF A LITTLE RED GIRL

Childhood days always seem insufferably long. Behind the closed doors of China in the Mao era, when we continuously had to sing "Long, Long Live the Greatest and Dearest Chairman, the Reddest Sun in Our Heart," the long days seemed even more excruciating. If the old chairman was to live forever and stay the way he was, then we kids would probably never grow into adulthood, let alone get old. It was fun to dance mock ballets and play hide-and-seek, but I also admired the teenagers and adults in the lane who volunteered or were sent away to the country or cities in faraway places. Their destinies as well as their destinations seemed so dramatic, and romantic. For a while, the lane was filled with incessant crying of mothers and wives who had to bid farewell to their loved ones. That kind of melodramatic excess only evoked in me a powerful longing. I wanted to embark on a train for an unknown future and exotic landscape, leaving behind the confines of my home and the city. But, alas, I was too young for that. I had to wait until I at least finished junior high.

Shortly after Rotten Apple went back to school and later left for the countryside for reeducation, I found myself enrolled in a school next to the No. 1 department store. The historical building that housed our school, as I learned only recently in my research on early Shanghai film culture, used to be the headquarters of the Association of the Ningbo Natives and hosted one of the first film showings in Chinese history. Now come to think of it, our troupe actually performed on that very stage in the large auditorium. I could not care less about the history of our school back then: I thought the classrooms too dark and the ceiling too high. On the whole, I did not enjoy school as much as I had expected. In fact, I found school oppressive. The lack of an open track field forced the gym teachers to hold classes on the rooftop of the building. Gym class was the only time in a long day when we could breathe some fresh air and savor the view of Shanghai's skyline.

The school was oppressive partly because some of the boys in the class were nasty toward female teachers and girls. It was a time when the authority of teachers had just barely been restored. Students were supposed to continue the revolution in the classroom while learning how to read and write and calculate. Those boys constantly disrupted the class, and even used foul language toward some female teachers. They seemed to have inherited the aggression of their Red Guard brothers and sisters. Once, to my horror, I even saw a boy slap the teacher of our class. Her face went instantly red. She cried and fled the classroom. It was hard enough to concentrate on studying, let alone enjoy it. I longed for the school day to end, so I could go home and play with my friends in the lane.

Two boys were particularly hard on me. They were the naughtiest and toughest in our class. Because I was elected as a member of the class committee in charge of things such as Ping-Pong rackets and cartoon books, each claimed I was his "best" (girlfriend).

Of course, they did this without my consent and made my credibility as a good student dubious in front of the whole class. (How could a student with the best grades and the status of a Little Red Pioneer be the "best" of a worst boy in class?) They verbally abused me if I did not give them the best rackets or their favorite cartoons. Boy A even sent to my home address a blackmail letter, in which he threatened to beat me up if I did not discontinue my "friendship" with the other boy. It all seemed like a big conspiracy. I was scared to talk to anyone about it. Young as I was, I had learned that to be involved with the other sex in such a "complicated" way would only bring political disaster to me as well as to my family. I was living in fear. I missed our all-girl performing troupe; things were so much more carefree and simpler then.

Things continued to develop from bad to worse. Boy B shared a desk with me. Not only did he force me to let him copy my answers during exams, he also demanded that I buy him snacks with my pocket money. If I resisted, he would pinch my thighs. It felt like living with a tiger in the same cage everyday. I reported to our teacher a couple of times—the same teacher who was slapped by one of the boys. It was useless.

I eventually managed to mobilize all the girls in the class. As it turned out, many were also being harassed by these and other boys. It might have been a twisted form of expressing their budding, yet repressed sexual desire on the boys' part, but it was hard to take, let alone appreciate. Since the teacher was weak and powerless, we resolved to defend ourselves. The boys made us feel inferior even though many of us had better grades. But grades did not mean anything back then. It was time to prove we could be physically strong as well. One day, our Russian teacher ordered us to self-study because she had to be at a meeting. Boy B coerced me again to do his homework for him. When I refused, he pinched me. I could not put up with it anymore, so I stood up and called my female comrades to arms. It was incredible. For about ten minutes, each girl grabbed a boy and the whole classroom turned into a battlefield. As girls at that age tend to be taller than boys, we were no mere lambs at the mercy of those aggressive boys. When the teacher returned, we quickly rushed back to our seats as if nothing had happened. That day, for the first time ever, I walked home with a sense of triumph. We were girls all right, but no one could dominate us on account of that fact.

That victory gave me the courage to tell my parents about boy B's harassment. Immediately they took me over to that boy's family and had the matter settled. Boy B apologized to me in front of the concerned adults and promised never to pinch or coerce me again. I had no knowledge of feminism back then; but in retrospect, I can see it was perhaps the first—and quite literal—war between the sexes I had experienced and won with the little "detachment of women." I could not have done it alone. Who knows? Perhaps the androgynous heroines in those model operas, highly improbable (and superhuman sometimes) as they were, inspired us. I am quite sure that they did.

Because schoolwork was both light and bland, I developed an insatiable appetite for reading, especially literature of all kinds. I read all the books and magazines I could find at home, including a book about the ABC of sex and pregnancy hidden on top of the tall, ornate armoire (a quaint piece of furniture from an unknown past). I was intrigued by a love story by an author called Zhang Ailing—only many years later did I learn that she was one of the greatest modern Chinese women writers—printed in a yellowed magazine from the 1940s. It was a wonder it had survived two decades of socialism. (Did it come with the armoire when my parents purchased it for their wedding from a consignment store?) Besides a couple of novels, however, our home library mainly consisted of technical books and foreign language readers that my dad used before the Cult Rev. I had to hunt for literature elsewhere.

Fortunately, the neighborhood library opened its door in the early 1970s. Its collection was very limited, but it had at least all the Chinese and foreign classics that had been redeemed from the historical "trash bin." Still seen as loaded with poisonous elements and potentially dangerous to unguarded minds, the more recent editions of these classics all carried a foreword or introduction of sort that spelled out the political "shortcomings" of the books. But they also affirmed their usefulness in "exposing" the evils of either the feudal or bourgeois society. I devoured all the Shakespeare and

Molière that the library had. Zola was another must-read. And I adored Pushkin's poetry. As with many girls, my favorites were the novels by the Brontë sisters. I read *Jane Eyre* at least three times. I was so drawn to the heroine that I secretly adopted "Jane" as one of my pen names. (What I loved about the name was in fact the Chinese character for Jane, which means "simple.")

Reading became an addiction and books almost an appendage of my body. As soon as I got home, I would rush to the library and exchange a new book at the fee of one penny each. Then I would sit on a little stool in the courtyard of our building, burying myself in the pages. Nothing could distract me from those dramas made up by writers dead or alive, Chinese or foreign. The books transported me to remote times and places. Both my mind and body were under intense metamorphosis. They were plasmatic, susceptible, and impressionable. I felt that I was literally growing up; I heard my joints crack as my limbs grew longer and stronger. My breasts were also bulging, hurting me with a kind of sweetness. As I read, I grew into a dreamy teenager with increased romantic yearnings and stores of secondhand knowledge about the mixed blessings of love and marriage.

Meanwhile, our lane continued to be a sanctuary for play and fantasy away from official domains. But it also began to function as a hotbed of disillusionment and cynicism. With the loosening of the revolutionary spirit, young people began to return to the city from hardship and alienation in the country. They brought back experiences, stories, and books. I was eager to befriend them so that I could gain access to those stories and books. I was no longer the little girl tiptoeing in the lane, dreaming of becoming a ballerina. My appetite for books and my precocity won me the trust of some of these returned youth. They lent me books that I had not seen in the neighborhood library, such as Chinese translations of Dostoyevsky's *The Idiot* and Stendhal's *Red and Black*. The oldest son of the family living in the middle unit of our townhouse was a tall, good-looking young man with a mustache. In my eyes he resembled a Russian hero in a movie I saw, and I secretly adored him in a platonic way. One day, when he handed me *Crime and Punishment* after my persistent begging, he looked into my eyes and asked: "Can you really understand a book like this?" I eagerly nodded. I was a bit disenchanted by his question and wanted to prove that I was his intellectual equal. Of course I could not understand everything, but it all added up to something.

A book, or rather a hand-copied manuscript, I was able to secure from another young neighbor was the famous underground novel *Second Handshake (Di Erci Woshou)*. The novel was widely popular. It depicted a Chinese woman's quest for knowledge in the male world of science, or, precisely, astrophysics. The heroine was supposedly based on a real-life figure. She left China for America to become a renowned expert in her field, taking with her the memory of an unrequited love. Looking back, the romantic plot of the novel is contrived and hardly convincing; the expression of love was limited only to handshakes. What inspired a girl like me was its portrayal of a sentimental journey of a female scientist who achieved world fame at the cost of her emotional life largely due to historical happenstance. The novel, with many of the hand-copied pages missing, made a profound impression on me.

Gradually, the real world around me began to merge with the world of fiction. With bewildered eyes, I began to see romantic melodramas unfold. The good-looking "Russian hero" in our building began to date a petite young woman next door, the daughter of a party secretary. She was a worker in a factory, but because of her musical talents, she got involved in the performing troupe of the factory and walked around with a cocky air. Her parents were opposed to the liaison because the boy did not have a real job and hence no future. The girl was upset for a while, but she obeyed her parents and eventually began to date an artistic colleague of hers. One quiet afternoon, while I was reading again in the courtyard, I was surprised to hear the Russian hero and the girl laughing inside his home. They sounded very intimate together. Feeling ashamed of my involuntary eavesdropping, I quickly stood up and moved my stool outside of the house to continue my book. The book happened to be the first volume of *Dream of the Red Chamber*, a classical romance whose central plot revolves around the impossibility of "free love" in the "feudal" society. At least that's how it was presented in the foreword. The love affair between the Russian hero and the girl ultimately came to a predictable, sad end, with the two families becoming estranged from each other. It created a tense and uncomfortable atmosphere in our building. My Russian hero became rather cynical and began chain smoking and drinking, something that, strangely, only augmented his Russian aura in my eyes.

An event in my own family shook me greatly and made me realize Chinese society's cruelty toward youthful love. My youngest uncle, who was living in the country and taking care of my grandparents, suddenly began sending several urgent telegrams to my father. One day he and his girlfriend showed up in Shanghai and stayed at our place for a whole week. Initially I did not know what was going on. My parents seemed very serious and secretive about the visit of the uninvited couple. After we kids went to bed, the four of them engaged in long discussions with lowered voices. Only after my uncle and his girlfriend left was I told that they had eloped to Shanghai to escape the pressure of the girl's family. To begin with, it was not customary or auspicious for two people from the same village, which is essentially a loosely related extended family, to marry. But the main reason for the family's objection was my uncle's class background. He had been working intermittently as a school teacher when he was sent back to the village due to my grandfather's "problem." To protect my uncle, my grandfather also objected to the marriage. It must have taken a lot of guts for that girl (who later became my aunt) to fall in love with and pursue her love for my uncle.

After returning to the village, the story had its ups and downs. One day, another telegram arrived. In it, my uncle said the two of them would drown themselves in the village pond if both families continued to force them apart. My father hurried to catch a train to his hometown to help settle the matter. Somehow it worked out. They eventually got married, at the cost of my aunt being disowned by her family. I never came to know her well. She died unexpectedly just before I visited my grandmother and uncle about ten years ago. She had overworked herself in the rice field, and her chronic illness was not treated properly in the local hospital. I bowed in front of her portrait as directed by my grandmother. Looking at the incense smoke rising to the ceiling and the ashes falling on the ritual table, I suddenly remembered that afternoon when she arrived at our lane. She was young and had long pigtails. The scrutinizing look of the fashionable urban youth did not intimidate her. In fact, she carried a certain tragic and heroic air about her. Back then I did not know that this small country girl fought a big war with her family and society.

I grew up quickly in those years. Reading and watching how young people in fiction and real life struggled for love and happiness against an oppressive environment inspired and strengthened me. But the pain inflicted on themselves and the people who cared for them (for better or for worse) also made me aware of the danger or the potentially transgressive nature of sexuality. I was not ready to emulate them yet; but I thought to myself, someday, when I grow up, I will choose my own destiny and do anything to defend my love.

The year Mao died and all of China was turned upside down was the year I was officially (or biologically) admitted to womanhood. The arrival of my first period did not shock me. I had learned enough about a woman's body and its growth in the book I found on the top of the armoire. (It was so high up that I had to use a ladder to reach it.) I had a strange premonition earlier that year that my life would go through a dramatic change. In an uncanny way, I felt my bodily change was connected to the pulse of a larger movement in history. Until then, much had happened; but now things strangely seemed to stay the same. We were in a perpetual "continuous revolution," as Mao put it for us.

That fall, we did not go back to school right away. We were dispatched to different locations to learn about society firsthand. I was assigned to a model food store across the street from our lane. I liked that location. I could see all kinds of people coming by every day. Besides, it was so close to our lane that I could go there during breaks.

Only a few weeks into my internship, on September 16, the incredible news broke. Mao had died. Some female shop assistants started crying loudly right away, as though it was women's duty to mourn for the passing of the nation's head in an expressive, theatrical way. But, strangely, I had no tears, although I thought I ought to be sad. I only felt a strange excitement, as if something bigger was about to happen. We took turns watching Mao's corpse displayed on TV in the manager's office. (TV had begun to emerge as a new mass medium, although only few people had them at home.) I stared at the screen and thought to myself: Is this the man we saw as the nation's father, who we wished to live forever and ever? I sang songs and danced under his gigantic portrait surrounded with radiant rays, but I never knew who this immortal man really was. Some great chain of being had broken. I finally outlived my girlhood. A history had come to an end.

I watched the mourning masses passing through the thoroughfare in front of our store, on their way to the People's Square—the common place for mass assembly in central Shanghai. A few weeks later, I found myself watching another hysteric mass parade, this time celebrating the downfall of the Gang of Four, which included Mao's widow, Jiang Qing. In my memory, everything that happened that year was of epic proportions and took place at a dizzying speed. Yet daily life came to a standstill; everyone was busy figuring out where he or she was going and with which flow. There were people everywhere on the street. The business at our store boomed from selling sodas and snacks, box after box.

Our internship ended as soon as the euphoria over the rupture of history receded. We were ordered back to school and told that we were going to study English instead of Russian, to be in line with the ideological reorientation. I opened my English textbook and looked toward the horizon of an uncertain future.

OUT OF THE PAST

More than two decades have elapsed since I watched Mao's corpse on a black-and-white TV screen in the model shop where I wrapped candies and sold sodas. The scandalous lore of the Gang of Four has been all but forgotten. And there have been other releases of mass energy in the intervening years, especially in the wake of the student movement in 1989. But even the memory of the latter—and its human cost—has become eclipsed by recent waves of large-scale commercialization and urbanization.

Several days into my stay in Shanghai in the fall of 1996, I realized that the fate befallen my old neighborhood was actually a citywide phenomenon. The center of the city, the infrastructure of which had stayed virtually untouched for decades, was being radically remapped. Vernacular residences like ours were forced to give way to elevated highways, subway stations, sleek office buildings, and fancy shopping plazas.

One day, when I rode a bus on Yan'an Road on my way to the Shanghai Municipal Archive, I was shaken by the sight of the destroyed Huguang (Light of Shanghai, literally) Cinema. The facade, foyer, and auditorium had been reduced to rubble; only the foundation of the stage and the bare wall on which the screen used to be remained. Just a little more than a year ago, I sat inside this theater and saw *Annihilated Youth (Qingchun de Yanmie),* a film about moral bankruptcy and sexual confusion among urban youth, directed by the young Shanghai director Hu Xueyang. I remember taking a cab there so that I would not miss the beginning of the matinee. The theater had a medium-sized rectangular auditorium with two columns of seats divided by an aisle in the middle. The theater was not packed, but there was quite a crowd. It was also a theater where I had had several dates in my youth. These flashbacks passed quickly in my mind as the bus passed the theater. I heard several other passengers lamenting about the vanishing theater. They counted the names of the theaters that had been taken down that year. They also commented on the recent closing of the Da Shanghai theater near my old neighborhood. Listening to their words and sighs, and watching the ruined street, tears welled up in my eyes.

The disappearance of the Huguang theater is not just a side effect of the urban facelift to which Shanghai has been subjected. For me it symbolizes a profound disjuncture in time and space. The imminent demolition of my old neighborhood did not sadden me as much as the brutal eradication of public spaces like theaters and street corners. Residential places like our lane have, as people do, come to the end of their life. We have outgrown the old lanes, the houses, the kindergartens, and the schools; they have been used up. The residents and their children will move on, forming new kinds of communities and bonds.

The theaters are different, especially those beautiful and sturdy large structures where dreams and fantasies were projected, recycled, and remade. In those politically turbulent and materially impoverished years, they functioned as anchors and provided food for the fantasies of many. They were not only sanctuaries for forbidden romance, but also spaces for imagination and a repository of collective memory. Seeing the empty, half-torn wall on which *Annihilated Youth* was projected the last time I was inside Huguang, I realized that another epoch had ended. It stood for the larger historical stage on which the ideals and life dramas of my parents' and my generation were enacted and transformed. With that stage and the screen removed forever and the entire city center remapped (or emptied out), it becomes much harder to trace our recent past, let alone understand it. The past has become a foreign country.

YANMEI WEI

"CONGRATULATIONS, IT'S A GIRL!"

Gender and Identity in Mao's China

FAMILY TREE

One night in 1996, my elder sister Lili called from China to inform me that my father's relatives were compiling the Wei family genealogy. "That's great!" I exclaimed. I have heard numerous stories about my mother's ancestors, but I did not know much about my father's large extended family. I was therefore very excited by the news. What a great source to satisfy my curiosity! I remember thinking. But my enthusiasm was quickly dampened when my sister told me that our names would not appear in the genealogy. Apparently the book's compilation would follow the time-honored tradition that leaves out the names of any female offspring of the family, despite the fact that my sister and I are probably more accomplished than any of our male cousins.

"How unfair!" I groaned.

"Yeah, can you believe this?" My sister's voice was indignant and bitter.

Although our paternal grandparents did not shower us with affection and attention as my sister and I were growing up, we have always been under the impression that they loved and cared about us. It was such an eye-opener to realize that their love is not enough to wrestle with the forces of tradition. We thought my father's family would be proud of us. Instead, we were excluded from the family book. It was assumed that we would get married one day and join another family. So what is the use of keeping us in the family record? As daughters, we are outsiders, external elements to the family tree. Ironically, both my sister and I kept our names after marrying. Chinese women no longer adopt their husbands' surnames after marriage—a practice that began among educated Chinese women in the early twentieth century and became standard after the founding of the People's Republic of China in 1949. While I got married in the United States, where a large percentage of women give up their family name after marrying, I had made a conscious decision not to do so. I wanted to hold on to a name of my own (even though, come to think of it, it is just a name I inherited from my father). When the news came that my sister and I would not be listed in the Wei family genealogy, I had such an acute sense of irony that all I could do was laugh. I felt like a martyr for a defunct cause, embracing something that does not accept me in the first place.

The news was unpleasant but not entirely shocking. I suspect that subconsciously I expected something like this to happen. In graduate school I developed a strong interest in feminism. One book that keeps coming up in my women's studies classes is Maxine Hong Kingston's *The Woman Warrior,* a memoir of a Chinese American woman. It begins with the story of "The No Name Woman," whose family attempted to deny her existence and erase her memory after her alleged extramarital affair. In our discussion of the book I was always ready to condemn the repression of women in traditional China. Strangely, when such a tradition returned to haunt my sister and me, my reaction was not so much anger as resignation. Despite the initial disappointment, I was more concerned about my father's position in the book. What would his entry look like now that his two daughters, his only offspring, would not be listed? Will his entry be blank then? Will he need to find a surrogate son to fill in the blank? How could later generations of the Wei family find out he fathered and raised two daughters if they relied solely on this genealogy? With our exclusion isn't an important aspect of my father's life buried too?

My sister, on the other hand, took the omission of her name personally. At family gatherings Lili likes to emphasize the fact that she is the eldest granddaughter of my paternal grandparents *(zhangfang zhang sunnü)*. Although not taken seriously by the family, it is a meaningful term for her. She feels special because of it and demands the same kind of treatment bestowed upon a *zhang fang zhangsun* (eldest grandson). The genealogy snub was an assault on her self-esteem. Needless to say it caused a mini storm in her emotional world.

This situation both united and divided my sister and me. We both felt the slap of tradition, yet we reacted differently to it. Although I was fascinated by the idea of a family genealogy, I did not attach too much importance to it. As a young feminist, I am searching for my own identity rather than my place in family history. However, it seems to have taken Lili a longer time to get over the sense of pain and betrayal. It was she, rather than my parents, who broke the news to me. She also did not hesitate to protest to our parents.[1] Such a difference in attitude, I believe, can find its roots in the circumstances under which we were raised and, by implication, the larger social and political environment of our childhood.

My sister and I are only three years apart. Yet we grew up in very different historical and geographical landscapes. Our temperament and experiences are likewise divergent. My sister is restless, driven, and self-assertive, which she attributes to the nomadic childhood she spent with my mother in the army. My childhood was passed in a quiet, unassuming, and isolated rural village in northern China—an experience that has shaped my personality and worldview to be dramatically different from my sister's. By the time my sister and I were born, around the beginning of the 1970s, the furor of the Cultural Revolution had subsided and the so-called Mao era was about to enter its last phase. Neither of us was caught in the center of the political and social movements that had been sweeping across China since the 1960s, yet it seems that from the very beginning our lives were inevitably blended into the social and political fabrics of the time. We moved frequently as children and as a family. When the whole family finally reunited in the city in

1978, our disparate journeys had taken us across the northern, western, and eastern regions of the country, from the mountainous west to the "rice and fish" eastern plains, and from the rural to the urban.

The fact that such dramatic events occurred in the first few years of our childhood may seem quite extraordinary, but it is really not that uncommon among our peers. We, particularly my sister, are surrounded with friends and relatives who identify with our experience. To tell our story, in a way, is to evoke the memory of our generation—the generation that was born in the early 1970s, came of age in the immediate decade after the end of the Cultural Revolution, and is the product of two different yet interconnected eras: the Mao era (1949–1976) and the post-Mao era (1976–present). Through speaking to each other, and to ourselves, we hope our voice can reach others who share our memory or our desire to understand and to remember.

"CONGRATULATIONS, IT'S A GIRL!"

When I was born, in an army hospital in southwestern China, my father was teaching in a city in eastern China. My mother, an army doctor, was stationed at an army base thousands of miles away from him. Due to professional needs and administrative restrictions, they lived apart for more than thirteen years. For more than a decade their vacations were spent crisscrossing the country for family visits. Each one-way trip meant sitting for more than twenty-four hours on crowded and uncomfortable hard train seats. My parents were just one of the tens of thousands of couples who endured *liangdi fenju,* that is, living separately in different cities/regions for years, if not decades—a situation prevalent enough to warrant a special term.

The phenomenon was especially common in the army, which recruited members from all over the country and moved them to wherever they were needed. The compound where my mother lived had about twenty families and boasted a colorful assortment of dialects, cuisine, and customs. Such a diverse group was melded together by its members' military identity, language, and careers, and also the fact that almost all the families were in the state of liang di fen ju. It was particularly difficult for the women, who, while striving to establish themselves professionally, were often the designated caretaker of the children. When asked why my mother, rather than my father, was responsible for child rearing, my parents would cite the realistic restraints. As a young faculty whose family did not live with him, my father was at the lowest priority for university housing. He lived in university dormitories, sharing a room and facilities with other young male teachers. He could not possibly take care of his daughters under these circumstances. I wonder if it ever crossed the minds of the housing committee that a male employee might need a room of his own to raise his kids. In any case, my parents did not burden them with such a request. It was presumed that as a doctor and female, my mother would be a better caretaker.

Liangdi fenju may have disrupted the stability of the nuclear family, but, interestingly, it seems to have strengthened the traditional (extended) family relationships. My mother's best friend had her sister move in and help take care of the kids. My mother turned to her parents, who were watching my sister and now gladly took me under their wings.

A year after giving birth to me, my mother made a trip to her hometown to pick up my sister and drop me off. A few years later, my mother, who visited regularly, brought my sister along. As they approached the entrance to the village, they were greeted by a rosy-cheeked girl who started to dart toward the village at the sight of them. Her hair went flying in the wind and all the front buttons of her jacket were wide open. She screamed at the top of her lungs as she dashed toward my aunt's house: "Auntie, Grandma, Great Aunt, we have visitors!" That was me, in my first encounter with my elder sister after being sent away. I, of course, had no recollection of this. I heard the story from my sister, who remembers thinking at the time: "Is this tomboy really my little sister?"

My sister may have exaggerated a little, but I was indeed flourishing under the loving care of my mother's family. Probably because it is so remote from the political epicenter, life in my village was not as politically charged as some other parts of the country.

We did not have sent-down youths from the city. My childhood memories are not haunted by rallies, slogans, or posters. Rather, I remember it mostly as a fun-filled time when I roamed the wheat fields and daydreamed under the enormous peach tree behind my aunt's house. Spring brought the sweet, juicy taste of the ears of wheat that shot up almost to the sun. Summer nights were spent among the symphony of cicadas and crickets, and the animated chat among the villagers who gathered to cool off from the heat of the day. There was always a lot of storytelling during these gatherings. As I lay in my grandmother's arms, I listened intently to the eerie adventures of the ghosts or the tragic fate of the lovesick fairies. I remember distinctively my grandmother's heartbeat, since she liked to hold me very tight. I remember feeling at once concerned and reassured in her arms. I often worried that my head was too heavy and I was putting too much pressure on her chest. At the same time, however, I felt safe and happy knowing I was loved and cared for.

The village I grew up in was a serene and protective environment, if only a little bit superstitious. One day I was yelled at for squatting down to watch a sheep giving birth while the boys continued to cheer the baby lamb on. According to local custom, for a girl to observe the birth process is indecent and inauspicious. But how about the boys? There will be no consequences for them?! I can hear myself scream now. However, at the time of the incident, I obeyed, even though I did not really believe what I heard. At that age, I had no resources to question and challenge. It will be many years before I realize how, little by little, incidents like this formed my sense of self and womanhood.

I don't know if I would have gotten a satisfactory answer had I expressed my doubts. The elders were merely reciting gender beliefs that had been circulating for centuries. I doubt if they ever took sayings as such to heart. Our family matriarchs seem to be ambivalent about the whole gender issue. On the one hand, they understand and live by the power of the patriarchal arrangement. Despite the fact that my grandfather was the founder of one of the first high schools in the county, his wife, my grandmother, who was as sharp and articulate as "a college professor," did not receive any formal instruction until after the revolution, when they were sent to night classes established by the government to eliminate illiteracy. My great aunt used to take her brother, my great uncle, to school every day, yet she herself was never enrolled. Later she taught herself a few characters through reading holiday couplets. After becoming a widow at the age of twenty, my great aunt had a number of opportunities to remarry. Yet each time her father, my great grandfather, who had a concubine himself, objected to it, and she ended up widowed for the rest of her life. She became a surrogate mother to many of us in the family, taking care of my mother, aunt, and their cousins when they were little and then helping to raise their children.

Because of their personal experience, the two elders in my family naturally think highly of the status and opportunities offered to a male. They often accept the gender hierarchy without much questioning. On the other hand, conventional gender beliefs are not necessarily carried into the daily practice of life. My grandmother, for example, sometimes lamented the fact that she did not have a son. However, it never crossed her mind to disregard her daughters' well-being or neglect their education. When my sister was born, my great aunt congratulated my mother for being so smart, citing that a daughter will become the best friend and caretaker of her parents when they are old. In the countryside, an individual or a family without sons is often taken advantage of. Many parents will therefore try anything to beget a male child. At the same time, however, the peasants are practical thinkers who understand that their best hope for a comfortable old age rests with the daughters. While sons boost the status of the parents, those with many daughters are considered in possession of "good fortune" (fuqi). People like my grandparents, who did not have a son of their own, generally move in with their daughter(s) in old age. Those who are "lucky" enough to live with sons still depend on filial daughters to provide them with a stable and plentiful old age. My grandmother was looked after by her two daughters so well that she became the envy of her friends, many of whom had sons who could not be relied on for support.

As my mother was telling me my great aunt's comments after

my sister's birth, I wondered if the same compliment was offered at my birth. After all, the subtext of that remark is not that my mother does not need a male child. Rather, now that she has a daughter, she needs to go for a son, or, in my mother's words, to *"huanhuan huayang"* (change varieties). By the time I was born, birth-control policy was in effect and it was no longer politically correct to have a house full of children, as was the case in the 1950s and 1960s. Had the policy not shifted, would they have continued to try for a boy? My parents are educated and liberal parents who invested in every way they could in our well-being. Yet when I was in elementary school, my father used to call me "daughter-son." Would he have resorted to such coinage had there been a real son? My parents could never explain why they called me "daughter-son," except that it was a term of endearment. Some would say that I might have been treated as a "surrogate son"—a child that can hopefully fulfill the parents' dreams and bring glory to the family name. My parents would vehemently object to this suggestion, and, frankly, I think they treat us equally, that is, with equally high expectations and strictness. But had there been a son, would it have dramatically changed my life?

"WHEN I GROW UP, I WANT TO SAVE THE WORLD!"

During the first six or seven years of my sister's life she lived with my mother on a compound for army doctors and nurses. The mother-daughter unit led a hectic life. My mother worked full time at the hospital. As a young doctor, she was frequently on call at nights and on weekends. It did not matter much that she had a young daughter at home. Nor would my mother ask for any special treatment. My mother's service in the army had taken her to some of the most remote and harshest regions of the country. She was proud to be able to overcome the arduous conditions.

My mother was a very caring mother, yet she could not find enough time to spend with her daughter. In addition to a busy schedule at work, every week she had to devote two afternoons and three nights to the study of Mao's writings with her colleagues. My sister remembers some very lonely nights. She was enrolled in a kindergarten and was always the last one to leave at the end of day, since my mother was often delayed by work in the hospital. Some days my mother would pick her up and, instead of going home, they would go to the hospital, where my mother was on night shift in the emergency room.

As an army doctor, my mother moved quite frequently. One of my sister's earliest memories was during one of her many trips. When the train climbed an extended and treacherous range of mountains, the light inside the train flickered as it crawled in and out of the tunnels. She sat inside and watched the light change from bright to dark to bright, and then back to dark—kind of like the journey of her life, she later commented to me. If life in the army has left her with many moments of loneliness and pain, it has also brought out some of the best qualities in her character. In the army she neighbored with doctors and nurses from all corners of the country and truly enjoyed such diversity. As my mother transferred from unit to unit, my sister moved from one elementary school to another and made different sets of friends. As a resilient child, she quickly adapted to whatever situations she and my mother were subjected to. Contrary to popular wisdom, the instability in my sister's childhood has not made her long for a peaceful, sedentary life. Rather, she is a restless dreamer who refuses to settle down and is always in search of the next challenge.

Given the circumstances, my sister did not grow into a pampered, enervated, and coquettish girl. Instead, she learned to be independent, assertive, and ambitious. Like many of her girlfriends, she was a tomboy: "we have to be. One-half of the population in the world is suffering and we need to deliver them out of their pain when we grow up!" To save the world. That was my sister and her friends' dream at that tender age. Such an ambition instilled in my sister the kind of self-confidence that has sustained her throughout the many ordeals in her life. She formed an intense relationship with my mother and taught herself to be self-sufficient.

"I AM SORRY THAT I LET YOU DOWN, CHAIRMAN MAO"

My formal schooling started at the age of five, when I entered the village school, a one-room school built by the villagers. I remember coming home one day and announcing proudly that the school was now equipped with an outhouse, which the students had helped construct by drying the mud walls. The room was furnished with hard, mud desks and benches that stretched across the room. In the winter the benches became so cold that we would bring blankets or pillows from home to sit on.

Only the first two grades were taught there. Third grade and beyond was taught at a larger school ten miles away from the village. There was a number of girl students. The villagers generally do not mind sending their daughters to elementary school for a few years of basic education, but they are more reluctant to put their daughters through middle or high school.

Aside from lessons in Chinese and math, there was little instruction in "lofty" political and social ideals. There was, for example, no picture of Mao hanging above the teacher's desk or daily recitation of Mao quotations. It wasn't until I went to the city that I became aware of such terms as *the little red guard (hong xiao bing)* or *the young pioneer (shaoxian duiyuan)*. As a good student I received certificates of merits. But I did not receive a *hong ling jin* (the red scarf)—a triangle-shaped piece of cloth, which, as every young pioneer in the city could tell you, is red because it is symbolic of the blood shed for the revolution.

The simple condition and curriculum of our school was made for the life lessons we learned in the fields. After class we all worked on the farm. Our teacher, an amicable peasant woman, toiled alongside many of her students. The children are normally assigned to collect grass for the livestock or pick ripened fruits and vegetables. Compared with the boys, the girls were generally more disciplined, hardworking, and productive. Somehow little boys were permitted to be naughty and playful while the girls were expected to help out at an early age. At dusk one could often see the lonely and silent figure of eight- or nine-year-old girls returning home, weighed down by a basketful of grass two or three times their size.

Meanwhile, kids in the city were growing fast, too, but in a very different way. The atmosphere in the urban schools seemed to be much more politicized than that in the countryside. In my sister's city school there was a huge portrait of Mao in her classroom. For fifteen minutes every morning, before instruction began, the teacher would lead the entire class in reciting Mao's quotations, and whoever committed misdeeds apologized to Mao's picture on their own initiative. A written confession would be posted on the wall afterward. At the time, this was considered a "progressive" act, a way of showing loyalty to Mao. Competition was fierce. Students would rack their brains to find things to confess, even resorting to fiction at times. My sister remembers the time when she walked to the front and confessed between sobs that on the way home the day before she saw an old peasant pushing a coal cart up a bridge. The old peasant needed some help, but because of her "bourgeois thought," my sister walked right by him without even stopping (It was questionable how much help a third-grader could offer in this situation). However, after returning home and studying Mao's quotations, she felt so ashamed about her lack of "class consciousness" that she rushed out of the house to give the old peasant a hand. Upon hearing this, the entire class broke into applause. Many years later, when my sister ran into her elementary school teacher, she confided that she had made up the whole thing. Her teacher laughed forgivingly: "how much truth was there then?"

When Mao passed away in 1976, I was still in the countryside. The villagers' reaction to the news was nothing like the humorous but deadly serious portrayal in the story "Leader's Demise." Changke, the protagonist, agonized for days that he would not be able to cry at the village's memorial service for Mao. As a former teacher with a "bourgeois" background, Changke "was afraid of being noticed, but he was also afraid of not being noticed" at the memorial service, which he mistakenly referred to as a "celebration" to the village head. As it turned out, he "was the first adult at the memorial service to cry" and achieved instant celebrity status in the village.[2] Had Changke been living in my village, he would not have been so worried. I do not recall any public memorial service or staged demonstration of grief. My grandfather shed tears upon hearing the news, but as someone who retired to the countryside after becoming a "rightist," he was not under any internal or external pressure to showcase his political consciousness like the paranoid Changke. In the village, there were crops to tend and mouths to feed. As the initial ripples of shock receded, the farmers went about their business as usual. The only memorial service I remember was the funeral of my grandfather, who died from a stroke a few months after Mao.

For my sister, it was another experience. She was in class when Mao's death was announced over the school wire. She remembers the whole class, actually the entire school, bursting into tears. One teacher passed out from the grief. It was reported that at the state funeral, numerous people fainted and had to be taken by the ambulance to the hospital. On the day of the funeral, my sister sat with our mother in the apartment in silence for a long time. As she recalls later, it felt like the end of the world, as if there would be no hope or future.

IT WAS THE BEST OF TIMES?

Interestingly, time went by and the future did come. After years of separation, my family was finally reunited in Nanjing in 1978. I was enrolled in my sister's elementary school. The Cultural Revolution had ended two years before, and China was entering a new phase of development. One departure from the Cultural Revolution era is that school education gradually became less political and more academically oriented. In the late 1970s the university entrance examination was reinstated, and merit, rather than family background and political consciousness, was now the ticket to college admission. While during the Cultural Revolution students were told to quit school and fight the revolution alongside the workers and peasants, in the post–Cultural Revolution years every parent used the grim tale of a street cleaner as an incentive for their children to study hard.

During my sister's elementary school years, *hong xiaobing* (Little Red Guard) was the title awarded to an honor student. The criteria for the Chinese schools' honor system are generally centered around the three *hao* (goods): good in academics, good in physical education, and good in character. As its name suggests, hong xiaobing, a replacement of the young pioneers in the early years of the Communist state, was very much a product of the Cultural Revolution. During those years a good student would become a hong xiaobing in elementary school and then a *hong weibing* (Red

Guard) in middle school and high school. A title like this was handed out as recognition of an elementary school student's political progressiveness. However, *hong xiaobing* became less and less a meaningful title as I moved up the grades in the same elementary school. When I was eligible to become an honor student, the title had been changed back to *young pioneers*. The criteria for selection, although still the three "goods," had become heavily academic.

In terms of the advancement of knowledge and mind for the female students, the message I received from the school and my family was loud, clear, and consistent. Every night my whole family gathered around the dining-table-turned-writing-desk and worked together, my parents with their books and my sister and I with our schoolwork. Calluses soon started to grow on the middle finger of my right hand, the finger that the pencil rubs against. Homework took longer and longer, and playtime became shorter and shorter. My parents, like the parents of all my girlfriends, cooperated fully with the teachers, who in turn, regularly gave them feedback on our academic performance. Together, parents and schools created a congenial environment for the development of our intellect and self-confidence.

For the most part I have fond memories of my elementary school years. It can be said, without much exaggeration, that girls were the stars of our school. We outdid boys in almost every aspect of school life: we were better students, performers, and athletes, we had neater handwriting and behavior, teachers loved us more, and we occupied almost all of the important posts in the student body. When my sister and I were in elementary school, in addition to grades and classes, the student body was organized into military regiments. Accordingly, there were student leaders for *dadui* (big-team, battalion), *zhongdui* (middle team, squadron), and *xiaodui* (small team, squad). It was not uncommon for girls to occupy all leadership positions in the hierarchy, not to mention the positions as class representatives for academic subjects. In a co-ed elementary school, where girls and boys are paired up to share desk and bench, well-disciplined girls were often assigned to sit with naughty boys in an attempt to reform their behavior or, at the very least, to keep a watchful eye on these troublemakers.

In elementary school we did not feel inferior as girls. On the contrary, we were a very proud group who found boys alternatively amusing, pathetic, and annoying. Such girl pride, however, is not really gender consciousness. Although we saw ourselves as better, we did not see ourselves as very different from the boys. Girls were not educated to be the "sugar and spice." Instead, we were taught to aspire to the ideal of "the little red guard" or "the young pioneer." Each year the boys and girls in my elementary school made a pilgrimage to the Platform of Rain Flowers (Yuhua Tai) in southern Nanjing, where, under the reign of the Nationalist Party, Communist prisoners were tortured and executed. We would gather under the famous monument to swear in new young pioneers while stories of the martyrs were recounted. A friend of mine told me that she used to have nightmares after each visit, since graphic details and pictures were generally not omitted from the speeches and exhibitions, not even for the "delicate" psyche of elementary school students. The goal of these trips was to foster the children's loyalty to the revolutionary cause. Like the boys, the girls had plenty of role models to emulate, since there were a lot of tales about the female martyrs.

At school, girls and boys played the same kinds of games and competed in the same kinds of sports. We danced together and took turns leading the dance at the school's playground on National Children's Day. When teachers assigned chores at the school or for the community, such as sweeping the leaves, washing the floors, watering the plants, wiping the windows, or cleaning the bathrooms, in no way would girls be given favoritism on the basis of their gender. On the contrary, we were encouraged to do as much and as well as the boys.

In its effort to promote gender equality, the school took pains to curb the development of feminine traits and vanity in the female students—a continuation of the Mao era tradition. In doing so they showed remarkable attention to details. We were told, for example, not to gossip, nibble between meals (chi lingshi), or wear such outlandish clothes (qizhuang yifu) as blue jeans. One year, the day after we returned from winter vacation it was discovered that one of the girls in the class had permed her hair. She was ordered to stay at home until the perm straightened, even though this meant she would have to miss classes. This episode also put an end to my parents' effort to have my hair permed. My sister, who was in middle school then, had it even worse. They were not allowed to wear their hair long, not even in a ponytail.

However, this puritanical and rather reductive view of femininity proved to be inadequate to address the issue of gender difference and thus created much ambiguity, mystery, and contradiction about the meaning of femininity. The official position notwithstanding, good-looking girls continued to be favored and certain stereotypical feminine behaviors were subtly or not so subtly encouraged. One day a good friend of mine told me about her mother's suggestion for her to *da ban,* that is, to fix herself up. My friend is smart and personable, but she is not a natural beauty, just a regular, wholesome girl. Her mother was apparently worried about her attractiveness. My friend and I were both mystified by her mother's advice. Hadn't we just heard that we should be judged only by our intelligence and achievement?

My friend rejected her mother's suggestion outright because, as she put it, she wanted to be herself. I too decided that I would remain true to my self. But what was my true self?

During my elementary school years my family lived in a university dormitory. Since we did not have a kitchen, every evening after supper my sister and I were sent out to fetch hot water for the family from the university hot water center. This was normally the busiest time on this part of campus, when hungry students and faculty poured out of classrooms into the dining halls and dorms and into the living quarters. Sometimes the traffic was so thick that we had to maneuver our way in the sea of legs and bicycle wheels like two headless flies. It was, however, my favorite chore because I got to open my mouth and sing the songs I liked. My sister may have joined me on occasions, but I remember it mostly as my solo performance. I started to sing the moment I stepped out of our dormitory building and would only stop when I had to conserve my energy to carry the thermos up to our fourth-floor room. I sang whatever tunes happened to come into my mind and remember feeling pleased with myself. I did not feel embarrassed by being so loud or self-conscious about singing in front of total strangers. The world was a stage, and I was the most exuberant participant. I was completely happy and content with my voice, my behavior, and, essentially, my being.

Unfortunately, this period of solid and comforting self-definition was not to last long. My optimism would be subjected to reality checks as I grew. A happy-go-lucky chatterbox, I was friendly with the twenty or so families that were living on the same floor of our dormitory, and I often played with my neighbors after dinner. One night when I was in the third grade, as I was getting ready to go out, my mother pulled me aside and with a serious look on her face, said, "Yanmei, don't play so much anymore. You need to concentrate on your studies. Besides, it is not good for a girl's reputation."

While my friend was able to resist her mother's suggestion, I did not disobey my mother's request that I stay home after dinner. I had been suspecting that something was going on, as I saw fewer and fewer girls of my age at our nightly playtime and sensed gossip in the air. The painful message that my mother delivered confirmed that I could not be a tomboy forever. As a girl, with a reputation to worry about, I had to learn to draw a line between the world of boys and the world of girls. For many years I had been blissfully oblivious of the issue of gender and did not really concern myself about the meaning of femininity. My mother's request, clearly well intentioned, left an indelible mark on my sense of self. It can be called, I guess, my initiation into the world of femininity and gender consciousness. Upon reflection, I am struck by how powerful and anonymous the process of gender indoctrination can be. A quick and casual remark from my mother was enough to make the message abundantly clear to me. We did not argue, nor did it seem necessary to discuss the matter further. I started to distance myself from my playmates and immersed myself in my study. A few years later, with an elementary school diploma and my first pair of eyeglasses in hand, I walked into middle school.

THE THREE HOLIDAYS

Like in elementary school, my life in middle school was marked with a grueling schedule and strict discipline. There were few political rallies or activities. Only occasionally did we debate about when Communism would be realized all over the world. Would it be in fifty years? One hundred years? Or two hundred years?

Boys and girls went separate ways in middle school. Girls no longer shared a desk with boys; instead, we sat with someone of our own gender. During the annual work-study week, female students were sent to help out at the cafeteria, library, or labs, while male students were assigned to posts that required more intense physical labor. The male and female students formed their own interest groups and codes of behavior, yet they also gravitated toward each other by mutual fascination and secret admiration.

We also tried to invent ourselves. One year my friend and I came up with the idea of the three holidays: the day of "fairy-like elegance," when we would behave like ladies, all proper and polite; the "carnival" day, when we could entertain and enjoy with utter abandon; and, finally, there was the day of "pouring one's heart out," when we would share our most sincere feelings and opinions. Thinking back, I am struck by the meaning of each holiday and the order of its appearance on the calendar. The first holiday was designed for the spring, while the second, its opposite, was set for the summer. The day of honesty was scheduled for the end of the year. It seems that no sooner than we decided to be a nice Chinese girl, we wanted to move away from it. So we created the two holidays, giving outlet to both the desire to conform and the desire to rebel. But the interesting thing is, I don't think we really observed these holidays. Or if we did, it was not for long. In real life, when the struggle between the two impulses occurred on a daily basis, how could we separate or move between the selves at will?

I don't remember why we decided to have the third holiday. As teenagers we were naturally forthright. At least I was. So why a designated day for honesty? Does that mean we could be insincere during the rest of the year? Obviously this holiday was set up to fill a certain void. But what was it? As I remember it, it was a rule of the holiday that we were entitled to say the bluntest and silliest things on our minds, as long as they were our true thoughts. It was to be a day of listening, questioning, and examining. Although we were required to be completely honest with each other, the rule was not to be abused for the purpose of personal attack. Rather, we were looking for reflection and affirmation through each other, and we gave both positive and negative comments. I guess this holiday provided us with a means to battle the insecurity that plagued us all at that tender age. We strove to find comfort and guidance in the solidarity of our friendship. As I realized many years later, such bonding is vital to my well-being.

As the decade progressed, there was more and more questioning and reevaluation of the mainstream ideology and value systems in China. A rather popular kind of essay writing in my middle-school years was to take a clichéd situation/statement and analyze it from a different perspective. So a previously negative trait or behavior would now be endowed with some redeeming features. I once read an essay that tried to give an alternative interpretation of "only sweeping the snow on one's doorsteps and not caring about the frost on the neighbors' roof." Normally this kind of behavior was condemned as selfish and not conducive to society, but this essay wanted to defend it from the perspective of guarding one's own privacy. Such type of writing quickly became a cliché itself, but the fact that we could easily find materials to challenge and come up with counterarguments bespeaks an era of reflection and examination.

However, as the old belief systems were being challenged and dismantled, new, well-articulated replacement was slow in coming. Communist ideals were still a staple of our moral education, but they no longer seemed to impact our lives in the way they had previous generations of youth. This, together with the physical and psychological changes my girlfriends and I were experiencing, made it an exciting but confusing period of time.

Although in the early 1980s my friend and I scoffed at the idea of da-ban, by the end of the 1980s it seemed that makeup and high heels were indispensable components of the new womanhood. And while in junior high we waited for the thermometer to hit thirty degrees Celsius before daring to put on a skirt, in senior high there emerged more and more self-proclaimed fashion experts. Dancing parties, which inevitably gave girls (and boys, too?) an excuse to da-ban, were a unanimous choice for end-of-the-year celebrations.

I remember watching a student disco dancing at one of those parties and admiring her figure and movement. I had admired many things and people before. However, this was different from the kind of adoration I had for a string of colorful beads, my most treasured possession in junior high, or the esteem I held toward some of my classmates, who were smart, funny, or kind. Looking at her, so healthy, energetic, and graceful, I became aware of a new kind of femininity, the kind that is physical and spiritual, unabashedly beautiful and confident. It seemed a century had passed since the time my elementary school friend and I rejected the idea of da ban. Sitting at the party and watching my classmate perform, I wondered what my childhood friend would do now about her appearance.

During this period, literature, film, and public discourses featured a more feminine and self-assertive female image. At the same time, commercialization and the resurgence of conservative gender ideology also subjected females to increasing sexual exploitation and stereotyping. I had a friend who became a slave to her makeup, who could not feel that she was herself without putting on a whole ensemble of cosmetics and jewelry. As the world turned, I fumbled along the crossroad between the old and the new. Often I felt that I was being pulled in all directions. One minute I was convinced that I could accomplish anything that a boy could; the next minute I felt very vulnerable and uncertain about my status as a woman. It was a long time before I resolved my identity crisis, but by then I had traded in much of my childhood enthusiasm and pride.

Of course I was not the only one who endured such growing pains. In my feminist readings I was surprised to learn so many girls in the United States (and probably all around the world) were tomboys just like me before they were groomed into "proper" women. We probably all go through certain common perils in the transition from girlhood to womanhood. However, I came of age in the 1980s, the immediate decade after the end of the Cultural Revolution in China, and an era of profound change and dynamics. The growing pains I experienced, while a natural component of the process of growing up, may very well have resulted from the particular time and circumstances I was in.

NOTES

1. My mother, herself a victim of the same kind of double standard, dismissed it as something not to be taken seriously. My father, who never misses an opportunity to foster ambition in his children, advised, "Why don't you try to get into other books, since you cannot be admitted into this one [the family genealogy]?"
2. Shaogong Han. *The Leader's Demise,* trans. Thomas Moran, in *The Columbia Anthology of Modern Chinese Literature,* ed. Joseph S. M. Lau and Howard Goldblatt. (New York: Columbia University Press, 1995), 387–398.

About the Contributors

NAIHUA ZHANG is an assistant professor at Florida Atlantic University. She received her Ph.D. degree in sociology from Michigan State University. Her research interests include social movement and social change. She has published articles on the contemporary women's movement and women's organizations in China.

 WANG ZHENG is an associate professor of Women's studies at the University of Michigan. She is the author of *Women in Chinese Enlightenment: Oral and Textual Histories* and *A History of Contemporary Feminist Movement in the U.S.* (in Chinese). She is the coauthor of *From the Soil: The Foundations of Chinese Society* and coeditor of *Selected Works on Gender Studies* (in Chinese). Her research interest is in Chinese gender and feminist histories.

XIAOMEI CHEN is an associate professor in the department of East Asian languages and literatures and the division of comparative studies at Ohio State University. She is the author of *Occidentalism: A Theory of Counter-Discourse in Post-Mao China* and numerous articles. She is currently completing another book titled *Acting the Right Part: Cultural Performance in Contemporary China.*

BAI DI is an assistant professor of Chinese literature and culture at Drew University.

JIANG JIN is an assistant professor of history at Vassar College. Her publications include "Liang Shuming and the Emergence of Twentieth-Century New Confucianism," in *The Chinese Historians* (autumn 1993), and *June Fourth: A Chronicle of the Chinese Democratic Uprising* (cotranslator).

LIHUA WANG is affiliated with the women's studies program at Northeastern University and is an associate in research at the Fairbank Center at Harvard University. Since completing her Ph.D. in sociology at Northeastern University, her teaching and research interests have been in Asian studies, race, gender, family, and development. She is currently completing her

manuscript *"The Iron Girl" and the Obedient Wife: Competing Constructions of Femininity in Twentieth-Century China.*

XUEPING ZHONG is an associate professor of Chinese literature and culture at Tufts University. She is the author of *Masculinity Besieged? Issues of Modernity and Male Subjectivity in Chinese Literature of the Late Twentieth Century.* Her other writings have appeared in such journals and collections of essays as *Modern Chinese Literature and Culture, Chinese Historians, Engendering China, Gender and Sexuality in*  *Twentieth-Century Chinese Literature and Society,* and *Chinese Women Traversing Diaspora.*

 ZHANG ZHEN is an assistant professor of cinema studies at New York University. Her scholarly and creative writings have appeared in a number of journals and volumes, including *Public Culture, Asian Cinema, Cinema and Urban Culture in Shanghai, 1922–1943, Spaces of Their Own,* and *Chinese Women Traversing Diaspora.* She is currently completing her book on cultural history of early Chinese film and urban experience.

YANMEI WEI received her B.A. in English from Nanjing University in China in 1992. She holds a Ph.D. degree in comparative literature from SUNY-Stony Brook. She has taught literature, women's studies, film, and language and is currently co-chair of the Chinese Society for Women's Studies in the United States.

Index

Anderson, Perry, xviii
Anhui Province, 115–118
Annihilated Youth, 177
Association for Asian Studies, xvii

Bai Di, xiii-xxxiii, xxx, xxxi, 77–99
Ba Jin, xxii
ballet plays, 166–167
Beidahuang, 69, 70–75
Beijing, 3–5, 20, 105, 107, 121–126
Beijing Foreign Language Institute, 54
Beijing Jingshan School, 62–68
birth-control policy, 186
books and reading, 106; "bourgeois
    literature," 127; Chinese classics,
    103, 109, 171; confiscated by
    Red Guards, 92; picture books,
    41–43; propagandist, 34—35,
    93; romantic novels, 43–44, 93–
    94, 173; science, 92; taboo, 151,
    153; Western classics, 43, 44,
    45–47, 114, 171–172
Brigham Young University, 53

Cao Xueqin, 139

capitalist-roaders (*zouzipai*), 3, 67,
    80, 87, 104, 124, 148
*Changing Identities of Chinese
    Women: Rhetoric, Experience, and
    Self-Perception in Twentieth-
    Century China* (Croll), xxv
chastity, female, 39–41
chi ku (bearing hardship), 124–125
Children's Palace, 142
Colleges and universities: admis-
    sions, 22–23, 134–136, 150,
    151–152, 190; under
    Guomindang, 108; WPS (worker,
    peasant, and soldier) students,
    150
Complete Works of Lu Xun, 103
Croll, Elisabeth, xxv
Cultural Revolution: children's
    activities during, 87–90, 143–
    144, 163–165; end of, 22, 151;
    family class origins in, 3–5, 44,
    161, 162–163, 174–175; family
    surveillance in, 112–113; gender
    equality and, 14–15; performing
    troupes in, 66–68, 69–70, 71–72,
    155, 165–168, 173; power
    seizure struggles in home, 81–

CPSIA information can be obtained
at www.ICGtesting.com
Printed in the USA
FSOW02n1447210115
4683FS

9 780813 529691